For The Sake of Mrs.

Africa Cooper

ISBN: 0692797920
ISBN 13: 9780692797921

Introduction

Why do I continue to keep making the same mistakes over and over again? As intelligent as I think I am, I have not managed to master the game of marriage. One would think, after several husbands and divorces, I would have a PhD in the field.

Marriage, for many women, is seen as the ultimate goal of a romantic relationship. And why wouldn't it be? We're brought up dreaming of Prince Charming, wondering when we'll find that elusive Mr. Right and spending hours upon hours planning the perfect wedding, regardless of whether or not there's a potential groom in the picture.

To make matters worse, if you're like most women these days who've discovered that finding Mr. Right takes a bit of time, and a lot of luck; friends and family will likely have peppered you with constant questions – *When are you going to bring home 'the one'? What's the holdup?* They wonder aloud about your fate, or even worse, encourage you to stop being so picky and just settle already.

Well, I have always had fabulous weddings - but no real marriages... Whoever issues wedding licenses should revoke my privileges of ever saying "I do" again!

Lord knows that, after several legal attachments, someone should have investigated my motives or examined my head! Yet, I know that, first and foremost, I should have delved deeper into my own reasons for walking down that aisle, time after time. Asking myself before – not after! – why I wanted to get married and why I continually made the same mistake of falling in love and truly believing that marriage is always the second step...

Nevertheless, I've realized as I spoke to my friends, and other women that I met, that I was not alone in questioning my choices, and repeating the same disastrous cycle over and over again, despite having suffered firsthand the consequences of failed marital relationships.

The pressures and expectations are part of the problem, adding stress to an already important decision. *"If he really loves you, he'd marry you."* I've heard it, you've heard it. Is it any wonder then that marriage is often seen as a marker of success and worth? And who doesn't want to prove themselves, prove they're worthy of love, that they are in fact easy to love. We're left screaming at the top of our lungs: *"Of course he loves me, of course he wants to marry me!"* True or not, the subtle implication that we need to defend ourselves against this type of attack can push many women forward – right to the front of the church, exchanging vows at the altar – against their better judgments. All for the sake of being Mrs.

Today, with divorce rates sky high, it goes without saying that something isn't quite as idyllic as the blissfully married couples on the covers of wedding magazines. While there are the clear-cut examples of why people might separate, such as abuse or infidelity, there are still many cases where it's more complicated than that, or even more simplistic, like you aren't well-matched. And you're left asking yourself: *how did I get into this mess in the first place?* Or perhaps even, *how did I get into this mess – once <u>again</u>!?*

But, as I discovered, you shouldn't only be asking yourself, when there are others who are going through this mess, too. Take for instance, the story of Darla, with a PhD in Philosophy, who's been married five times; Rachael, a motivational speaker, with her first divorce still pending; Marilyn, a psychologist, twice divorced and currently engaged to beau # 3. These are educated, intelligent women and their stories are our stories, their mistakes are our mistakes, and their lessons are lessons we can all learn from.

No matter what stage you're at in life—whether you're a newlywed for the first time, or you're half-way through your second marriage, or maybe you're single or recently engaged—this book is for you. (And of course for any of you men who are curious, too!)

By taking a closer look at real actions and reactions, choices and their consequences, exploring how our past (and current) relations have played out; you'll have the insights to help identify these key moments that define every relationship and the perilous pitfalls that can be found along the road to "I do" and beyond.

Unfortunately, I've learned the hard way that knowing where things went wrong is only step one. It's time we take control of our relationships and their outcomes. I know I should have dug further into my own reasons for walking down that aisle, time after time. I know I should have asked myself before—not after!—why I wanted to get married at all and why I wanted to believe that marriage is the inevitable next step in a relationship?

None of us are completely in the dark to what might go wrong when dating, marrying and divorcing our partners. But I found, along with the women in this book, that something integral was still missing, something that let us keep making these same mistakes as if blind to the outcome.

What was it? It was isolation. Isolation in the sense that we were all looking at our relationships as single entities. It wasn't until we pooled together our collective experiences to learn from our mistakes that we could identify these pitfalls and challenges in our relationships.

More specifically, have you ever watched a close friend begin a new relationship with the wrong guy? Could you tell it wasn't going to work from the first time you saw them together, but she had no idea? Taking a look at the relationships of others can be the beginning of looking more clearly and subjectively at our own decisions, and the real reasoning behind them.

At the end of the day, it's always going to be easier to perceive someone else's poor choices than our own. It's not a simple act to look deep within ourselves and answer hard questions, like: *why did we join into a union with this person?*

Naturally, everyone has their own version of events, but for so many women, marriage is for the sake of Mrs. This book shares the true stories of marriage and separation, and the lessons learned along the way.

They're taken directly from the mouths of the women who went through it. From all of the joy and happiness that was put into the wedding day, and then the long cold lonely nights after the honeymoon; this book details it all, from the perspectives of three women, from three different walks of life.

All three of whom – Darla, Rachael, Marilyn – have tasted a piece of the marriage vow, which has soured in the years that followed. Their stories are here to learn from, as each woman eventually discovered why their marriages fell apart. Learn from their troubles and tears, feel their pain, and grow along with them as they learned from their experiences, and you too can avoid these issues in your own relationships.

And by the end of this book, will you still want to find Mr. Right and get married? That's certainly your choice. Since I have not found my perfect fit, I have made a conscious decision to refrain from the institution of marriage until God Himself speaks in an audible voice telling me to go ahead! But whatever you decide, by thinking honestly and openly about what you want, you'll be one step closer to knowing why you want to get married and why you want to couple with this person, starting a life together.

For some it might be the search for that "perfect" mate. For others it's the hope of a happy-ever-after. For others still, they're chasing the dream of being given away in a white dress. This book isn't here to judge. It achieves nothing to stand on the sidelines and cast stones; instead, through sharing, we can help each other on the journey that lies ahead, and ultimately help ourselves to make the best choices we can, be the best partners we can be, and build the strongest marriages we possibly can.

Darla

Marriage is a skill. One which I've never possessed, though I've tried my luck plenty--five times. And although I've had many beautiful weddings, I've never once actually been married. The way I see it now; marriage is like a partnership--two people on the same team with the same goals. And I've never been on the same page as my husbands.

Every time I wed, it was like I somehow knew things weren't going to work out. I had my doubts from the beginning, but something kept pushing me forward, propelling me to walk down the aisle one more time and dismiss these "pre-wedding jitters."

While I can see the definite faults in my relationships now, I certainly couldn't (or didn't want to admit them to myself) at the time.

Reflecting back, I saw being married as the ultimate goal in a relationship and part of me felt compelled to see things through. Unfortunately, that's not a good reason to get married. And even less of a reason to stay married.

Bottom line: there was no good reason for me to get married. The only argument for the official union: It was all for the sake of being Mrs...

I wish I could say it started with a spark. I wish I could blame some burning passion. I wish I could say I'd been swept off my feet, fallen for my husband(s) at first sight--any of them! But it was nothing like that. Nothing like a fairy tale.

In my experience, real life isn't very much like a fairy tale at all. There's certainly no guarantee of a happy ending. But that didn't stop me from looking for one... This is my story:

1

I stared at my books, sprawled across the library table, as I tried to shake off the feeling that someone was watching me. But I couldn't.

My first inclination was to look up. I lifted just my eyes, hoping to subtly catch whoever it was. But all attempts at subtleness were cast aside when I couldn't spot anyone out of place. My head turned, checking all around me, but again, there was no one. Nothing out of the ordinary, just rows and rows of bookshelves in every direction.

I sighed to myself, enjoying the sense of relief that washed over me. I could finally relax and focus on my studies. It had been a summer from hell and I was grateful to be back at university, even with the heavy workload of a double major in political science and philosophy. Sure it was a challenge, but after the summer that I'd had--anything was easier than that.

My head ducked back down into my books as I tried to delve into the material at hand. Yet, there was still one part of my mind I couldn't rein in. The part that was still trying, in vain, to process everything that had happened, that wanted answers, that wanted to understand why.

I couldn't help but wonder how it had all turned out so wrong? Six months ago I was walking down the aisle to be married. And now, I was a divorcee. What kind of woman has a six month marriage, I thought, feeling my self-esteem dropping by the second. The whole thing had been a nightmare. My stomach rumbled as if in agreement. Or out of hunger--I shouldn't have skipped lunch.

I shook my head, fanning out my long brown hair as I tried to ignore the sudden feeling of a set of eyes upon me once again.

I was dreaming, I told myself, as I tried to pretend it was all in my head. Whoever it was, surely they weren't looking at me--it must be someone browsing the shelves for books. But regardless of what I told myself; instinctively, I looked up again, determined to pinpoint whoever it was this time for sure.

I saw him right away. His rich, dark brown eyes were fixed in my direction, staring right back at me.

Quickly, I looked back down at my books--why was he staring at me? I looked back up again, certain he would've moved on, having been caught peeping. But there he was, still staring straight at me!

What was his problem? Why was he staring? I shook out my hair as if I could shake away the unwelcome stares and forced myself to look away once more. Whatever game he was playing, I didn't have time for it. My course load was too heavy to waste time on this sort of thing. I needed to ignore him and pretend this wasn't happening.

In theory, that was the plan. In reality, some plans are not so easy to keep. Every few minutes, my eyes would peek up just the smallest amount to check if he was still watching. And he was. Without a doubt, he was focused on me and hadn't stopped gawking!

Strange thoughts danced around in my head. Why would anyone behave like this? What kind of man would just sit and stare?

My body shifted awkwardly in the stiff library chair as I felt his eyes holding their gaze. The attention was intense and I was beyond uncomfortable with the situation.

Maybe he's a stalker, I mused, looking for any rational explanation. I looked up again hoping he'd finally got bored--no luck. Maybe he was just plain crazy. Who knows, I thought, as a frustrated groan escaped from me. And another rumble from my stomach.

I slammed my books shut; no way any real work was getting done now. Not that it mattered--I was tired and hungry. Today was definitely not the right time to start my diet. I really shouldn't have skipped lunch. But at least I could fix that problem fairly easily. Something nice and spicy would be perfect. I knew just the place.

It was getting easier to ignore his longing stare as I packed up my things. Books, notebooks and pens were all thrown haphazardly into my bag, speed more important than tidiness. I wanted out of there, out of his line of sight. For all I knew, he had some scheme and was just waiting for his moment, I thought to myself.

It was then, when I turned to see where he was one last time, that I noticed--he'd finally left.

I exhaled loudly, feeling better by the second. Staring strangers were more often a start to a horror film than a romance movie. And I wasn't interested in either.

At least that was over; I told myself. And now surely I deserved a treat for getting through it in one piece. As I walked to the corner pub, I dreamed of ordering one of their yummy, tangy fish fillet sandwiches.

My shoulders had lost all of the tension from the library on the walk over to the pub. That was more than enough drama for one day, I thought as I pulled open the heavy wooden door, hearing the sounds of laughter within.

But I stopped in my tracks as soon as I crossed the threshold--there he was--the first set of eyes I saw were the same ones that had been staring at me in the library! Right here, again. Sat at a booth over to one side; the man watched my every move.

Well, this time he was going to face the music! You can't very well just go around staring at people, I thought to myself. And I certainly wasn't being chased out of a second place because of him! The smell of the food wafted over as another customer walked by--it sang to my empty stomach. No doubt, I was staying.

Still, even knowing I was in the right, my heart was racing--anger and fear mixed with confusion as I tried to figure out what to say to this man. I paused, to compose myself, smoothing out my hair to calm my nerves.

The nerves didn't settle; if anything, they multiplied with each step I took towards his table. But I held my head up high, determined not to be intimidated.

"You again! What are you looking at? What's your problem?" I said, my voice rising in volume as I got going. I tried to keep it level, but it was impossible to hide the severity. At least he'd know exactly how freaked out I was feeling about all of this, I thought. "You're creeping me out!"

I stared right back at him ignoring the impish grin that was now crossing his face. But other than the childish smirk, the man didn't react and said nothing in reply.

"Well, what are you doing? It was the same nonsense in the library! Do you think you know me?" I pressed, much to his amusement. The man grinned wider as my irritation grew.

We stared at each other in silence for a few moments; no way was I going to break the stand-off--he was the one who needed to answer for his actions, not me.

The man waited until he was sure I was finished venting before answering in a soft voice, "Don't be angry. I only stare at things that are delightful. And you are so much more than that. You're absolutely gorgeous!" He smiled again.

"Who are you?" I asked incredulously. Flattered as I was for a split second, this guy was still a stranger who'd been spying on me.

"Adam Gilmore," he said, holding out his hand for me to shake. "We share chemistry class together."

My lips pursed for a moment as I pondered all the faces I could recall from the large class. But his wasn't one I could place amongst my fellow students.

"I sit behind you," he paused, waiting to see if that jogged my memory.

But it didn't.

"I guess you never noticed me..."

I shrugged, feeling unexpectedly bad for not remembering him. But he kept talking, unaware of my sudden shift in emotions.

"Anyway, I did not mean to scare you. I was only admiring you," Adam said.

I felt my face flush involuntarily; I was unaccustomed to random compliments from strangers.

Adam smiled as he continued his flattery. "I read your article in the school newspaper and I liked it. You're a strong activist for human rights--I respect that."

"Uh, thanks," I said quietly, growing more and more confused by this man who had totally disarmed me. I wasn't sure what I'd been expecting when I approached him; maybe a confrontation, maybe an apology, but certainly not a wooing.

"My intentions are not to be rude. Let me apologize if I came across that way," Adam continued.

"Sure," I replied, not really sure at all how to answer.

"Would you please join me for a meal?" he asked, pointing to the bench opposite him in his booth. "Let's get to know each other, shall we?"

"No. I can't. I've got so much to do. But maybe some other time," I answered, regaining my composure.

"Oh, Darla, please. I've seen the back of your head in class and now resorted to staring at you from a distance, just to admire your beauty. Won't you please indulge me and stay awhile so I can see your face, close up." He was silly and foolish with his words, but there was something sincere about him. I laughed awkwardly at his persistence.

"Really, I can't," I said again, though my stomach groaned in opposition to my words.

"You're hungry. You want to stay. Just for a quick meal. My treat," he said, waving the waitress over with one hand. "Could we get another menu and--" he paused, looking at me as he continued, "What would you like to drink, Darla?"

I sighed. "A coke." Just a drink, Darla, I told myself.

"A coke and another menu, thank you," Adam reiterated before the waitress left.

"Just a drink."

"You have to eat," he pressed, not letting up an inch. "Come on. It's just a meal and you do have to eat. You can't win that point. Please, join me," Adam pleaded. He stared at me with his big brown eyes as if they were trying to convince me, wordlessly. He was not going to take no for an answer.

"Fine," I conceded, mainly out of curiosity I think. I put my bag down gently on the floor and sat opposite him in the plush booth.

"Thank you, Darla," he said smiling, like he'd just won a prize.

I smiled back, feeling strangely excited by this unexpected turn of events. "So, tell me, Adam," I started, feeling bolder by the second. If he wanted to get to know me, he would see the real me, I thought to myself with a laugh. "Are you a student at the university? Really? Or do you just hang out there to stalk young girls like me?" I asked playfully though still ever serious.

Adam smiled back unfazed. "No, I truly am a student. I do sit behind you in chemistry."

"I hope so. I'll be checking in class on Thursday. What are you studying then?"

"Petroleum Engineering."

"Sounds hard."

"It can be. What about you?" he asked.

"Poli Sci and philosophy."

"That sounds like quite a handful as well," he joked.

I smiled again, feeling the tension release a little more every minute we were together.

"Where are you from, Adam?" I asked, his accent clearly suggesting he was an international student.

"The Caribbean. It's lovely here but nothing compared to my home. There it's beautiful--the ocean, the beaches, the colors... Have you ever been?" he asked, leaning in across the table.

"No. But I love to travel," I grinned playfully.

"Well then, Darla, I'll have to take you there some day."

Adam's whole disposition was cool and relaxed, an embodiment of the carefree Caribbean attitude come to life.

I smiled in response, unsure if he was serious or not.

"Tell me more about yourself. Are you an undergraduate? You look so young and are so beautiful, surely you must be."

"A graduate student actually," I answered.

"Myself as well. See we have something in common already," he grinned, looking pleased with himself.

"One thing anyways."

"Well, perhaps there's more?" he said. "Not that there's much time to ourselves in graduate school, but what do you like to do for fun? I'm so curious about you."

His sincerity brought with it a genuine sense of comfort and I started to relax, chatting freely with him, forgetting all my anger towards him.

"Nothing too interesting," I said dismissively. "I like to cook, I go to church. And I wasn't kidding about liking to travel--exploring, a sense of adventure, I guess."

Adam stared at me again without saying anything as if he was trying to ferret out if I was telling the truth. "Really?" he questioned.

"About which part?"

"All of it?"

"That's easy--yes. To all of it. I love to cook... whenever I have the time," I said, laughing at the fish sandwich that was now placed in front of me. "And I'm really active in my church," I said with a shrug. "Why?"

"I am as well."

"Christian, you mean?"

"Yes, I'm very involved in my church community. And in the kitchen, too. Who would have thought--we actually have quite a bit in common, it would seem," he added. His grin was wider now; he looked as if it would be impossible to dampen his spirits at this point.

As it turned out, we did have a lot in common and we started to see each other regularly, meeting at the pub for dinner and hanging around on campus together.

"Darla, where've you been? You were meant to call me hours ago," said Fatima as soon as I picked up my phone. Friends always keep you honest.

"With Adam," I replied. "We had lunch again today."

"Isn't that the second time this week? I thought you weren't interested in him."

"I'm not," I said defensively.

"It sure doesn't sound like that..."

"Fatima--I'm not attracted to him. There's no warm fuzzy feelings or sparks of any kind. And he's twelve years older than me!"

"Be serious, Darla. You've been spending a lot of time with him for someone you're not--"

"There's no chemistry," I explained, cutting her off. "None at all!"

She paused briefly before answering, "Maybe not, but there's something about him you like."

I sighed, not sure how to explain our relationship--it wasn't romantic in any sense of the word. "I do like him. But we're friends. We hang out. That's it, Fatima. He's a simple, plain, old fashioned kind of man. He's not a boyfriend, nothing like that."

"If you're sure," she said.

And I was. Adam wasn't my type, if I had a type. Despite all the fun we had together, the last seven or eight months enjoying each other's company, I never saw myself with Adam in that kind of way. He was the boy in school who no one noticed; someone who blended in with the woodwork--and I was looking for someone who stood out, someone who was the center of it all.

Yet, despite Fatima's constant reminding, I still remained friends with Adam, even though it wasn't leading anywhere in my heart. And he didn't seem to mind. In fact, I think he just liked spending time with me.

I smiled as I looked in the mirror of the dressing room. "What do you think?" I asked Adam, as I opened the door.

"Very nice. It brings out your beautiful eyes," he said without pause.

"You're too much, honestly," I said, laughing at his liberal compliments, not taking him too seriously.

Adam smiled in return. "Now was there one more you wanted to try? The one I picked out for you? Take your time, of course."

"I'll try it on. I'm not in a rush, don't worry about that," I said. Both of us loved to shop and shopping together was even better--an extra pair of eyes for a second opinion, or an extra set of hands to carry the bags. We had so much fun, and somehow we never seemed aware of the time--it just flew by whenever we were hanging out. It was an easy, comfortable way of life.

"Are we really seeing that movie tonight?"

"The comedy?" I asked, as I tried on the last outfit.

"Yes," Adam answered sternly. While we generally shared the same tastes in movies, I enjoyed comedies much more than he did.

"Oh come on--It'll be fun! I bet even you will laugh," I said with a quiet chuckle. "What do you think?" I asked, stepping out with the most ridiculous hat on to brighten up the dullest of outfits. The large brimmed floppy hat might have been tasteful if it hadn't been so garishly colored, or clashed so dramatically with the proper, old-fashioned dress that Adam had picked out. I laughed out loud as I opened the door.

"Darla," Adam frowned.

I laughed louder, unable to help myself. Sometimes a good laugh is just what you need. For me at least. Adam didn't feel the same way.

"Shhhh," he shushed me with a scolding look. "Darla, you aren't a child. Stop behaving like one," he chastised.

I nodded, biting my lip to muffle the giggles and quickly closed the dressing room door. Once behind closed doors, my laughter escaped once more.

I heard Adam groaning just outside. He wasn't fond of laughter. He'd often get upset if I laughed too loud or too long. Silly, really--what an odd reaction to happiness. It was as if he hadn't heard the old adage that laughter is the best medicine.

Perhaps he was saving the best joke for last? Only he wasn't joking when he said to me, with all seriousness, "Marry me, Darla."

I smiled, flattered but much more rational than Adam, I shook my head. "Adam, we've been over this."

"I thought you would have come to your senses--now that you've had a chance to think about it some more."

"How many times do I have to tell you--I like you. A lot. But not in that way. A hundred percent, absolutely--no. No, I won't marry you. I can't. It would not be fair to either of us. I don't love you like that, like I believe a wife should love a husband."

I was beginning to feel like a broken record, Adam had proposed so many times over the past few weeks. Still, even as I said those words, visions of white dresses, of roses and bows, and fancy invitations danced in my head for the briefest of seconds. And that word--Mrs... But I wasn't in love with Adam--I couldn't pretend to be even if I wanted to.

Nevertheless, he was persistent, just as he was at the pub that first night when I met him.

"Are you ready?" Adam asked, waiting for me outside my office at the university.

A few undergraduate students walked by, their curiosity no longer piqued by this familiar face in this part of campus. Adam was always around as much as he could be. He was keen to know what I was doing, interested in spending any free minute he had with me.

"I'm just packing up."

"Here, let me help you," he said, stepping into my tiny office space. The room was cramped, three desks for all the graduate students in the political science area to share. Thankfully it was just me here today.

"Where to tonight? What restaurant should we try?" I asked, as I looked around the room for my things, which were sprawled everywhere.

"Well, there's that new Thai place downtown, or we could go for a curry?" he countered.

"Maybe Thai. You've spoiled me with your Indian cooking, you know," I said, rifling through my papers on the desk, looking for a notebook absentmindedly. "You're a superb cook, Adam. You've got all my favorite Indian dishes mastered. I love it when you fix me up a curry," I said, smiling to myself--at the thought of a warm spicy meal and because I'd just found the notebook I'd been looking for.

"Got it," I said, turning around. And then suddenly, Adam was right in front of me.

There were no words spoken on his part. He simply grabbed my waist and pulled me towards him. His lips found mine and he kissed me. Funnily enough, I wasn't as angry as I thought I would be by his forwardness. Not that I was into the kiss, my heart wasn't there; but I was naturally curious as to what it would be like, what it would feel like. And it felt okay. A regular kiss, but without any of the desire or passion I'd come to expect from the act.

It was not the only time we kissed. But each time was the same for me--the spark, the chemistry, the attraction simply wasn't there. This wasn't a romantic relationship now or ever in my mind. There was no way I could see him in that light, or anything other than simply a good friend.

However, Adam wasn't on the same page as me. In his mind, we were 'together' and every moment we spent with each other was filled with tension brought about by the impromptu kisses and his recent proposals.

I remember that it was a warm day, the sun was hot outside, casting a bright light into my small dining room. Adam was over and he'd worked his magic in the kitchen.

"Thanks for cooking tonight, Adam. The curry was delicious."

"Anytime, my love," he said, naturally.

"Adam, please--"

"I'm sorry, I'm sorry," he said cutting me off.

"It's just--"

"I know," he answered quickly, as if he didn't need to hear my answer again. He'd heard it before. Or maybe he hadn't. He just didn't want to hear it. Yet, I'd said it hundreds of times before it seemed--we weren't right for each other, I didn't see him that way--I couldn't even recall how long I'd been trying to convince him of this.

"Darla," he said my name softly. "Darla, I know you don't see it now--yet--but I have been praying, and listening to God."

I looked over to Adam, who was seated in the opposite chair; the sun beams shining on his smooth skin. They gave him an almost angelic glow.

"What did he say?" I asked, suddenly calmer than before. It was as if the sun and the rays had mellowed my spirit, suspending me in a different space of some kind.

"Darla, I know without a shadow of a doubt that I want you to be my life partner, my beloved wife."

I look back at him, unable to mount a defense this time. For whatever reason, my guard was down. And I was listening, truly open to his words on another level altogether.

"My Darla, will you marry me?" asked Adam.

At that moment, in a different zone than ever before, the words I never expected came from my lips: "Yes, Adam, I will."

2

As I looked into the mirror in the dressing room, my eyes couldn't focus on the woman in the white dress who was staring back at me. What had I done, I wondered, running the silky fabric through my fingers. Sure, I might be ready to get married again, but to Adam Gilmore? My hands shook, like a physical reminder of my shaky resolve in going through with this.

The marriage didn't make much sense when I thought about it; as a result, I rarely did. Only when I was on my own. Only when the reality of afterwards crept in. After the white dress, after the ceremony, after the reception and the celebrations...

My breath hitched as I unzipped the dress and changed back into my everyday clothes. Why *had* I said yes, I asked myself, thinking back to his proposal. How had we gotten to this point of walking down the aisle?

I closed my eyes, trying to feel the same feeling I had on that day. I remembered those feelings, though I didn't seem to have them now. That split-second when I'd said yes, it was like an out-of-body experience, as if someone else had taken over my actions and thoughts. My heart pounded with adrenaline. There was such a surge of emotions coursing through me--was it love, all of a sudden taking hold of me? Or was it something else entirely? Maybe--it was possible--it could be love?

That was the best answer I could sum up at the time. And even now, I was no further ahead.

Perhaps, over time, the engagement would at least please my parents on some level, I thought, trying to see the positive in all of this. They'd been quite surprised when we told them, and not entirely supportive. At least whenever I was alone with them, they hadn't shied away from voicing their doubts as well. Maybe they thought I'd done this because of them, I thought, trying to work through everything in my head. Only the week before I'd finally agreed to marry Adam, they'd spoken to us both about the subject.

Pausing before I left the dressing room, it dawned on me. Was that it? Is it possible that this was actually why I was going ahead with marrying Adam? I replayed the conversation back in my head...

The four of us had just finished dinner at my parents' home. They'd watched us throughout the meal; I could see it in their eyes even though they said nothing up until dessert.

"You know you two--" started my mom. "I can see that you're very close to each other. *Very* close."

"Please, mother," I pleaded quietly, blushing as she spoke.

"No. No. Come on now, Darla. We only have your best interest at heart," said my father, backing her up.

"I know," I mumbled.

"Well. There comes a point when you need to handle things responsibly. And I think you're probably there," said my father, as I blushed an even deeper shade of red. My mother carried on without missing a beat.

"You know once you start that heavy petting, one thing leads to another. Remember, our aim is to please God." My mom spoke softly, but there was no mistaking the seriousness in her voice.

I could feel myself blushing again in the dressing room, overcome by the sensations of reliving the embarrassment and guilt from weeks ago. Was that it then? Had their sermon set me on this course to run down the aisle once more? This would be my second marriage and Adam's third--surely by now, we were both smart enough to recognize real love and not repeat the same mistakes again. No matter what pressure and guilt was thrown at us from third parties.

Besides, nothing was ever clear cut. The engagement hadn't really appeased my parents anyhow. Just today we'd had another awkward lunch together, right before my dress fitting. It was lose-lose with them at the moment.

I poked at my food, unable to look my father in the eye. Visits with my parents hadn't been good since we'd announced our pending nuptials.

"What are his intentions, Darla?"

"Dad, stop. He proposed. He wants to get married. Those are his intentions. Isn't this what you want? Isn't this the right way to do things?"

"I want you to be happy, to settle down, yes. But I don't want you to settle..."

"I'm not," I said quietly, unconvincingly.

"Are you sure?"

"Of course I'm sure," I snapped defensively. But my palms were sweating.

My father paused a minute before continuing. He put his fork down and waited until I looked up.

"Darla, you see him almost all the time. Every day, every other day--you must enjoy his company, but something isn't right. You're not... happy. I don't want to see him take advantage of you. And I don't want you to waste your time with someone you don't love."

I sighed, wanting to defend our relationship. But the words wouldn't come out. I couldn't defend it. Not really. "I'm not being taken advantage of. I'm making the decision to get married, Dad. I'm calling the shots. The wedding will be lovely."

"I don't care about the wedding, Darla," he snapped. "What about after--can you see yourself with him after the ceremony? Living here, living there? Do you even have a plan as to where you'll live? This is forever, Darla. It's *supposed* to be for forever. Is this really how you see your life?"

I nodded, not really hearing his words. It was a heady sensation--I was elated but frightened by the thought of getting married again. Elated about the wedding, frightened about the marriage.

We were planning to live in the Caribbean--but while Adam obviously knew what to expect, I simply had no idea. Images of turquoise water and white sand beaches flooded my mind... Yet, truthfully, it was impossible to picture the reality; there was so much unknown about this future, our future.

"Darla. Darla!"

I shook my head, my father's voice intruding on my mini-daydream.

"Listen, Dad. Don't make a scene, okay? This is going ahead--we're having a wedding. Please try to be nice to him," I pleaded.

My father said nothing in return. He looked away from me--not wanting to concede in any way.

"Mom, talk to him, okay?" I added desperately, looking to her for support. She was usually a quiet bystander in these conversations. But her motives weren't out of support for me. She had her own plans--grandchildren--and the best way to achieve them was through me becoming a wife.

Of course, there was another person who had a say in this matter. And that was Adam, who clenched his jaw and looked firmly at me that evening. He had questions for me, too.

"Darla," Adam started, "have you thought any more about the wedding? I can't wait to be married to you."

I smiled at the start of the sentence but was flinching on the inside by the end. The wedding--focus on the first step, the best step, I thought, smiling to myself. I hadn't told him about my impromptu visit to the wedding dress shop. It was more about me dipping my toe in the water than making a decision on what to wear.

"I don't need anything too flashy. Just something small, intimate even. What were you thinking?" I asked, stirring around the pad Thai noodles on my plate.

"Is it okay?" Adam asked, pointing to my food.

"Delicious. I was just distracted by your question." If nothing else, there would always be a nice meal on our table--there was no denying, Adam was a whiz in the kitchen.

"Good, I'm glad. As for the ceremony, Darla, whatever you wish for, we shall make it happen. A small gathering sounds lovely."

"Will anyone come from the Caribbean?" I asked, wondering aloud.

"We can invite them, if you like."

"Yes, I would like that. But let's keep it small, just a few friends and family," I said, a picture already taking shape in my head.

"Your church seems like it might suit better than mine," Adam said raising his voice like it was a question, like he was searching for whatever option I most wanted to hear.

"That works, Adam. I'm sure Pastor Talmadge will agree to marry us. And you're right, the church will be just perfect--cozy but tasteful. What do you think, it holds maybe 40 people? That sounds like a good number. And maybe right after morning service on a Sunday? Or is that--" I hesitated, not wanting to disappoint him.

But Adam jumped right in, completely on the same page as me. "That's perfect, Darla. I love it."

Thankfully Pastor Talmadge agreed as well. And we set the date.

In retrospect, that was the easy part--deciding to have a small wedding and actually having one were very different things.

"Fatima, I need your help," I tried to talk slowly, forcing myself to calm down a little so she'd be able to understand me. "Listen, this has gotten out of hand. It's nothing like Adam and I had planned!"

I had dialed her number so quickly, I wondered if I'd gotten it wrong. But then she finally answered, "Are you talking about your wedding?"

"Yes," I squeaked.

I heard her sigh from the other end. "I know, it's definitely getting ridiculous."

"What am I supposed to do?" I asked, while visions of white ribbons and roses still danced through my head. Even though I knew we were way off budget and the plan entirely, part of me didn't care, part of me still wanted it all.

"Let's look at this logically, Darla. I thought you said you wanted a small, quaint wedding. Am I right?" Fatima waited patiently until I answered.

"Yes. That was the plan," I agreed, cringing already at the stern voice that was coming. Fatima could be so pragmatic, so focused.

"Well, that doesn't seem to be what you're arranging. What started out being quaint is fast becoming more like a wedding for the rich and famous," she said, chiding me.

"I know," I answered, sounding more and more timid by the second.

"Okay, okay," she finally said. "Let's look at it together. We can figure it out, Darla, not to worry."

"Oh thank you, Fatima. Thank you."

"Now where do we start? Hmmm. Let's meet up later today and sort this all out, okay? Bring the budget and all the wedding plans you have. We should be able to work from that."

"Thanks, Fatima. I mean it. You're a life saver. Our usual coffee shop? Two o'clock? That should give me enough time for a good chat and to stop by to pick up the invitations on my way home. Did I tell you they're ready?"

"Oh Darla," said Fatima. She sighed before she continued. "Okay. Two it is. See you then."

Well, if there was a way out of this mess, Fatima would be able to help me find it. She'd managed to stay on budget and stick to the plan for her own wedding--she'd been a real stickler about it, too. Hopefully she could help me get my own back on track.

Only, we were so far gone from the original plan, it was hard to even see a way back to it. I knew what my problem was and so did she--my free-spirit attitude. Instead of making me stick to my plans, Fatima had been indulging me in a little flexibly. And rightly so--it wasn't like I didn't know that I should stick to the plans and budget, I just didn't really care about doing either. I wanted to spread my wings, and my wants cried out so loudly they seemed like needs; as a result, I was now in this mess.

Unfortunately, even after Fatima and I met, we could only do so much to rein in the purse strings. Almost everything had already been booked. The game plan was to simply stay on point for any other decisions that came up. Secretly, I crossed my fingers than none would--sticking to that decision would be a challenge.

Even if we weren't able to stick to the original budget or plans, at least I'd managed to pick up the invitations on the way home from the coffee shop.

I opened the lid of the crisp white box; Adam peered over my shoulder curious himself at how they'd turned out.

"Oooo," I sighed as I lifted the tissue paper from the top, exposing the cursive, old-fashioned print of the writing below. I held my breath as I picked up the thick paper, my eyes soaked in the red and white colors as my fingers ran over the classic design. They were perfect.

"Beautiful, Darla. Aren't they?" said Adam, still watching over my shoulder.

"Yes. Beautiful. Just perfect. And our photos--" I added, picking up one of the engagement prints we'd selected to include with the invitations. "They turned out so well." I smiled, remembering what a fun time we'd had that day. The photographer had suggested the pose--our cheeks were pressed together as if they were kissing--it was sweet. And it looked so happy, so carefree, so far removed from where I'd been this afternoon. Reality rarely lived up to moments like that.

"Come on then, let's get started, shall we?" asked Adam. "I can put the package together and you can go through the invite list and address the envelopes?"

"Sure," I said eagerly. "Let's get set up on the floor. That might be easiest."

And so we spent several hours sitting on the floor, stretched out in front of the coffee table, addressing wedding invitations. This is what a marriage should feel like--working together as a team, I thought to myself.

Though, those happy times seemed worlds away as I stood at the back of the church, my heart racing, my palms sweating as I tried to smooth out the wrinkles in my white satiny dress. They wouldn't disappear, and neither would my doubts and concerns. Yes, everything was ready, every detail decided, every little thing in its place. The wedding was perfect, would be perfect, if only I could calm myself down.

Suddenly, it felt like my feet were locked in place and the walls of the church entrance were closing in on me. I closed my eyes, willing every part of my body to get with the program. This was it--time to get married. I just had to put one foot in front of the next and get down the aisle. I could do this, I thought. Who was I trying to convince--only myself.

My eyes opened as I heard my cue. Mrs. Greenwood was playing the organ pipes, the wedding march; my guests were on their feet, turning to catch the first glimpse of the bride, to watch my grand entrance.

My heart pumped faster and I struggled to catch my breath once more.

"You ready?" my father asked, taking my arm.

I nodded, unable to pull together even a simple answer.

Somehow I managed to make my feet move, shuffling forward, and we walked down the aisle. One foot in front of the next. Step after step until suddenly my feet had a mind of their own. Again, they just stopped, as if they'd been cemented to the floor. My body jerked to a sudden standstill in response. I was paralyzed by fear, or doubts, or some sort of inner protective state of preservation.

My father turned to me, a worried look in his eye. "Darla?" he whispered, fraught with concern.

My stomach twisted and turned, the contents threatening to come back up, right there in the aisle, on the floor of the church, in front of everyone. I pushed aside the urge to heave and forced myself to ignore every other emotion that was invading my weak sense of calm.

Heavy tears rolled quickly down my face; the veil, now wet, stuck to my cheeks. This wasn't what it was supposed to be like, I thought to myself, unable to suppress the next round of tears that fell.

It was my father's voice that broke the spell of this quiet panic attack. Still looking at me, he squeezed my arm a little tighter and smiled softly. "I know what you're feeling, sweetie. You don't love that man. You don't."

"Daddy," I whispered.

"Who are you fooling?" he said sternly. "Come on, now. I can send you on back to the dressing room. I'll gladly stop this charade." He nodded, as if he somehow thought that was what I wanted.

"No, Daddy! Please!" I said in a hushed voice.

"You know in your heart--"

"Stop--look at all the people," I said, cutting him off. "Look at Adam. He's waiting for me."

"It's your choice, Darla. We can do this your way," he agreed reluctantly.

And we did. I inhaled deeply, as if I could suck in a dose of courage, and resumed our walk down the aisle. All the way to the front. To Adam.

Instead of listening to the warning signs, I plowed ahead towards our wedding vows; instead of respecting intuition, what I look at as the presence and guidance of the Holy Spirit, I chose to label it as wedding bell jitters, simply a case of classic cold feet. My feet were so cold, they literally froze to the ground beneath them. But, truly, I wasn't fooling anyone. My body didn't want to be here anymore than my feet. And still I wouldn't listen, I didn't want to. I had to do it Darla's way. I was determined to be married.

Most of the people in the crowd looked puzzled and had started to whisper as they'd noticed my less than composed façade. I'm sure they were curious as to why there was an unannounced stop in the middle of the wedding march, but with each step forward, the curious whispers gave way to the usual ooos and ahhhhs. Somehow I'd managed to regain my composure and pushed my nerves aside; I looked every inch the part as we proceeded down the aisle to my future husband.

Though I remember every word of the ceremony, in the moment, it seemed as if time stood still. One minute I was walking down the aisle and the next thing I knew, the minister was announcing us to the full house of our friends and family.

"It is my honor to pronounce you husband and wife. You may now kiss the bride."

Adam leaned in quickly to kiss me. I smiled in response, suddenly feeling giddy that I'd made it through the ceremony. And that was the hardest part. I was now Mrs. Adam Gilmore.

The rest of the afternoon passed without another incident--it was easy to brush aside any hesitations or worries now--we were married, it was done. My cold feet were left far behind as I'd dived in headfirst. And with the reception up next, there were so many details to see to that it was easy to forget my earlier anxieties.

As we turned around, I got my first real look at the crowd of people sitting in the pews, supporting us today. All of our friends and family had come out to be there for us. Almost all. My eyes ran over the faces, looking for those whom I'd recognize only from photos--they weren't there. None of Adam's family had shown up for the ceremony. Not one. How could that be, I wondered. How could no one from Adam's list turn up? Not even his own children? A little red flag tried to pop up in my mind but I ignored it; we were married now. It didn't matter. They were missing out, not me.

Our wedding had been absolutely out of this world. And the wedding reception was even better. "Please put your hands together and welcome for the very first time - Mr. and Mrs. Adam Gilmore," said a voice over the loud speaker, welcoming us to our reception.

We held hands as we walked into the hall; though beautifully decorated, the faces of our family and friends took the spotlight. It was like a United Nations gathering--so many different cultures and countries were represented.

"Congratulations, Darla. And you too, Adam." Fatima smiled and gave us a warm hug as soon as we stepped inside. "What do you think? It's turned out beautifully, hasn't it? Everyone is wearing their traditional outfits, just like we asked."

"It's amazing'" I agreed, looking around at all the colors and costumes. My group of friends was quite international, with most originating elsewhere in the world. Fatima and I thought by suggesting they wear their traditional clothing it might create a more interesting and worldly atmosphere, and indeed it had.

"Ladies, you outdid yourself--it's so wonderful. Truly, a beautiful atmosphere in here," said Adam, a bit in awe of the spectacle.

"It was all Fatima. You're the best matron of honor ever. Thank you, Fatima."

My father joined the rest of the family, smiling and chatting with them. Only he knew the secret of my hesitation going down the aisle. It seemed even Adam hadn't noticed the pause. Perhaps it wasn't as long as I'd perceived it to be. Just a split-second, a tiny hurdle that I'd overcome. At least, I'd hoped I'd overcome it. But as I scanned the sea of faces, everyone from my past, yet nobody from Adam's, I felt the resurgent of my doubts over our future together.

As I was whisked around the room, talking to everyone, the noise of the reception clouded any thoughts that I was having. Besides, I honestly thought that once Adam and I returned from our honeymoon all of my doubtful feelings would finally vanish for good. Though, like seeds, they grew instead and took root inside my mind. Could I really spend the rest of my life with this man?

3

"Will there be tiny feet running through the house soon, you two?" My mother wasted no time in asking us about grandchildren.

I turned to look at Adam, begging him with my eyes to not make this conversation any worse.

"What she means is: when are you two going to start a family?" my dad clarified, though there was no need. We knew exactly what my mother had been asking. She'd mentioned her hopes before the wedding and even on our actual wedding day--it was to be expected. She brought it up at every visit.

"I know what she means, Dad. And no, there's no news. We're not having kids right now," I explained, trying not to sound annoyed.

"I'm ready and willing," Adam added. "And I'm trying to convince your daughter. It's just a matter of time," he said, smiling like he knew he was going to win and that someday he'd be able to say yes we were having a baby.

"We're about to move. *I'm* about to move to another country, and all you want to know is if we're having kids?" I sighed, my stomach dropping as I thought about the next few weeks--moving to the Caribbean, to a house I'd never seen, living next door to Adam's family, most of whom I'd never even met.

"Darla, you're married now," my mother said, as if she could guilt me into procreating.

I ignored her, closing my eyes to calm the sudden onset of nerves.

"I've told her hundreds of time too--our children will be lovely," Adam said, still grinning from ear to ear.

"I know, I know--you already have the names picked out," I mumbled.

"For both boys and girls," he added, with an even wider grin.

"Ugh," I groaned. It's not that I didn't want to be a mother. But there was so much I wanted to do before then. There was more to me than having babies! "It's like everyone suddenly forgets I was going to be a professor. At the university," I moaned feeling a world away from my goal.

"Of course you *were*," my dad said sympathetically, but his tone was almost condescending, as if my professorship would never happen now.

I sighed again, tuning out the rest of the conversation. I'd miss my family, but in some ways, it would be nice to have a change of pace, a different life. With the exception of my career goals being tossed, everything I'd heard about the laid-back tropical life of the Caribbean made it sound like it would fit the bill perfectly. Sunshine, here I come...

I could feel the heat the moment we stepped off the plane. A bright glare shone in through the windows of the small airport that I'd never seen before, as if everything was sun-kissed.

"Adam!" Voices cried out as we stepped out into the open. Within seconds there were people all around us, welcoming us both with open arms.

"Darla? You must be Darla. Oh, we're so glad to finally meet you!" The cacophony of voices blended together, I could hardly figure out who was saying what, there were so many of them; so many faces.

"Come, come, let me take that," said a man, grabbing my bags. "We're family."

Adam smiled and nodded in appreciation to the man, a brother I later found out.

"We're so excited to have you here. We're so glad you came. I can't tell you what a help it will be with the business."

"We're glad to be here," I said, reminding myself to smile. Not that I wasn't happy, it was just a lot to take in.

We stepped out of the old worn-looking airport into the brilliant mid-day sun of the tropics. The beauty of the clear sky, the salt water breeze wafting in from the coast--it was another world. Paradise, perhaps.

When Adam's family first invited us here to help with their diving business, I wasn't sure what to expect. Of course, I knew moving to the Caribbean was a very real possibility when I married Adam, but now we'd gone and done it--suddenly everything seemed surreal. Like I was living in a postcard. My life not my own.

Packing up my things, starting a new life in a different country--it was all very exciting and appealing, but that was on paper. Right now, with the hot sun beating down, warming my skin to the touch; the plan was much more real than ever before.

"Thank you, Darla. Thank you for coming to help out with the diving school," said another voice. Adam's mother came up next to me and took my arm. She was greying and short, but her eyes were full of life. It was written on her face--she was a woman who had lived a full life.

"Of course," I answered automatically.

His mother smiled. Warm and genuine.

"What's it like? Lots of tourists?" I asked, trying to make chit-chat on the way home.

"Yes, mainly tourists, but there are some locals. Did Adam tell you what we do?"

"A little."

"Adam!" she said, reproaching her son. "Well, for the most part, we give tourists diving lessons and then certify the divers once they've passed their course. The waters are beautiful, dear. An exquisite turquoise. And they're as warm as a bath. Everyone comes here from all over the world too, just to dive in our sea." Her pride was evident in her voice--she loved her country, loved her home.

"I'm sure they do," I added, feeling the nerves die down a little and the excitement starting to build again.

"Ah, home," Adam said quietly as we drove along a small winding road towards the oceanfront.

"Your home," his mother said looking at me. She pointed silently to a large house coming up in the distance.

"Is that the family house?" I asked, guessing from the size of residence we were headed towards.

She shook her head. "It will be yours and Adam's."

I felt my mouth drop a little, and then some more as we came nearer.

There on an island adjacent to the beach was a huge house, bigger than I had ever imagined.

"That's ours?" I whispered.

His mother nodded with a smile. "All yours."

"Welcome to your new home," said Adam.

On the surface, an eight-bedroom home just a stone's throw from the beach would be a dream come true for almost anyone, myself included. And superficially that was still true. The islands were beautiful, my home was beautiful. But those two things aside, not everything was dreamy. While I had whiled away hours before the wedding thinking about the ceremony, there was no denying anymore that our relationship had cracks. Time will tell, I thought to myself, hoping for the best as I opened the car door, opened this next chapter of my life.

It was balmy outside, apart from the caress of the gentle breeze of the sea--a welcome relief from the heat. There was so much to do, so much to clean in our large house.

"Darla," Adam called out.

"Yes?" I answered, sipping a coffee as I looked out of the large windows towards the beach. It was the first break I'd taken all morning. I'd managed to clean half the house--of course that meant I was only half finished.

"Darla, have you seen the sand in here?" Adam called from the main entrance.

Of course there was sand, I felt like calling out. We lived by the beach, we lived on the ocean. What did he expect?

"Yes, dear. I'm getting to it."

"What have you been doing all morning?" he asked. I could hear his footsteps coming closer. Surely he wasn't coming to chat just about this?

I sighed, not wanting the fight that I could feel in the air. Tension had replaced the refreshing breeze.

"Well, first I made the coffee. Then our breakfasts, do you remember? But if you mean since you've been at work--I've been cleaning, Adam. That's it."

He looked at me like he wasn't sure if he believed me.

"Why is there so much sand still in--"

"Because I didn't start there," I said, cutting him off. "I decided to start in the bedroom today. Is that okay?" I asked, daring him with my tone to say anything to the contrary.

He didn't answer, but headed for the bedroom.

"You're checking up on me? What--don't you believe me?" I pressed, angered by his ridiculousness.

He said nothing as he came back out. "I do believe you, Darla. I just wanted to check the time." He smiled innocently.

I could feel my skin prickle with anger. "Two years, Adam! We've been married for two years! What on earth would I be doing if I wasn't taking care of things here?"

Adam walked over to me, rubbing his hand along my arm. It was meant to be soothing, or comforting, but it did neither. "Honey, come on. I believe you. I just thought you would have got a little more done by now."

I stared at him with amazement--he couldn't hear it in his voice, the offensive undertone of his comment. Or maybe he could and didn't care. I growled under my breath. "That's all I could manage. Why don't you see what you can get done this afternoon? I think I'll head over to the gift shop. I bet they could use a hand," I said, throwing a few things in my bag.

"Darla, don't," Adam started.

But I ignored his protests.

A minute later, I was out the door.

As soon as the fresh air hit my lungs, it was as if I could finally breathe again. It felt like the first real breath of fresh air I'd had all day, compared to the stifling environment of our home.

It didn't matter that Adam didn't like me working in the small gift shop. I wasn't going there to spite him. I liked working there. It was my escape. In fact, my only escape from the dreary reality that had become my daily life of cleaning, cooking, housework, taking care of my husband--and repeat. Again and again.

"Darla!" shouted my mother-in-law from the front of the diving school. "Good to see you, dear. You coming this way?"

I smiled at her. "I thought you could use an extra hand in the shop?" I offered, walking towards her.

"Of course, dear. Always. You're such a help."

"Thanks," I answered, returning her smile.

"You're welcome here anytime. We hardly see you round," she said, opening the door for me.

"I know, I know. Wow, it sure looks busy," I added, casting my eyes over the people on the beach, diving classes in session.

"Always is in the winter. I don't blame them--who'd want to stay in the cold when you can come down to the islands."

"I know," I agreed. It was easy to fall in love with the Caribbean.

Time flew when I was working at the gift shop, which was constantly bustling with tourists. But it wasn't just the lively, happy atmosphere, the colorful ambiance that was in such stark contrast to my life that made me love being at the shop. There was something about mixing with other people, chatting freely, intelligently, casually; it made me gravitate there whenever I could. The conversation with the divers was stimulating, the company--both diverse and intriguing.

However, today I was still so uptight, it was harder to unwind. I didn't force it; instead I let myself succumb to the task at hand, folding a stack of t-shirts, one after another, as the divers milled around the store.

"Excuse me, Miss?" a deep British voice called out.

I looked up automatically; there was no one else working in the area. "Yes?" I answered with a smile. Good, I thought, something to take my mind off things. I turned around to look for the man who'd called out to me and there before my eyes was a tall, dark, handsome man.

"Can I help you?" I asked, even more willing than usual to offer my assistance.

"I'm looking for an extra towel actually. The guys outside said you might have one behind the counter?" He moved closer as he spoke, as if there were some sort of magnetic attraction between us.

I blinked twice, trying to get my thoughts together to reply, hypnotized by his dark, smooth skin. It was a rich mixture of black coffee and cream that was hard to place.

"Uh, sure thing," I answered, pausing a second too long. "This your first time to the islands?" I asked as we walked towards the counter.

"That's right. Why? Is it that obvious?"

"No, not at all," I answered quickly. "I just don't remember seeing you around here before. I know most of the repeat customers. And the locals." I smiled.

"Well, I'm Collin. Collin Kennedy," he said, holding out his hand formally. "I'll be around for at least a week or so; that'll make me a regular soon enough."

"Nice to meet you, Collin," I answered with a smile, shaking his outstretched hand. "Let me guess--you're from England, aren't you?" I asked unable to stop myself from checking out his taut firm body. Muscles rippled beneath his cotton shirt, padding out his masculine stature.

"Ya, I am actually. Well, to be fair, not originally. My mother's from Ghana and my father's Irish."

I reached down behind the counter, pulling out an extra towel for him.

"What an interesting background. And what do you do there?" I asked, not caring that my question may have come across as prying—some part of me felt beyond compelled to keep the conversation going, embracing this surprise attraction between the two of us.

Collin laughed, maybe a little taken aback by my forwardness, I wasn't sure. "I teach Art History, actually."

"Wow, that's exciting. I love art. Where do you teach?"

"At the University of Bath." He smiled, showing off his brilliant white teeth.

"That's incredible. So what period is your specialty?" I asked, still staring at this beautiful man in front of me.

"Are you serious?" he asked.

"Definitely. I wasn't being polite—I really do like art," I answered, unable to stop smiling myself.

"Impressionism, actually. I didn't catch your name--"

I smiled broadly. "Darla."

"Well, Darla, it was lovely to meet you. Will you be here again tomorrow, before we head out for the dive?"

"I can be," I answered coyly, without thinking about my words.

"I hope to see you then," he said with a nod, before picking up the towel and heading towards the door.

And we did see other again. For every day of Collin's vacation, I found myself working in the gift shop at exactly the right time, an hour or so before the afternoon dive.

The initial sense of magnetism between us only grew with each second spent together. But, it wasn't good for me though. It wasn't good at all for my lonely heart, or my unloved soul, to feel this deeper connection, to see this strong, masculine man, day after day after day, our attraction building to a crescendo.

"Hi, Darla," called out Collin's now familiar voice.

I looked up to see Collin walking towards me, his t-shirt clinging to his wet body. "Hi," I said quietly, having a hard time controlling my thoughts. His chiselled body, already hot and wet, his gorgeous coffee skin, piercing brown eyes; it was all too easy to imagine how things would have played out under different circumstances. How our bodies would have melded together, how his hands would have felt around me, how incredible it would have been to let our emotional connection play out physically in a night full of passion.

These images swirled through my mind, lingering on the details, both real and imagined. I fanned myself with a diving brochure as my thoughts got carried away with themselves.

Darla! What are you thinking, I chastised myself. My cheeks were flaming red, my heart pounding inside my chest, I was beside myself. I felt like a schoolgirl, instead of a married mother! And maybe that was exactly it— neither of those women should be having these passionate thoughts! Get it together, I said to myself, forcing a deep breath through my lungs, praying that would be enough to clear my head. I looked around me discretely—had anyone else noticed my blushing, I wondered? Thankfully, it didn't seem like it. My eyes scanned the shop, looking for anything else to focus on, to give me a chance to pull myself together. There—on the display table, off to the side of the store—I exhaled as I spotted the stack of t-shirts that had been shuffled out of order. I walked with a purpose to the table and busied myself with the trivial matter of neatly folding and refolding the shirts.

I refused to look up from this task, even when the bell rang as the door opened, not wanting to catch his eye again.

"Later," said a quiet British voice, from the other side of the room.

That sweet accent, the thought of those chocolate eyes--I couldn't help myself—I looked up just in time to see Collin wave from the doorway. My cheeks felt like they'd flushed red in the same instant.

Needless to say, after that drama, the rest of the afternoon passed slowly. Even without the visual reminder, Collin's features were engrained in my mind. It took longer than I care to admit to get him out of my head.

But while one minute there was some sense of calm, a feeling of order, a purpose in my life, it switched in a snap as I watched the clock tick down--stress mounted; I'd be expected at home soon. Even on the best of days, I never looked forward to going home after working at the gift shop. And with our earlier spat looming, like it was simply 'paused' until I returned; I hated the idea of going back to Adam even more. Still, as I watched the minute hand inch towards the twelve, I knew it was inevitable. *Unpause.*

"Darla! Where have you been?" Adam snapped, the minute I walked through the door.

"At the gift shop, like I told you before."

"There's no reason to go there. They don't need you at the shop. Anyone could work behind the counter."

"I like going there. It's nice to work a little outside of the house."

"It's completely unnecessary. You should be at home," he said. "You have a hard enough time taking care of this place!"

"Adam," I cautioned, not wanting to go down this road again.

"Darla--you could be the best housewife on the island if you tried a little harder."

I glared at my husband. "I don't care if I'm the best housewife. I don't want to be, that's not my goal in life, Adam."

"You're being so stubborn. You have everything you could want for, but you--"

"I'm what? Not taking care of it? Not enjoying it as you see fit?" I argued.

"You could do so much more, that's all."

"Yes, I could--I just don't envision it being in the housework department, Adam. I didn't go to school to spend all my time dusting and washing and sweeping and cleaning. Who did you think you were marrying?" My voice was raised much higher than I'd planned.

"A woman who loved me," he said curtly. "Who wanted to take care of me and our home, together," he countered.

I closed my eyes, not wanting to admit that maybe we were both at fault, maybe neither of us had thought this marriage through. "I'm going to have a shower," I said, defeated from the argument.

"Good idea. The calendar has a circle on it today," he added as I walked out of the room.

As the water dripped down, washing away the stress of the day, I could feel my anger subsiding, as my tears started to flow. What had happened to my life, I wondered, as I struggled to breathe. It was suffocating here. Each day with him was one day more that I was losing another part of myself. He was always angry when I worked at the shop. When I talked about going out. Whenever I shared any dreams or interests that would take place outside of these four walls. And I'd tried everything to ignite the sparks again, but maybe there just hadn't been any to begin with, I wondered. If we weren't spending time in front of the TV, or in the bedroom, he just wasn't interested. And even though I refused to give into his restrictions, still it felt like I was losing part of myself each and every day I stayed with him. I was listless; I was anti-social--neither by choice. I had lost my zest.

As much as I loved the islands, paradise had become a prison.

"I just want a bit of spontaneity!" I sighed, cradling the phone against my shoulder as I talked to my sister; knowing that in reality it was a lot more than just that. But maybe if something small changed, that would be enough. It would be something anyway.

"What do you mean? Everything can't always be planned. Come on, Darla."

"Everything. Every minute of every day if he could."

"God, that sounds awful."

"You don't know the half of it," I mumbled.

"Pardon?" my sister asked.

I sighed again. "I'm just fed up of it. I feel like I'm on a leash, like every little piece of my life is under his control."

There was a pause on the other end of the line. "Darla, he's always been a bit odd, hasn't he?"

"What do you mean?"

"You know--different. A bit of an airhead, if I'm honest."

"What?" I laughed, having never gotten even a hint that she'd thought that before.

"Sorry, Darla. We all think that. I was talking with Mom the other day--it is kind of what everyone says."

I laughed a little more to myself. Somehow, rather than upset me, the fact everyone else thought this made me feel a bit better about myself. Maybe I wasn't crazy. Maybe it wasn't me in the wrong here. Sure, my initial decision to get married was my fault, but this daily tension, this constant arguing--maybe I wasn't being unrealistic, maybe he really was asking for too much.

"Can I ask you a question?" I asked my sister, hesitating a little.

"Sure. Anything."

"Ugh," I sighed, not wanting to admit this to anyone, but wanting to hear her thoughts at the same time. "Is this normal? He schedules sex. He's so controlling that he circles the days on the calendar that he's free to have sex. Have you ever heard of anything like that?"

There was no answer on the other end of the line. "Sis? You still there?"

"That's a joke right?" she finally said in reply.

"No. Totally not. The calendar's all marked up."

"You have to be kidding. No one does that. No one."

"Adam does," I admitted, quietly.

"Scheduled intimate time! That's insane! What happens on days that aren't circled?"

"I know, right? Nothing. If it's not circled, nothing happens."

"Oh, Darla. That's just crazy. I don't even know whatever to say."

"I know. I used to look forward to those circled days in the beginning, but it's hard to have your desires match a calendar."

"I couldn't do it!" she added. "That's got to be adding to your stress. I see what you mean about no spontaneity! What an absolute airhead!"

I smiled to myself, feeling a little bit more confident in my own sanity. "It does add a bit of conflict. We're supposed to be married, right? I thought it was a partnership of some sort, not his schedule only. What about me, right?"

"It's definitely not supposed to work like that, honey."

"I mean, if I had my say, I'd schedule some exercise time for him--he's starting to get that 'husband gut,'" I added with an impish smile, as my sister laughed aloud.

And that was the problem. He'd become too content, too comfortable, and everything was set to his schedule, his way

Looking back, I often wonder if I would have played my hand differently, if I could do it all over again. Even now, after all this time, I still don't know for sure. Nevertheless, I knew it couldn't go on like this.

Several weeks later, a warm wind blew in through the open doors of the patio. I could taste the salt in the air as it swirled around the house. But something was different this morning--I could just feel it. I wasn't interested in hearing the familiar sounds of the ocean, the waves lapping against the sand, the birds singing in the morning, the people walking along, starting the day.

Soon, this wouldn't be mine anymore. I wasn't as sad about that as I thought. In my heart, I knew I couldn't stay here forever; I could barely stay here much longer at all or I'd lose my mind; I'd lose myself completely.

I'd been up for hours--knowing today was the day. The first day of the end. Soon, I'd no longer be Mrs. Adam Gilmore. My lawyer was ready to file the divorce papers.

Suddenly, a gust of salt air blew through the doors, hitting me with an unexpected force. Woah, I thought, feeling off balance. My hands found their way to the soft white floral couch. My legs buckled as they made their way to it; it took longer than I expected to get my balance back, to feel like myself again. Woozy, dizzy, and, nauseous even--from the wind? No, I argued with myself. Stress, it must just be the stress, I rationalized.

"Darla, where are you?"

"Just out here, Adam."

"Weren't you going to make the coffee? What happened?"

I sighed, wondering if I should rock the boat prematurely or wait until the filing was official. My stomach heaved. "It's coming," I called back, grabbing my abdomen. Not long left--I might as well make the best of it for the time being, seeing as how there's so little time remaining of this life with Adam.

I closed the large double doors overlooking the beach before heading into the kitchen. Grabbing the coffee pot, I quickly put it on the stovetop to percolate. But the smell of the coffee as it brewed rolled my stomach again; I folded in half, covering my mouth with my hand. A groan slipped out through my lips.

"Darla? What's going on?" Adam called out again. Thankfully, he was still in the bedroom.

"It's coming," I answered with as much force as I could manage.

Using whatever energy I could muster, I righted myself, but the nausea hit me once more the moment I smelled the coffee.

"It's ready. It's out here," I called to Adam, taking the pot off the element. Even if I'd wanted to, and I didn't really, there was just no way I could've made that drink for him.

Holding my breath as I left the kitchen, I headed back to the patio doors and opened them again, hoping to usher the coffee smell away.

The sea air quickly did the job, wafting away everything in its path.

I was back on the couch by the time Adam came into the main space en route to the kitchen.

"Darla, what's wrong with you?" he asked, unable to hide his accusatory tone, or maybe he didn't even realize it was there.

"Nothing," I snapped back at him.

"Darla," he said, softer now. "Darla, have you seen yourself? You're green."

"Thanks."

"No, I'm not being rude, I swear. Go look at yourself. Do you feel alright?" he asked, walking over towards me, his mug in hand.

Just then the sea breeze picked up the smell, blowing a gust of coffee scented air towards me--and once again I was doubled over with nausea. I ran for the bathroom, knowing my breakfast wasn't going to stay down this time.

"Darla?" Adam called out after me.

I couldn't be bothered to answer. To hell with him, he didn't need an answer, I thought, wishing whatever this was would just stop ruining my morning.

And then it hit me. I was never nauseous, I was never sick. Don't jump the gun, I thought to myself, refusing to believe in my rash, snap assumption. I closed my eyes and put the guess aside, until I could check, vowing to carry on my day as normally as possible until then.

Thirty minutes later, I'd been to the pharmacy and back already. I watched the minutes on my watch tick by. Two minutes. It seemed like an eternity--it was as if every second that passed was one second closer to sealing my fate.

Positive--and my life would change forever; negative and my life stays the course, which at the moment meant a huge change regardless.

Two minutes were up. I walked over to the stick. I closed my eyes, not wanting to see the result. It didn't have to change my plans, I said to myself, trying to believe that. It didn't matter; either way, I had to know. And there it was: the two thin blue lines starring back at me. Two lines--positive. I was pregnant.

I stayed in the bathroom for what seemed like forever; the decisions to be made floating around in my head--stay, or go. Go or stay. Could I fix this future here with Adam? What would be better for the child inside me? Was it even a choice? Going out on my own felt insane and Adam would make it impossible once he found out I was pregnant. A child needs their father, I rationalized, thinking back to my childhood, of how valuable my own father's presence in my life was.

I sucked in a big gulp of air, steadying my nerves, and left the bathroom.

"Adam?" I called out.

No answer. He was probably at the diving school helping out.

My stomach twisted and turned in tune with my emotions. It was better this way, I thought, heading for the door.

My heart pounded as I made my way to the city, weaving in and around the thin streets awash with color.

I knocked on the big blue door, praying I hadn't missed him.

There was no answer; I knocked again.

"Come in," said a voice from somewhere inside.

I turned the handle, letting myself into the office.

"I'm just in here. Can I help you?"

I smiled as I recognized my lawyer's voice, praying he hadn't had a chance to file the papers yet.

"Mr. Turner?" I asked, walking towards the ruffling papers.

"Yes. Is that you, Darla? I haven't filed it yet. Just on my way--"

"You haven't?" I said, cutting him off.

"No. It's been a hell of a morning. Next on my list."

I sighed with relief, a weight visibly off my shoulders.

"Don't. I'm going to put the divorce on hold." For the child's sake, I added to myself.

I ignored the next few words of advice my lawyer shared with me, bemused at my sudden u-turn as he was unaware of the bigger picture. As well, I ignored the feelings of bitterness that were mounting inside me. Though it felt like I'd be trapped here forever, it wasn't true. That's what I kept telling myself. That's the reality I made myself believe. I had to believe it.

This wasn't just about me anymore. Or Adam. There was someone else to consider now--our baby.

4

Time took care of itself, passing at a speed I'd never known before. Overwhelming and centering, the very idea of a new life forming; a physical creation, a person, because of my union with Adam. This idea, this reality shaped every facet of my being.

"Adam," I started, walking back into our home. "Adam. Please, sit down, we need to talk," I said, instinctively holding my churning stomach.

I heard his footsteps from inside the bedroom as he headed out to join me. "Calmed down, have you?" he asked, unable to contain his smirk.

I bit my lip, refusing to get into another argument with him. This wasn't the time. Not if I was going to try to make this work.

"Adam, please. Just sit down and listen to what I have to say," I asked him again.

It was his favorite position. Of course, he sat willingly.

"What is it, Darla?" he said, now looking a little suspicious of me.

I sucked in a deep breath and closed my eyes. "I'm pregnant," I said, almost whispering.

Adam stared back at me. Not responding for more than a minute. "Pregnant?"

"Yes, Adam."

It was another full minute before it had sunk in, before he showed any sort of response whatsoever. But then, he was hard pressed to hide his obvious excitement. "Darla, honey, are you sure? I mean, really? This is incredible! Darla, you're pregnant?" He jumped up, grabbing me by the waist and swung me around. He cheered with delight. "Are you sure?" he asked again, setting me back on my feet.

"Of course I'm sure. A woman knows, and in this case, I've checked with a test." I laughed, unable to stop myself. This was a happy time. I was meant to be a happy, I reminded myself, as I tried to forget my earlier meeting with the lawyer and the plans that I was about to set into motion, yet stopped at break-neck speed. That path was for a different life. Things change, Darla, I told myself as Adam celebrated, blissfully unaware of how close I'd been to ending our marriage.

"How far along are you? When? How?" The questions poured out from his lips as he squeezed me tighter.

"I don't know yet," I answered honestly. "We should probably make an appointment with a doctor just to get me checked out," I said thinking aloud.

"Of course, we'll book it today. Wait. Have you told anyone else?" Adam asked.

I hesitated. Again thinking about the lawyer. But I hadn't told him. I hadn't told anyone. "No one," I answered.

"Come on, we have to go find my mom. She'll be thrilled! They all will be," he said, grabbing my hand and pulling me towards the door. "This is amazing. Maybe this will finally keep you at home, right?" he laughed, though he was serious.

My heart stopped for a moment at his words. Was that what he equated with kids? That I'd be a housewife, a stay-at-home mom? Forever at his beck and call?

Indeed, I wanted what was best for my baby, and if I would be at home for them, then I would make that choice for myself. But in this case, with Adam, I could see it now: he was always trying to make those decisions for me. And once again, he seized the chance to remind me: housework was "women's work."

Months later, I sighed before turning the handle to open the front door. Tired and stressed, I knew what I was going to find--the house would be a mess. It would look exactly as I had left it. Every unwashed dish, every unfolded sheet, every dust bunny in its place. It didn't matter that I was seven months pregnant, that this baby was coming in a matter of weeks. Nothing had changed. And nothing would.

The breeze from the ocean ran through the house as I entered, the sweet smell of salt water bringing a smile to my face.

My eyes panned the room as I walked in; I spotted Adam easily--he hadn't moved.

I closed my eyes, willing the tears to stay inside for the moment. It was my own fault, not Adam's. It was me who as foolish, who kept hoping something would change. But why would it? It hadn't yet and even news of a baby hadn't stirred Adam out of his rutted opinions.

Adam looked over at me for the briefest of seconds, just enough for a small smile.

Maybe he just didn't know, I thought, trying to rationalize with myself. Maybe if I told him, he'd actually help out, or do *something.*

"Adam," I said, looking over at him sprawled out on the couch. I took in a deep breath to keep the frustration out of my voice.

He turned his head reluctantly away from the TV.

"Adam, I need more help around here," I said, rubbing my growing belly subconsciously.

He nodded, his eyes flitting back to the screen in the same second. "Sure," he agreed. "Anything you need." Although the words were right, the tone was one I'd heard countless times before--dismissive, empty, meaningless.

"Ugh," I sighed, not worrying about whether he heard me moan. He didn't notice things like that. At least he hadn't in years.

"Oooo," I groaned, feeling the baby kick from inside me. Suddenly, it was as if the baby was trying to nudge me into action, spurring me to speak up for myself.

"Adam," I snapped again.

"What is it, Darla? The game's on."

"Adam, can you please stop watching that for a second. Would it kill you to listen to me?" I barked, unleashing my mounting frustration on him.

"Sure, Darla, you just had to ask," he said, though he waited for a commercial before turning to face me.

I practically growled at him.

"You're stressed, honey, I know you don't mean to be acting like this," he added, coming over to me. He stroked his hand down my arm as if he could smooth out my anger somehow.

"Yes, I'm stressed. I'm pregnant. Seven months pregnant and nothing's changed. You still expect me to do everything around here, while you do nothing. Nothing, Adam. We've got to work this out."

"Here, here," he said, rubbing my arm some more. "Don't worry, Darla. It'll all work itself out. You'll see."

"I don't want to see," I snapped back. "I want you to help, or get me help," I said. "I don't want to just let this go. I need you to be on my team, Adam - but you're not. It's just you calling all the shots, and I'm expected to just follow along."

"Darla," he cautioned, not wanting me to get carried away. I knew that tone.

"Don't, Adam. Don't shut me down. Don't cut me off."

"Honey," he pulled back, looking me over before pulling me in for a hug. "It'll all work out, okay? Trust me." He patted my back with a sense of finality just as I heard the announcer's voice come back on the TV.

I closed my eyes as he stepped away. I could do this, I said to myself, willing myself to believe it.

I made it as far as the bedroom before the tears started to fall. I didn't bother to wipe them away; they dampened my shirt and soon the pillow where I was resting my head.

Later, I pulled myself together just enough to make us dinner. But it was an early night for me. What was I supposed to do, I wondered, feeling as trapped as I'd ever felt before. Had I made the wrong decision, staying here, when my marriage was falling apart?

I looked over to where he lay, unable to help myself from staring at my snoring husband just as another set of tears streamed down my face. He never heard my cries, and tomorrow would be like every other morning--back to normal, as if I hadn't spent the night crying myself to sleep, as if he hadn't heard the sniffles, as if he couldn't see the sadness in my puffy eyes.

And true to form, he didn't.

Two months later, nothing had changed, except for the fact that I'd given birth to a healthy, beautiful, baby girl. Aila, our daughter, was a true blessing. It's incredible really how something so innocent, so pure could come out of our marriage.

As I held her in my arms, it was easier to forget the world around me, still crumbling into a million little pieces. Our marriage was still dismal but the future seemed bright in a way I'd never imagined.

And so, things were better. Superficially, at least. With a baby at home, there were things to do, things to look after besides Adam. And for the first few years, staying home didn't feel like a chore. Cooking and cleaning and taking care of our family--I'd learned to enjoy the daily humdrum of my routine. Well, almost.

Within a few years though, reality hit hard; and when Aila headed to school, I struggled to keep it together.

It was just the monotony of it all, I tried to tell myself. That's all it was, all that was getting me down; but in my heart, I couldn't deny the tension, the arguments, and the conflict that were part of our everyday life.

"But, Adam," I cried.

"What is it this time? It's always something! Something every day with you, Darla. You've got to get over this. What is wrong with you?" he snapped back at me.

I sighed, not wanting to get into it, but knowing I had to. How else would things change if I didn't at least try to deal with it?

"I'm tired. Tired of doing everything around here, tired of -- tired of being here and no wherever else. We never go anywhere, Adam. Ever. Nowhere," I whined, feeling myself drifting further and further towards a complaining child. But I wasn't a child and this wasn't some petty complaint. I was growing weary and restless with this life we'd created.

"What'd do you want me to do? Take you out more? We have a child."

"You think I don't know that? You think that's what this is about? Darla wants to go out? Ugh," I sighed, frustrated even more.

"Do something about it then. Stop complaining! You don't even have Aila here in the day anymore."

I stopped arguing, looking out the front window instead, waiting to see her little pigtails bopping down the driveway. It was nearly 3:30. She'd be home any minute.

"You're right," I agreed after a long sigh. Best we not be arguing when she came home. That wasn't the kind of house I wanted to raise her in. Not that we could be perfect all the time, but there didn't seem it be any obvious answers anyhow. I was miserable, restless, frustrated and now all alone during the days.

Furthermore, despite my snoring husband lying next to me, it seemed I was alone at night too. Tears pooled in my eyes--what had my life become, I wondered, taking stock of where I was and how I got here. That I was a happy, doting mother was a blessing. But for me, for my life, where was I?

A loveless marriage, a controlling husband, and responsibilities I'd never imagined being solely responsible for--I was a free live-in housekeeper. What happened to the team work, I wondered, feeling the trickle down my cheek, soaking into my pillow. I sniffled lightly, not wanting to wake Adam. Like that would happen, I laughed at myself through my silent tears.

The self-pity didn't last too long--by morning, there were still sniffles but thankfully no tears--I was all cried out.

"Morning," said Adam, rolling over to look at me.

I smiled. Today would be a better day, it had to be, I vowed. "Morning, Adam."

He smiled back at me as I wiped the corners of my eyes.

He reached up, touching the dry patches on my cheekbones. "You using a new moisturizer?" he asked.

I sighed quietly, as he let his hand drop. Yes, I wanted to say--it's the secret moisture called midnight tears. How could I save a relationship that was so far gone; my husband thought dried tears were a new moisturizer!

Another day passed. And another. Housework filled my days while tears filled my nights.

It was the nights that were the hardest. No little feet running around the house, no meals to prepare, no expectations to be met. And I felt even more alone, night after night after night.

Lying in bed my gaze flickered from the moonlight out the window and the still form of my husband next to me. Sweet dreams perhaps, of a life and marriage that maybe was working for him, but certainly not for me.

Had I been wrong, I wondered? Staying in this marriage for Aila's sake? It was hard to look at the situation objectively. I'd made the best choice that I could; certainly the choice I'd thought was best at that moment. But would I make the same choice today? It didn't matter, I argued with myself. No one could turn back the clock, nor should you spend your whole life second-guessing your decisions. I'd made my bed. But if I wanted to revisit the issue, I could do that too.

"Another cup, please, Darla!" Adam called from the breakfast table. He barely looked up.

I paused in the kitchen, staring out at him, staring at our daughter just finishing up her cereal. I took a deep breath, steadying my nerves as I grabbed the pot of coffee and brought it over.

"What, were you making another pot?" he asked, a small smirk threatening at the corners of his lips.

"Why?" I asked, pretending I didn't get his subtle commentary about my timeliness.

"It's probably cold now, it took you so long," he added, not backing down.

"Can I go play now?" asked Aila, immune to the tensions, at least I liked to hope as much.

"Of course, sweetheart. You've got a few minutes and then it's time to get ready for school," I said with a smile, as I sat down at the table for my own breakfast. I watched her leave the dining room, the tension almost melting away as I focused solely on her.

"So, honey," Adam started.

I turned to look at him, every ounce of irritation returning in that same second. "Yes?" I answered, trying to contain my emotions.

Adam didn't seem to notice. Of course not, he never did, he never noticed anything. "Are you planning on getting to the living room today--it's such a mess. There's dust everywhere and it's just not up to the standard we keep around here. Really, I thought you'd have dealt with it by now."

I gawked at my husband. My mouth gaping open. "You did, did you?"

"You have responsibilities, Darla. We can't live in squalor."

"What did you just say?"

"Come on, Darla." Adam barely looked up at me while he continued talking. It was as if everything he was saying was gospel. Like it was taken for granted; like I was taken for granted. Of course I was. I'd known that for years.

But this morning, I'd finally reached my limit.

"No, you come on," I snapped, jumping up from my chair. "Listen here, man, enough is enough! I officially resign as your housewife."

He looked up now, pulled from his laisse-faire attitude into the present by my tone. This time it was different and he could tell.

"Adam, I have a PhD in Philosophy and I am going to use it. I have allowed your foot on my neck too long!"

I stood back, waiting for him to say something in return.

But, Adam was too startled to say a word. This was the first time that I'd completely stood up to him. And I wasn't going to back down an inch.

"What's happened to you?" he whispered, clearly taken aback.

I shook my head, feeling the strength inside me growing. I knew why he was uneasy. Normally we'd discuss things quietly and come to some kind of compromise. But I was no longer playing by the rules, no longer playing a game he recognized as us.

He stared, speechless.

But it did nothing to shake my resolve. Not today, there was no compromising. I had made up my mind. I was finished with allowing anyone to tell me how to live my life!

"Adam, this is it. I want to travel the world. I want to teach."

"How? What do you think we'll do? That Aila and I will just follow you around? Globe-trotting until you're happy?"

"No, actually. Aila will be happy with me, wherever I am, but you--you'll have to live with whatever you decide."

"I'll never leave, Darla. This is my home. You have to stay here, we all do," he countered, his emotions building.

"Adam, I know you are accustomed to us doing everything together but this time--this time it is all about Darla. I am sick of living like this!"

Adam just stared at me, speechless once more as my resolve set in.

"You can come or you can stay. That's up to you. But I'm doing this. I'm going to get a job and go wherever it takes me," I explained.

"But, why? You have it so good here."

"In your eyes I do, but I'm weary, I'm tired, I'm restless, Adam. I need more from my life that just this."

"Just us, you mean. You're tired of me and Aila?"

"No, of course not. I love Aila. I love you too," I added as an afterthought.

"What's this about, Darla. You're being ridiculous! You've got an eight bedroom home on an island, steps away from the beach, and the best, most supportive family anywhere."

"I know," I agreed.

"Plus, Aila's in school now. You're home all day alone. Why are you complaining? You have it so good! It would make any woman happy!" Adam stared at me, dumbfounded when I didn't reply.

Probably, from his point of view, he was right--on paper, I had it good.

But maybe that wasn't it. It was good; but it wasn't for me. In my heart I knew what I needed, what I was missing--life. A life of my own, a life shared. Though I loved Adam, his controlling, domineering methods, his domestic expectations, and his over-bearing attitude were simply too much for me. This wasn't what I wanted for myself, for my life. I had goal, I had dreams! And keeping the best house on the island had never been one of them.

He went on, talking as if he were trying to convince himself, or me, just how lucky I was.

"Darla, trust me--you'll never have it this good anywhere else. You don't have to worry about anything with me--it's all here, it's all yours. Even money--it's never an issue."

"I know, Adam," I said, losing my steam. I knew he was right, but it just didn't matter. This wasn't the life I wanted.

"So ungrateful. This is unbelievable," he muttered to himself, leaving the table.

"Adam," I said, calling after him. But he was long gone.

I sighed, sitting back done at the table, feeling more alone than before. What ever happened to working on things, I wondered. What happened to sharing and listening to each other?

Looking back now, I can see that maybe those were never qualities we shared--listening, sharing, communicating in general. No surprise then that, if the basics weren't strong, our marriage was in trouble.

I looked over to my daughter in the corner of the room, playing with her toys so sweetly. Whatever happened, she would feel loved, I vowed to myself, and her. That was a love that was unconditional, unwavering, and completely sincere.

My love for Adam on the other hand... I sighed, trying to think rationally as he came back into the room. Taking up his usual spot on the couch, I turned to look at him. He didn't look around, though he must have felt my gaze. Then again maybe he didn't. Maybe he didn't even know I was in the same room as him.

"Adam," I called out a little louder. "Can we talk about things?"

"Not now," he murmured, "You'll come around," I thought I heard him say.

I shook my head but didn't argue back. He was taking me for granted, taking our relationship for granted. But it didn't seem I was in a position to do much about it.

Weeks passed, maybe months. But that feeling inside me, the feeling of finality didn't fade. I knew I needed out of this relationship, out of this negative, unhealthy environment.

It was a sunny day when it happened. I was walking Aila home from school when we stopped to pick up the mail.

After flipping through the envelopes, I spotted the thick glossy journal, shoved in behind—it was a monthly education journal I received.

"Come on, honey," I called out, to my daughter. "This way. Let's go inside," I said, opening the door.

Aila quickly followed in behind me, eager to play with her toys.

Ignoring the housework, I decided to go through the journal, just so I was at least up to date on what was going on in the world of education

The advertisement stood out amongst all the other writing on the page: Wanted: English Teacher, University of Delhi, India.

My eyes honed in on the ad, focusing on it like no other. They were seeking a professor at a university in India--how exciting! I thought.

I stared at the journal for maybe ten minutes, thinking, dreaming about the possibilities of this new path in life before I sprung into action. That same night, I set about revising my CV and applying for the job. I crossed the t's and dotted the i's and submitted my application, and then prayed this was the opportunity I'd been waiting for.

Maybe this could be it; the job that would take me away, to the life of my dreams.

5

I walked over to the coffee pot, knowing Adam was watching me; I could feel his eyes on my every move. I exhaled loudly, trying to vent my frustration,

"What is it, Adam?" I asked, turning around to face him.

He was staring up from his breakfast with big, sad eyes. "Why, Darla? Why go? Why take our beautiful daughter away with you? You're my wife. We're a family. We belong together." He spoke softly, the sound of defeat resonating in his every word. It was like he'd already admitted to himself that this was a losing battle but that it still had to be fought.

I grabbed the pot and walked over to the table, filling up his mug without asking. "We've been over this. Time and time again. I want more from my life than just this, than being a wife."

"You're also a mother,"

"I know, but I'm serious. I want more. I need more."

"Darla, don't talk like this. You're being ridiculous. I can't speak with you when you go on about things like this."

I closed my eyes, knowing this was exactly the problem between us. I never got anywhere, he never let me talk, he never tried to understand. "Exactly, Adam. You don't want to hear it. But you have to. I've tried for days now. Days, Adam. You won't actually talk about this but you need to."

Adam turned his head, looking out towards the ocean as if he could get away from the conversation by simply ignoring me.

"Darla, I can't. I don't understand any of this. We're a family."

"We might be, Adam. But we're not a happy one. I'm not happy. Not at all. Can you understand that? Can you understand how I need more from this?" I asked, part of me genuinely curious whether he could empathize even a little.

Adam turned back to face me, looking calmer than I'd seen him in weeks. "I've never wanted you to be unhappy. If you truly are, then you're right, you should leave."

I stared at him, not sure if I had heard him correctly; this was the first time he had said anything like this. I kept my eyes on him, looking for any sign of double meaning in his words. I so wanted to believe him. Had he really accepted my decision? Had he finally understood my situation?

"You understand then?" I asked, unable to help myself.

"There's nothing to understand. If you believe you're unhappy, honestly, then go."

And so I did.

It was almost surreal as the plane landed in India; the thick heat that enveloped us as my daughter and I exited the airport was eerily familiar, just like the heat of the Caribbean. However, this was anything but the casual familiar life we'd come from.

Everything was new, everything was foreign. It was an adventure of ridiculous proportions, and just the sort of experience that would invigorate my weary spirit. It was a shock to the system - in the best way possible.

"Look at all the colors," gushed Aila as we rode in the taxi from the airport. It was a vibrant city, chock full of life and spirit, full of hope and opportunity.

"What are they wearing?" asked my daughter, pointing to the women on the streets as we weaved in and around the busy roads.

"Saris. They're beautiful, aren't they?" I said, in a daze. It was as if it all sank in at once--we'd made it, I'd made it. And our new world was welcoming us with open arms. I inhaled the rich fragrances of the city, breathing in this new life with an energy I'd long forgotten. The city was so bright and alive, teeming with people and humming with activity--I held my breath as we drove through a bustling market, savoring each new sensation. If the Caribbean way of life is laid back, then India is sitting up, wide eyed. It felt like I needed to pinch myself to be convinced this was our new reality. We were doing this - for real.

"This is the address, Miss," the taxi driver said in the Indian-accented English that we'd come to know so well. We looked out of the rolled-down window at a nice little house. A modest but well-kept property. The university had provided us with everything we needed for our stay, this house included.

I couldn't tear my eyes away from it, but it was time to exit the taxi and I felt Aila shoving me to get out and take a closer look. The house was beyond our expectations--surrounded by plenty of green trees, and loads of monkeys! It was like nothing I'd ever seen before.

"Mom, mom!" Aila cried. "Do you see them? There are monkeys everywhere!"

I smiled, exhaling loudly. I hadn't realized it but, up until that moment, I'd been mentally holding my breath--waiting subconsciously for something to go wrong, for something or someone to throw a wrench in the cogs of my dream. But it was really coming true. Right here, right now--me and my beautiful daughter were in India.

I turned to look at Aila, and smiled widely. "This will be home."

Aila looked over at the property; I could see my excitement mirrored in her eyes. She was as ready for this adventure as I was.

We quickly settled into our new lives, like two starving people excited to sit at a table full of food.

"Mom," cried Aila. "I'm just going to meet my friends," she called out to me.

"Sure thing. Stay close and be back in time for dinner," I answered. It hadn't taken us very long to feel at home in our house, and to fall into a new routine. It was as seamless a transition as it could be, given we'd moved halfway around the world, just the two of us. Thankfully, because of everything the university had handled for us, all we had to do was focus on adjusting.

I watched as my little girl ran around outside with her new friends--it calmed me, warmed me from the inside out, knowing she'd done so well here; she was still the happy outgoing girl she'd always been. I laughed as I saw her move away from a cheeky monkey dangling from a tree, careful to avoid them. So aggressive they were, Aila would sometimes be afraid to go outside. Thankfully that wasn't the case today. There were only a few around.

Smiling as I watched her play with her friends, I was unable to stop myself from overhearing their conversation. "Have you heard that new song?" Aila asked one of the other girls whose face looked puzzled by the question. "This one," Aila beamed as she opened her mouth to sing; a beautiful melody flowed out, one of the latest songs we had heard - we always had the radio on, so she knew all of the hits.

I watched as the other girls sang along, joining in. And for a minute it was easy to forget where we were--music truly does have the ability to transcend so many barriers.

Aila loved to sing and made a point to keep up with all the latest songs. She even sang on talent shows and never missed a chance to perform. I think it was an easy way to remind her of home; it was grounding in so many ways.

Yet, despite all the fun and success we were both enjoying, this adventure was still an adjustment, not just country-wise, but as a family--the new shape of us, just two instead of three--it wasn't easy.

Later that evening, I called out, "Aila, honey. Dinner's ready."

There was no answer, though I knew she was studying in her room.

"Aila?" I tried again.

Still no answer.

I turned off the element on the stove, and set down the wooden spoon I'd been using to stir our meal, a light curry. I was just a few feet from her bedroom--it was located just off of the main room. Aila's door was slightly ajar; I could hear the soft sounds of the radio playing in the background.

"Knock, knock," I said, rapping quietly with my knuckles on the door. "What's up, honey?"

Aila sighed, still not meeting my eyes.

"Is it something at school? Something going in with your friends?" I asked. In that instant, it seemed like the happy, carefree girl who I had seen playing, singing and laughing was nowhere to be found. Instead, my bright daughter was visibly lacking her spark.

"What's up, Aila?" I asked again, bending down to her level on the bed. She looked up at me, as a tear fell down her cheek.

"You'll be mad," she whispered.

"Whatever it is, you can tell me. I promise I won't be mad or angry or upset with you. I love you, honey. I'm here for you."

She closed her eyes and looked back to the book in her bed. "It's just hard, sometimes. I miss him."

"Dad?" I asked, though I knew that's who she was speaking about.

She nodded, still not meeting my eyes.

"I know you do. I miss him, too. It's quite a change, isn't it? From where we were to where we are."

Aila nodded. "We've been here for months now. It's fun and I love it, but--" she paused.

I sighed, part of me feeling the same longing for comfort and familiarity that my baby did. She needed her father--I could see that, and regardless of my relationship with Adam, it was never my intention of withholding that relationship from either of them.

"You've got a school break coming up," I started. "Do you want to go visit? Or should I invite him to come here?"

Aila looked up--it was a combination of disbelief and excitement on her face, like she wanted to believe the words I'd said, but didn't want to let herself in case she'd misheard them. "Are you serious?"

I nodded, smiling genuinely at her. While coming to India was something I needed to do, to get away, to spread my wings, to fly on my own; what my daughter needed was just as important. And she needed her father, both of us, in her life.

Just because I wasn't going to go back into that marriage didn't negate her relationship with him. I was more than mature enough to do whatever we needed to make this work.

"That's settled then. We'll call your father and set it up after soccer. Now come get some food--you need your energy for the game.

Aila smiled at me, like a weight had been lifted off her shoulders.

"Thanks, Mom," she said, giving me a warm hug as she got up.

Over the course of the next hour, it was such a transformation. By the time we reached the soccer fields, she was visibly relaxed, an air of confidence replacing her once worried face.

"Go, honey," I yelled out, as I watched the girls run across the field, basked in the warm evening sun. "You got it!"

Aila didn't look over, though I could tell she'd heard me. I was always there, at every game, happy to be a soccer mom--I'm sure my encouragement soon became background noise for her; though she always smiled, like she knew I was there for her.

As I watched the team play, watched my little girl run and chase the ball with such skill and talent, it was easy to think about the opportunity this sport could offer her. Scholarships maybe, at some point in the future. But more so, soccer, or football as it's known throughout much of the world, was right up there beside music with its ability to transcend differences and cultures.

Everyone in this part of the world had a favorite team, everyone could kick the ball and everyone was ready to play a quick game. If we continued down this international path, it was easy to see how her love of the sport would translate, regardless of any language difficulties or cultural clashes we might face.

Not long after that night it seemed, I was hopping out of the car and quickly running around to the trunk. I picked up the two bags and set then down on the ground at the curb of the airport drop-off.

"Now remember what I said, Aila. The stewardesses will be with you every step of the way. They'll keep an eye out for you," I explained, not wanting to think about the long journey she was going to make on her own.

We'd made all the arrangements--it had been decided that visiting Adam back home would be best for her. It was a chance to see not only Adam, but home and her extended family as well.

"You'll do so well, honey," I said, giving her a giant hug and kiss.

"I know, Mom. Don't worry. Dad will be there. I'll be okay," she said, trying to reassure me.

I laughed at my little girl trying to switch our roles, trying to be the one doing the reassuring.

This was the beginning of a new stage in her life, and our family. Aila made four trips back to the Caribbean during our stay in India, and Adam came to stay with us twice. This was our new norm.

It was a strange sensation being without Aila while she spent time with Adam. Strange, as during that time I felt almost free of a relationship. For so long now I had been a wife and a mother, yet for this brief period during her trips, I wasn't immediately defined by either title - even though I still thought of Aila for every minute from the second she walked out of my sight. Still, here I was - I was just me, responsible only for myself, my own happiness, my own well-being (for this short period).

How strange and different it all was; there were feelings of happiness mixed with a sense of uncertainty and loneliness. I missed my daughter but it was more than that; it was as if I finally had time to both grieve and celebrate the end of my marriage. Happy and sad; I struggled with this confusing mix of opposing feelings swirling inside of me.

Despite having our child's best interest at heart, and being thousands of miles apart; it seemed there were still issues between Adam and

I. He was just as determined as ever to set things right between us, and bring Aila and I back to the Caribbean permanently, to carry on as if nothing had happened. He still hadn't signed the divorce papers, given to him almost two years ago.

"It's been a nice visit, Adam," I said on one of his recent stays at our home in India, not wanting to broach this conversation but knowing I had to try. "But we're staying. I'm not coming home. I'm not going back," I said quietly.

Adam said nothing in return. Slowly, he walked around our house, taking it all in. How strange it must have looked through his eyes--his wife and daughter in this foreign land, comfortable, and at home here.

He turned to stare at me but still, he said nothing. I could read the words he wanted to say, the words he'd said so many times before. But today he didn't bother. "I can see it, Darla. I can see the same spark in you that I fell in love with. It hasn't been there for so long. But it's back now."

I looked towards him taken aback by this change of course by him. For so long now we'd been against each other; to have him admit that maybe I'd been right, that maybe this time apart had been healthy for me, was a shock. "Yes. Adam. It is back, *I'm* back in a way. I needed this--I knew it in my heart, I still know it now."

"It's just incredible, really. You have a real job. A real teaching job and are making it on your own." He either wasn't trying or was simply unable to hide the shock from his voice. He was amazed by the state we were in, that we weren't falling apart without him, I guessed.

"Yes," I answered, long past being offended.

Adam glanced at me, pausing before speaking again. "You're never coming back, are you?" he said quietly, disappointedly.

I looked up at him, hearing the pain in his voice. I didn't want to hurt him, but I needed him to understand. He deserved to move on, as I had accepted there was no future for us. "No, Adam I'm not," I said as gently as I could. This wasn't the first time I'd said it, but I think it was the first time he actually believed it.

It was the last real conversation we had during that visit, probably the most honest one we'd had in years.

Two weeks later, after he'd returned back to the islands, the divorce papers showed up in our mailbox in India. He'd finally signed them.

While I had no plans to return to Adam, before we knew it our time in India was almost up. Time flies as they say. And the lifestyle suited us. Traveling, experiencing foreign places, immersing ourselves in different cultures--it was an incredible life for us both. It rejuvenated me to such an extent that I couldn't bear the thought of giving it up just yet.

"It's almost been two years," said Aila, looking at the calendar.

"I know. It doesn't seem like that, does it? It went fast."

Aila smiled, but I could tell she was worried. "Are we," she started, but paused for a second. "Are we going back now?" she said.

"Do you want to go back?" I asked, knowing how much she had enjoyed the adventure here, but at the same time, knowing she deserved the opportunity to voice her preferences, share with me her needs as well.

"Yes and no," she sighed. "I miss Dad, but I love all the traveling, all the new places and people and things," she said, looking out the window as the monkeys swung by in the trees around us.

In the end, it was an easy decision to make--I had been bitten by the travel bug--I couldn't get enough. And the opportunity to give Aila such a rich, diverse, well-rounded education, filled with culture, languages, history and geography come alive--it was too hard to go back to the rigid structure that had ruled our life before. While Adam needed to play a role, it became simply a matter of finding the right balance for Aila. And we did.

And so it was our new life--a continuous adventure; nomadic and international in nature. Every two years, I would send out a round of applications to international universities, applying for a position on staff. And in no time, this revolving two year turnaround became our way of life. Aila and I became "international travelers".

For years, we travelled the globe together, venturing near and far, all the while immersing ourselves in the cultures and routines of our new host country. We enjoyed our time in Central America--staying in Haiti, Honduras, and Guatemala. We spent time back in the Caribbean, on the island of Jamaica. And we ventured much further from home during our stays in Jordan and South Korea and several countries in between.

True to my intuition, throughout our wandering years, soccer was a wonderful connection that Aila shared with the locals and other international students. Having honed her skills across the globe, racking up tricks and techniques everywhere we went, she became a brilliant player, one of the best on her team. More importantly, she enjoyed it--soccer became a constant in our every-changing life.

"Mom, Mom! It's here!"

My heart pounded as I ran to meet my daughter by the front door. We'd been checking the mail regularly lately--admission letters were due any day now.

"Where's it from?" I asked, eagerly trying to read the return address in the corner of the envelope waving in her hand.

Aila ignored my question and ripped open the envelope. "Dear Miss--" she read softly under her breath as she scanned the letter. With bright, wide eyes she looked up at me. "I'm in! They accepted my application!" she said, excited beyond belief.

I threw my arms around her, hugging her tightly, with every fiber of my being proud of her achievement. "Congratulations, honey. You deserve it. You earned it."

"Oh, Mom," she said, letting go of me. "Can you believe it? After everything, everywhere we've been? I'm in. I'm going to university!"

"I knew they'd take you, Aila. A bright girl like yourself--they had to take you."

Aila looked again at the letter, reading it a second time. "Want to see what else it says?" she asked, offering it to me.

"What?" I asked, holding the letter up to read aloud. "We have also been informed by the Athletics department-- They're offering you a soccer scholarship?" I looked back to my daughter for a short second before wrapping her up in another big hug. "Oh, congratulations, Aila! That's incredible!"

It took more than a few minutes to sink in that this was really happening, that my baby girl was about to finish high school, just days away from graduating from a renowned international high school in South Korea. In just a few short months, she'd be back in the United States starting university on a soccer scholarship. It was too much. Despite our unorthodox, international lifestyle, it was always her achievements, Aila's successes, that meant the most to me.

These years together were special--they marked the happiest of times--the two of us sharing, growing, learning from one another. In so many ways, this bond, this relationship between the two of us was the healthiest relationship I'd ever been in--that of a mother and daughter. In all my marriages, none has compared, nor even come close to the love and mutual respect, the understanding and compassion we share for one another.

In retrospect, perhaps there's a lesson in that--perhaps that revelation is the lesson--maybe one good relationship is all you ever get; be it with a parent, a spouse, a child or a friend. Or maybe it was just that this was the type of relationship I was good at--I knew my daughter, I trusted her and my trust was well placed; I loved her unconditionally and she mirrored that right back to me.

Certainly my relationship with Adam was lacking in these areas. If I was honest with myself, there was much lacking from the very beginning. Unfortunately, things rarely get better after the honeymoon stage; if my experience is anything to go on--once everyone gets settled and comfortable, sometimes the issues that were only hinted at, the little signs that were so easy to ignore, become glaring problems later on. Of course, perfection is impossible to achieve and compromise is integral to any marriage but there comes a point where, if you give in too much of yourself, you risk losing the very core of who you are. A core that you may need to go out and find again, like I did.

6

The car felt cold and empty as I drove away from the university campus, leaving behind my now grown baby. It was a strange sensation, leaving her to fend for herself. So much harder than leaving a marriage behind. As I looked back in the rear-view mirror, seeing the tall facades of the university residences behind me, there was little that could take my mind off of this feeling of being suddenly alone for the first time in years.

It wasn't like I hadn't been expecting it either. Much like my failed marriage to Adam, I could see this future reality coming, months, even years ahead. But, of course, knowing what's ahead doesn't always make it easier to deal with.

I pulled over to wipe my tears as soon as I'd left campus. Reaching into my purse, I fumbled through everything else to grab a tissue. In the process, however, I found something unexpected, but exactly what I needed. My fingers had stumbled upon an old postcard, from a few months back.

That was what I needed--a new adventure. Another world experience would help ease this transition. After all, traveling had been the only other constant in my life for the last twenty odd years. With my baby now starting her own adventure, perhaps this was the time for me to do the same.

"It's been an amazing first week, Mom," said Aila, the excitement plain to hear in her voice.

"I'm thrilled for you, honey. That's wonderful."

"And how about you? How are you doing? Have you decided where to go to next? Where will I be visiting you?"

I laughed at my daughter, ever the traveler, just like me. "Don't you worry about me, this is your time."

"I know. I'm just curious. We've been to so many places--are you going back to one of them, or somewhere new? I know you won't be staying around here much longer. You're a free spirit, Mom. Own it." She laughed warmly.

I smiled on the other end of the phone; my daughter knew me well. Too well. In the week since I'd dropped her off, I'd had time to research a few different places and had already submitted a handful of applications. Mostly to schools in the Middle East--we hadn't spent much time there, and the region intrigued me. I was curious about life in that part of the world; like everywhere, it seemed so different at first glance, but so similar in other ways. Of course, immersing yourself in any culture and community is the best way to fully appreciate these similarities and differences. And soon, I'd be doing exactly that.

In the end, it all happened rather quickly and before I knew it; my bags were packed and everything was sorted. I had accepted a wonderful university position in Jordan.

I expected the heat as I walked off the plane--similar to India in a way. The temperature washed over you like a warm ocean wave, seeping into every part of your body. But the nights turned out to be much cooler than I'd anticipated.

"Did you bring warm clothing too, Miss?" asked my cab driver on the way to my new home.

"Warm clothes? Like sweaters?" I laughed, looking out the window at the desert city, feeling the chill of the necessary air conditioning, as opposed to the hot sticky air outside.

"Indeed. You'll need them in the evenings. It gets cold here at night."

"Really?" I asked.

"Very much so. It can even snow in the desert," replied the cabbie to my surprise.

I smiled and nodded to his commentary, not sure if I actually believed him or not.

But it wasn't long before I felt the cool chill of the fall air for myself. And I hadn't brought the right clothes for that. Not enough, at least.

I knew I had to get my clothes sorted as soon as possible--it was only going to get cooler, I was told.

So, as soon as classes were finished for the day, I found myself at the local shopping center, with an aim to pick up a few extra sweaters. Despite all the work left to be done at my new home; browsing through the racks, store after store, sounded like a fun distraction and a great way to get a feel of the local culture, and see their traditions in action.

I took my time at first, wandering the mall, soaking in the world around me. I smiled to myself, thinking of all the times Adam and I had spent people-watching in the early days. But they were bittersweet memories; at the moment, thinking of Adam only reminded me of Aila. And as soon as I thought of her, all the fun seemed to disappear.

Turning my attention back to why I was here in the first place, I kept my eyes peeled for the items I was after. Soon, I spotted some lovely clothes on display in a shop window; I walked into the store, crossing my fingers they'd have what I needed. As soon as I grabbed a sweater or two, I could head home and finish unpacking.

I was not disappointed--inside were clothes perfect to my taste: classic and modern, but not ostentatious in any way. I browsed the store, casually picking up a few tops to see if they would work, humming a tune softly to myself as I went.

I picked up a nice red top, perfect for Aila, I thought to myself. A sigh escaped my lips in the same second. Aila--the fact she wasn't here next to me, but instead at university, an ocean away. How strange it felt being on an adventure without her. After all this time, we'd grown accustomed to having each other, to having a partner, a teammate, a companion for our constant adventuring.

"May I help you, Miss?"

I turned to look at the gentleman who had interrupted my thoughts. My eyes opened a little wider, as I took in his tall, ruggedly handsome frame. His deep caramel skin was beautiful, a native to Jordan, if I had to guess.

"I'm okay, thank you," I answered, smiling politely.

"Oh, you are an American woman! I love your accent," he said. "Are you sure there's nothing I can help you with?"

I smiled again and shook my head. "I'm good, really." I looked back down, browsing the shelf of sweaters in front in me, though I could still feel his eyes on me.

"Well, just know, I am the owner of this store. My name is Ali. If you need *anything* and I mean anything at all, please, please, just say my name, and I will be right there." He smiled at me, clearly wanting to impress.

"Alright. Thanks," I answered, before returning my attention back to the sweaters.

It really shouldn't have been that hard; I just needed to pick one and get out of there. As I continued to peruse the store, flicking through the items in display, trying on a handful of ones that stuck out to me, I didn't give much thought to the owner. I could still sense him watching me though, following my every move.

But thankfully, it didn't take long to find a nice sweater; I headed to the counter to pay.

"Did you find what you were looking for?" Ali asked, as I walked towards him.

"Yes. It's a lovely shop," I said politely.

"I own a chain of them actually. I have several retail stores in the region."

"Oh, that's nice. I'll just take this one, please," I said, placing a pretty blue sweater on the counter.

"A lovely choice. It looks beautiful on you too, by the way."

I looked up at Ali, raising an eyebrow at his comment. There was an undercurrent in his tone--like his compliment was more than just a salesman wanting to flatter a customer.

"Thanks," I said, my voice a little unsure.

I watched as Ali neatly folded the sweater and placed it in a nice soft bag with handles.

"Thank you and please come back," he said handing me the handles.

I took the bag from him, smiling politely but something was wrong. What was it, I thought to myself. "Oh, wait a moment, I haven't paid for it," I said, realizing the fundamental missing piece of our exchange. I placed the bag back on the counter, feeling myself blush with embarrassment.

Ali smiled at me, simply shaking his head.

I didn't have times for games, nor was I interested in trying to decipher what he meant. "How much is the sweater?" I asked point blank, getting my wallet out to pay.

Ali shook his head once more. "On the house, I think that's the phrase."

What? A free sweater from a stranger? Why? There was a catch, there had to be. "Ali, right?"

"Yes, that's my name. And what's yours?" he said quickly, throwing me off a little.

"Uh, Darla," I answered, automatically.

"Darla--that's a lovely name. I've never heard it before. The first and only Darla, I've ever met." He grinned as if he already knew me.

"Ali, how much is the sweater? I'm ready to pay for it. Cash, credit card, tell me how much," I said, determined to get this sweater and be on my way. Whatever he was up to, it seemed like much too much work to try and figure it out. I pulled out my wallet, waiting for the figure.

"Ah, did you not hear me, Darla? Don't worry about the price. If I wanted you to pay for it, I'd charge you. But I don't."

I shook my head in frustration. "I don't understand. How much is the sweater? I'd like to buy it. I'd like to take it home with me. I plan on wearing it—it gets pretty cold here in the evenings. I was not expecting that."

"It certainly does. Good to keep yourself warm. A smart woman," said Ali, still grinning. Though his comments remained professional, there was this air about him, a cockiness that came off as subtle flirtation. He was a confident man, undoubtedly very sure of himself.

Three times I asked Ali the cost of the sweater but he completely ignored me.

"How am I supposed to pay for it, if you won't tell me the price?" I asked, feeling frazzled by the nonsensical conversation I was having. I was in a shop, wanting to buy an item, but wasn't allowed to. What was I missing?

"That's exactly it--you don't have to pay for it. Don't worry about it. Forget the price. The sweater is yours; it looks fabulous on you. It really brings out your eyes."

"Ali--" I huffed, feeling exasperated.

"Let's just say it is a gift, yes? From me to you." Ali gestured with his hand, offering me to accept the bag once more.

I stared hard at him for a moment, looking for any doubt on his features, any sign this was a bluff of some sort. But I couldn't get a read on him past his pleasant, charming demeanor. And I wasn't in the mood to play a game of cat and mouse with him.

I raised my eyebrows, as if to ask if he was serious.

"Please, Darla," he answered, lingering on my name. "Please come back again."

"Thanks," I said, grabbing the bag. "Goodbye." I walked out of the store, and didn't look back.

Weeks had passed, and I thought little of my experience with Ali, until I found myself back at another shopping center. I laughed to myself as I passed through the main entrance, wondering if I'd wind up with another free sweater this time around. It had been a surreal experience--a first for me, and certainly the last.

I had walked past just a handful of shops before I wandered into one; my heart stopped when I spotted a familiar face, one of the few people I knew in Jordan.

"Darla? What a lovely surprise!" Ali walked over to me, beaming from ear to ear. "You've found another shop of mine. What a wonderful coincidence. I've been wondering when we'd bump into each other again." His words flowed easily. He was a charmer, a loquacious man. He ran his fingers through his hair, freshening up his appearance.

"Hi," I said quietly, shell-shocked at my luck--unsure if it was good or bad at that moment.

"What are you after today? I'm hoping I can help you find it. Whatever it is, I'm sure if it's not in my shop, I'll know just the right place."

I nodded, unsure if I really wanted to go down this path.

"Just browsing today. I'm out really to take a break from things at the university."

"Are you a student there?" he asked, trying to flatter me, I presumed.

"Professor, actually."

"A smart woman. I said that the last time we met, didn't I. And I was right."

"Ali?" a voice from the back called out, interrupting us.

Ali turned to look at a man in the back room.

"A call for you," said the man.

"Excuse me, Darla. I've got to take this. But then, if you're looking for a break, let me show you around. We have such a beautiful city here, so many wonderful things to see and do. I bet you haven't had the chance to see any of it yet."

"No, I haven't," I answered truthfully despite myself.

"Let me take this call and then I'll be right back," he said, before quickly excusing himself.

As I stood there in his shop, I found myself wondering what it was about him that made me just blurt out the truth? It felt as if the words had just escaped from within me. And now all of a sudden I'd gone from a day on my own, to a potential date? I shook my head, as if that could knock some sense back into it. I picked up a few pieces of clothing, pretending to consider them as I secretly tried to figure out if I should stay or go.

I was still deciding when Ali called out for me from the back of the shop. "Darla, how are you doing? I hope I didn't make you wait too long for me. Family--I'm sure you understand."

"Of course," I answered.

"Please, let me introduce you to Khaled, my younger brother," he said, nodding to the young man behind me.

"Khaled? Nice to meet you," I said, noticing the family resemblance at once.

"And you, Darla. How did you two meet?" Khaled asked curiously.

I shook my head, a little flustered. "At one of your stores. I was looking for a sweater and Ali was working," I said, cutting out the free part of that encounter.

My eyes flickered back to Ali who was smiling broadly at me. My stomach dropped, spinning with nerves; I was still unsure if I should be entertaining this idea of a personal tour of the city, or whatever Ali was thinking. But I could hear the hesitation in my own thoughts, one side warring with the other.

I didn't have any other plans and, there was no denying, Ali was a local so he would be able to show me some great places I'd probably never find on my own. But what would we do, where would we go? Was this a date, I wondered, not sure if I was even hoping it was.

I sighed to myself as I stared at Ali's caramel features--certainly he was charming and easy on the eyes. And that decided it--surely it was counter-intuitive not to try this out, I rationalized. What a great opportunity to get to know a culture and community, first hand.

"Ready?" asked Ali, sensing that I'd decided to give this a go.

Suddenly another man stepped out of the back room, waving at Ali and Khaled.

"Lots of people calling for you today. Are you sure you don't need to be here?" I asked, part of me hoping he'd take back the offer, and another part wishing he wouldn't.

Ali laughed. "Adanan is our accountant. He just happened to be here, but had offered to take care of things while we all go out. You ready?" asked Ali again.

"I'm not sure," I said, looking between him and his brother, my nerves still threatening to get the best of me. Going out with a stranger was one thing, but going out with two strange men by myself, seemed like another thing altogether. "Maybe another time," I hesitated, blurting out the words. But I didn't really mean them and Ali could sense my hesitation.

"No, come, it'll be fun," said Ali. "Khaled, here will join us, so it'll be just a nice little adventure. I promise. Do you want to see the sights, or head to the coast, or shop?" suggested Ali, not taking no for an answer.

"What do you recommend? It's pretty hot out there right now. Midday sun and all."

Ali laughed. "Let's start with lunch then. Maybe that'll give us a good chance to get to know one another."

"Like a date?" I asked, half-jokingly.

Ali and his brother looked at each other, eyes wide, a mixture of shock and surprise.

"What?" I asked, unsure where I had misstepped. In all my years of travel, this wouldn't be the first time it had happened.

"I'm Muslim," said Ali, looking at me with a knowing look.

"That's nice," I answered politely. "What am I missing?" I asked, trying to connect the dots. I had met and known people from all religions through my travels, but couldn't see where he was going with this.

Khaled looked away, stepping aside awkwardly. "Let me know if you need me," he said, excusing himself.

Ali nodded to his brother before returning his attention to me. "Darla, we can be friends but that is all. There is no dating in Islam. Nothing like they show on American movies. The very concept of courtship is foreign to us here."

"Oh, I'm so sorry," I apologized immediately. "I really meant nothing by it. I was kidding. Where I'm from, sometimes it's good to know someone's intentions ahead of time, so you're either both on the same page, or you can both get on the same page, if you know what I mean?"

Ali nodded. "I understand. I wish very much it could be that way between us, but there can be no dating in my life. It is simply non-existent because of my religion. It would be the same as me eating pork, or drinking alcohol. They're all forbidden in Islam."

"Sounds like you take your religion seriously. We have that in common--I do too." I smiled at him, wanting to reassure him that there were no hard feelings.

"Yes, I'm very strict about my faith."

"So, this would be like two friends going out, is that the idea?" I asked.

Ali smiled "Exactly. Why don't we enjoy a nice meal together? I know a great little restaurant just a few blocks from here. It serves regional food--have you tried any yet?"

"Not yet, that sounds great. Should we tell Khaled?" I asked, looking over to him on the far side of the shop.

"Yes. He'll be a chaperone," explained Ali. "It's customary for a man and woman to have one, so they're not alone together. So there is no chance to give in to temptation," he said, looking down at his feet.

I paused, trying to decipher the mixed messages Ali was sending. On every level he seemed to be interested in me romantically, but his customs seemed to dictate he must say otherwise. Maybe time would tell his real intentions, I thought to myself. "Well, you better get Khaled then--I'm starving!"

"Perfect, Darla. What a wonderful afternoon we will have. Here," he said, picking up a beautiful scarf off the shelf beside us. "It's windy today--to cover your hair, to stop the sand from getting into it," he said, passing the lovely silk cloth to me.

"I can't accept, Ali. You've already given me a sweater. Friends don't give gifts like this to each other."

"Yes, that sweater looked beautiful on you. And this will match it well. I insist," he said, extending the scarf until I accepted.

And that was the beginning of life with Ali. The gifts continued to come and he never took no for an answer.

We enjoyed a quiet lunch at a great little restaurant. Having a chaperone was a strange sensation. Though, thankfully, Khaled seemed to understand his role and stayed out of our conversation for the most part. And other than the chaperone element, mine and Ali's time together could have been considered a date by most standards--a meal together, intimate setting with just a few people, getting to know more about each other, and inadvertently assessing chemistry and compatibility.

"Come, let us order," said Ali, taking the menus in hand. "Are you sure you've never tried Jordanian food, Darla?"

I shook my head, more than curious about it. Looking around the busy restaurant, the sights were captivating. On every side of us, people were laughing, enjoying, and celebrating over a meal. Not just couples, but whole families were dining together. Generations gathered around tables, sharing food, conversation, and company. Hands reaching in, dipping, dunking and scooping food with their flat bread.

It was mesmerizing to watch their sense of community extend into their style of eating, but it did, and it was easy to admire. It was as if the people all around me embodied the spirit of giving, togetherness and love. And seeing their obvious affection for one another, it was hard to take my eyes away from their infectious happiness. I watched them, not even trying to hide my curious interest as families connected with each other over their food.

As I returned my attention to our own table, it was easy to wonder what we looked like to everyone else. Not a family, but maybe friends perhaps? I shook my head, trying to rid myself of any insecurities--yes, in our own way, we were a little group of friends, enjoying the process of getting to know one another.

"Let me order for us, Darla. There are so many wonderful dishes here," said Ali, waving for the waiter.

He glanced over the options quickly, before confidently ordering for our table in his native tongue.

I smiled as he rattled off dishes to the waiter. It was stranger having someone take charge like that, but exhilarating in a way. And it was perfect really--everything was so new and different, I would have never known where to start. As well, I certainly never would have ordered as much or as many different dishes as Ali did.

"Tell me more," I asked, curious to get to know Ali and his culture, as much as his national cuisine. "How do you get to know someone? How do relationships start out here?" I asked, grabbing a piece of bread from the basket in front of us.

Ali waited until my hand was clear of the communal space before he grabbed one for himself.

"I'm sure it's difficult to make sense of," he started. "I've traveled a great deal, all over the world and know how it is in other cultures, other religions. It is different here. Different in my faith."

"But how does it work?" I asked, trying to understand.

Ali sighed. "You simply get to know people in a group setting, in the presence of others. Like us with Khaled, for instance. If we were dating, he wouldn't be here, using your definition of a date, right?"

"Perhaps, though there are group dates," I countered. But I knew what he meant.

Ali smiled. "It is different though, is it not? In my faith, one does not live with another before marriage. There is no trying each other out, to see if it works. You must commit seriously, you must marry before ever taking that next step," he explained.

"How interesting," I said, leaning forward. "It used to be that way in America, but times have changed," I admitted.

"I know. They haven't changed here though," said Ali, as he looked over to his brother who had kept his mouth shut for most of our time at the restaurant. "Our customs are here to stay; they are part of who we are."

"That says a lot about a country. And its people. Having respect for your faith, for your history--I admire that."

Ali looked at me, a smile teasing on his lips though he raised an eyebrow as if he were taken aback.

"What?" I asked, feeling like our friendship or whatever it was would have many of these playful moments--sharing and learning from one another.

"I guess your respect surprises me, that's all. You seem much more open-minded than I expected. What a wonderful quality to possess."

I felt myself blushing at his words, ever more confused by them as well. It certainly seemed like he liked me; it felt that way, but on face value, he'd said this was just a friendship. Why did it matter, I asked myself as I matched his intense stare. It didn't. Because even if I did like him, even if he did like me, we were from different cultures, different religions, different countries. And even if we could overcome that, there was no way we could actively date like we would in the western world.

"Is anything else restricted?" I asked curiously, trying to distract myself from his dark brown eyes.

It was Ali's turn to blush this time. His cheeks grew just a shade darker, his lips turned up in an embarrassed smile. But Ali said nothing.

"What?" I asked, even more curious now.

"There's no physical contact between a man and a woman before marriage. None," explained Khaled, matter-of-factly.

"That's strange for you, hard to understand, I'm sure," added Ali.

It took me a minute to wrap my head around that concept before I could reply. "You're serious?" I asked, wanting to make sure this wasn't a joke they were playing on the foreigner.

"Absolutely," said Ali, no tone of humor in his voice.

"No contact? But what about a hug or a kiss, or even holding hands?" I asked.

"No. Nothing like that. No physical contact of any kind is permitted. There isn't supposed to be any type of physical activity what so ever before marriage," he explained.

"Well, that sure makes for an exciting wedding night," I laughed awkwardly, unsure how to get our lunch back on track, back to the light hearted topics we'd been discussing earlier.

Ali and Khaled exchanged a look between them before laughing along with me.

"Do people always gather like this?" I asked, nodding to a group of men convened on our left-- old and young mixing together, sharing in a joke as they munched on their flat breads.

"Not every day." Ali laughed, "But yes, it's a social thing here, and meals are a great opportunity to enjoy each other's company. Wouldn't you agree?"

I smiled back at him and Khaled. "Of course. It's wonderful, isn't it? I could get used to this," I said, watching the world unfold around us.

In no time, the waiter appeared with the first dishes. With a warm smile, he set down a beautiful plate of food in the center of our table, and laid out individual small plates in front of each of us.

"Oh, Darla you must try this," said Ali, his eyes lit up. "It's fattoush--delicious." He quickly dished out some of the salad onto my plate without waiting for my answer.

"Great. Looks good," I said, eyeing the mixed greens, tomato and fried pita salad before me. I quickly took a bite, happily confirming it tasted as good as it looked.

But before I could open my mouth again, the waiter reappeared with a handful of other dishes. And then some more. Within the course of five minutes, our table was covered in an assortment of delicacies that Ali had ordered for me to try.

"This is hummus. Have you tried that before? I know it's popular outside of the Middle East, too," said Ali, scooping a dollop of the puréed chick-pea dip onto my plate. "And you've got to try the falafel. They make it beautifully here. Nicely seasoned," said Ali.

I looked down at the small balls of food he was putting on my plate.

"What are they made of?" I asked, digging into one.

"Chickpeas and fava beans. You can have them in a pita too, a bit like a sandwich," Ali explained. "And this here is mansaf, the national dish of Jordan." Ali beamed with pride as he served me a portion of the rice and lamb dish in front of him. "It's Bedouin in origin. One of my favorites. Please, you must give it a try," he insisted, as he continued to pile small bits of each dish onto my plate.

I happily took a mouthful of the lamb and rice; it was easy to see why they adopted it as the national dish--it was indeed delicious.

Plates of grape leaves, olives and maddamis, which I found out was crushed fava beans served with olive oil and lemon juice, were spread out in front of me. All in all, we had a full table of every traditional dish Jordan had to offer.

"Mmmm," I said to Ali, as I took another mouthful. "This is all so scrumptious. I can't believe how much there is to try!" I said, looking at all the courses of food.

"I know. We haven't even tried the main dish yet."

"There's more to come?"

"Just one more: Bagdonsyyeh with seafood. It's the finest parsley blended with tahini and lemon juice. And then blended with fish. You'll love it."

And sure enough, I did. Still, there was so much food and way too many leftovers. Yet, I enjoyed every bite of everything that was placed on my plate. My first lunch with Ali was undoubtedly one to remember.

I sat there opposite Ali for the rest of the meal, pondering his words, his world, his religion. It was all so very different from my upbringing, yet by some strange coincidence it seemed the two of us had a great deal in common. He was a well-traveled, well-educated man, someone with a great deal of faith, and charisma--and in any other world this would have been a wonderful first date. Only it wasn't a date.

I watched him closely thinking about the rules and restrictions in his world, wondering if there was a place for me in it; and whether I wanted to be a part of it, as a friend or otherwise.

7

As fate would have it, I soon did become part of Ali's world. And he became part of my life and routine in Jordan. It was an easy transition--after that first lunch together, we made arrangements to see each other again the following week. And so this friendship, or courtship, or whatever this actually was, continued to bloom; whether it was a meal, or an activity, or an adventure, we saw each other regularly over the course of the next few months.

"Darla?" asked the voice on the other end of the line.

"Ali!" I smiled, joyous to hear from him again.

"Are you ready for our trip? Does tomorrow still suit?"

I looked at the calendar on my wall, already knowing I never had classes on a Saturday. Penciled in was my date with Ali. Not a date technically, but our planned outing--with him and I, and Khaled.

"Of course. I'll be ready and waiting," I said, unable to stop myself from smiling.

"Fantastic. I promised to show you the sights and I can't wait to get started."

"Don't worry, I'll hold you to it," I laughed.

After our lunch together, Ali decided I needed a personal tour of Jordan--all the top sightseeing sites but with the insights of a local. Of course I jumped at the chance, so we made plans to go out this weekend.

"Bright and early, yes? You'll be ready?" he said, double checking.

"I can be. And you won't tell me why though? Or where we're going?" I asked.

Ali laughed on the other end of the phone. "And ruin the surprise?"

"Please?" I said sweetly.

"What fun would that be?"

"So I don't get to find out now?" I asked, giving up on him, my mind racing ahead, going through the most likely contenders.

"Don't you want to be surprised?" teased Ali.

"I can take a surprise. A good one at least," I said, knowing there wasn't long left to wait anyhow. "Do I get a hint, at least?"

Ali laughed. "Sure. That sounds fair. We're going to a city made of rose."

"Okay, not much to go on," I teased. "See you bright and early," I answered, feigning ignorance before hanging up the phone. And then I couldn't help the size of the grin that spread across my face. Did he really think I hadn't done my homework, that I didn't already have a short list of possibilities?

My smile grew wider as I went looking for my camera. The Rose City--we must be going to visit Petra, Jordan's most famous historical site.

I looked out the window as Ali drove us towards the south of the country. "Is it far from here?" I asked, my eyes staying focused on the desert in the distance.

"Patience, Darla. But no, not much further." Ali laughed, looking over at me.

"I'm just excited!" I answered.

"I'm glad. We'll have to take you to a few other sites, too. This is just the first."

"Thank you, Ali. That's very sweet of you, both."

"It is my pleasure. Such good company; and it is so nice to get to know you better."

I looked over towards him, as my cheeks grew warm, even rose-colored, from his words. "I can't tell you how much I am looking forward to seeing this, Ali. Your country is so rich in history, I can't wait. It must be strange--growing up in a world where you're surrounded by reminders of the past, living proof of ancient eras, while you're actually trying to figure out life in modern times. Do you think that's why the culture here is so traditional?" I asked, trying to delve deeper into who he is and why he is how he is.

Ali smiled at me. "Perhaps. To be honest, I've never thought about it. We simply love our lives the best way we know how. Respect for our God, respect for our culture, our family, each other--it's a simple recipe for happiness. And what's yours, Darla? You strike me as someone who enjoys a happy life as well."

I laughed awkwardly, blushing even more than before. His tone, his words, they carried with them a sense of intimacy I was not expecting. "I like to think I live a happy life. It's not always picture perfect, but whose is? I don't have a secret formula though," I answered, shaking my head. "But I do think I'm getting a better idea of what works for me."

"And what's that?"

I smiled, looking down, suddenly feeling a little self-conscious. Ali wasn't just trying to make small talk; he was genuinely interested in my answer, in finding out who I am too. "I'm a bit of a free spirit. I love to travel, I love the world--exploring, discovering, a healthy dose of adventure," I rambled, fading out near the end.

"Sounds a lot like what we're doing today," said Ali, grinning with satisfaction.

"Yes. Like I said, I'm excited about our trip. I've always wanted to see Petra."

"Petra. You know?! Who told you? Khaled, did you tell her?" asked Ali, looking at his brother with mock disappointment.

Khaled shook his head, saying nothing.

"Please, Ali--your hint gave you away. A Rose City? Surely, I'd heard of Petra before. And heard of her nickname," I teased.

Ali smiled back at me. "You are a clever one, aren't you? I suppose there's no point keeping secrets from you, is there?" he said, with a serious look.

"Definitely not. I'll figure it out sooner or later," I warned playfully. "Why? Do you have a lot of secrets?" I laughed, looking out the window.

"Look, we're almost there," said Ali, pointing out the window to the village up ahead. "This is a Wadi Musa, the closest town to the site. We'll stop to pick up our tickets and then be on our way."

I nodded, looking ahead to the dusty silhouetted shape of a village in the distance.

Ali made quick work of everything, just as he had ordering in the restaurant. He took care of our tickets, and getting us a map to follow for our adventure.

"Here, let me have a look," I said, reaching out for the map.

Ali paused before handing it to me, as if he instinctively wanted not to, but thought better of it.

"You're very independent, aren't you? Darla, I can see this free spirit quality you spoke of."

My eyes flickered towards him before quickly finding their way back to the lines on the map. There was this subtle tension building between us, an undercurrent of heat, matched by the sun that was rising higher in the sky. Only the interest, the chemistry between us, was unlike anything I had ever felt before.

With a chaperone next to us, and strict protocol about any sort of physical contact, all my body's usual responses were off limits; and the entire situation, not being on a date, but feeling like we were on so many levels--it left my mind struggling even more so than usual to figure out what this was between Ali and I.

"Are we ready?" I asked. "Looks like it's this way. Am I right? You've been here before, I assume?"

"You're correct. And yes, we have been here before. Do you like history, Darla?"

I nodded to Ali.

"Then you'll love Petra."

Although it was a bit of a walk, soon, it became clear that we were getting closer. There were people all around us, funneling together as we got nearer to the site.

"Is this it?" I asked, eyeing the rocky passage way, nestled between the high walls of the mountain on either side of us. The dusty rose color of the stone was breathtaking, it shimmered in the sun.

"Yes, we're here. This is called the Siq," explained Ali, motioning for me to go first.

I smiled, instinctively reaching out to take his hand in mine, but he quickly shook his head. I dropped my eyes for the shortest of seconds before pushing aside the rebuff.

"The Siq," I said, looking down at my map.

A tour guide led a group up ahead as we made our way down towards the historical city.

I wiped away a bead of sweat from the hot sun as we followed behind them; I enjoyed listening to the guide spout off facts as we admired the rose colored walls around us.

"Situated in the southern part of the country, behold: our beautiful archeological city of Petra, famous for its chiseled architecture, carved directly in the rock and a brilliant water system, centuries before its time."

"How old is it?" I asked, looking ahead through the almost tunneled entrance.

"315 BC, give or take a few years," said Ali, his pride plain to hear. "It's in a valley that runs from the Dead Sea to the Red Sea. We'll go there too. Another day."

"To where?" I asked, turning my attention from the narrow gorge we were walking through towards Ali with interest. From the way he looked at me, and how he wanted to take care of me, plus all the time he wanted to spend together--I shook my head, trying to reset my Western frame of reference. But even still, it sure seemed like Ali was interested in me, in a way that was more than just pursuing a friendship.

"I want to take you all over Jordan. We can go to Aqaba another time. It's a little village at the edge of the Red Sea. You'll love it. It's beautiful."

"This. This is beautiful," I said, as the Siq started to taper off, before dramatically opening out onto the ancient Rose City.

"Yes, very beautiful," Ali said, agreeing.

"Shhh," I whispered with a smile, enjoying the silence around us. It somehow intensified the moment, transporting me back thousands of years, as if history was coming alive before me.

For right in front of us was the most magnificent stone carved structure I had ever seen. "The Treasury," whispered Ali after a moment. "It's a temple. Petra was at the center of everything back then."

"How so?" I asked, wandering around the beautiful rose colored stone carvings. The intricate, incredible Treasury stood before us, in pristine condition, as if it had been carved just yesterday. The incredible relic surpassed everything I had ever seen before.

"How did it work back then?" I asked, trying to picture a life more than 2000 years before my own. "This must have been an important place, to merit all this," I said, waving to the incredible chiseled detail in the rock face.

"It was. Petra was the hub of trade, and continued to be for centuries. It's all down to its positioning," explained Ali.

"Positioning?" I asked, raising my hand to shield the glare from the sun.

"You know the phrase, all roads lead to Rome?" asked Ali, with a knowing smile.

"I do," I said, smiling back at him. How strange that even in a simple conversation like this, the tension between us remained, like an electric current, constantly running through every interaction.

"Well, it is the same with Petra. Every commercial route passed through here; no matter which way you were heading--from Gaza or Damascus, the Red Sea, or across the desert to the Persian Gulf--everyone went via Petra."

"So, it's simply geography then? That's what made it so important?" I asked, trying to understand as I ran my hand along the smooth rock face.

The columns reminded me of Ancient Greece, yet the Middle Eastern feel was undeniable. A juxtaposition of east meeting west that was echoed back to my mind every time I looked into Ali's dark brown eyes. I turned to look at him again, wondering if I'd ever truly understand him, any more than I did this site. My knowledge of Petra was peripheral at best.

Beneath those lively eyes, there were secrets there, I could feel it. But unlike the Treasury before us, there would be no team of historians to uncover Ali's secrets; nor would I have centuries to figure him out.

"Geography? To a degree, yes, but it was also water--there was a stream, a constant trickle of fresh water that was available here. And that was invaluable to travelers," explains Ali.

"Oh I can imagine."

"Yes, I'm sure you can. The Nabataeans controlled the water as well, with dams and cisterns, so in a sense they created an artificial oasis, right in the middle of the desert."

"Amazing. No wonder it prospered."

"Come on, let's head over to the Monastery. It's a bit of a climb, but the view is incredible. And then we can explore everything Petra has to offer."

"800 steps, Ali!" mumbled Khaled, before Ali turned to stare at him, silencing him on the spot.

True to his word, it was a bit of a climb, but the views from the top of the Monastery, of the lush surrounding valleys, were outstanding.

"What a lovely day, Ali. Thank you so much for taking me here," I said, reaching out to touch his arm, but stopping a few inches short, remembering the rules.

"Honestly, the pleasure was all mine."

"So, is this going to be a weekly thing?" I teased. "Where will you be taking me next weekend? Or has someone else already staked their claim on you?" I laughed to myself.

Khaled and Ali exchanged a look between them before Ali subtly shook his head. "Hmmm. I don't think I can do next weekend, but the following one might work for me. Will that suit?"

"Definitely," I said, already looking forward to our time together.

"Darla, have you decided?" asked Ali, leaning towards me over the table.

I grinned back at him, and at Khaled, for we were never together without our chaperone. "No," I admitted, looking over the menu once more.

The men laughed at my indecision. We had been chatting so much, I hadn't taken the time to really look at the meal options.

"It's all so good, I can't decide," I said, making excuses for myself. But there was no point. It was always the same whenever we ate out--the conversation flowed so easily, the food seemed an afterthought. And while Ali and his brother could choose a familiar dish with just a quick glance, I was rarely able to order off the top of my head.

"Would you like me to order for you, Darla?" joked Ali.

He wouldn't have minded, happily ordering for all of us like that first time, but I shook my head and quickly settled on falafel.

"Now where were we?" I asked, trying to remember where we'd left off. "Oh yes, we were talking about traveling. So, tell me, in all your adventures, what is it that surprises you most about the world?" I stared at him as I spoke, getting lost in his dark brown eyes.

"What an interesting question, Darla. I'm sure you have your own observations. You've been to more places than me," Ali grinned. "Hmmm," he paused, giving careful thought to my question. "I'd be torn to narrow it down to one thing, but how about two?"

I nodded, interested in hearing his response. "I'm curious, please tell."

"Okay. Well, you know how much of a believer I am - how devoted to my prayers, how much faith I have, much like you," started Ali.

"Yes."

"Well, I admit, it struck me as strange, shocking even, how there are so many without that faith. I cannot imagine the emptiness in a life, or community, yet I've seen a great deal of people living without this belief in a higher power, or faith of any kind." Ali shrugged, though I could tell this concerned him more than he was letting on. "That surprises me about the world," he said, matching my gaze.

"And the second thing?"

Ali shook off his serious look and smiled widely. "Despite what I just said, I was even more surprised by our similarities—we are all the same, we are all just people. Most of us are seeking happiness on some level, striving to make a better life for ourselves or our families. That's interesting, isn't it? No matter where you live, most of us share a common goal. Of course, we're taking different paths, different approaches, but the aim is the same for so many of us. Did you ever notice that?" asked Ali.

I nodded, taken aback by his honesty and perceptiveness. I had seen this common goal in my travels; I had reached for it myself. "Definitely. It's amazing to see, really. Wouldn't it be nice if we could all work together to help each other achieve it?" I said, knowing that was perhaps an even harder task than imagining each individual attempting it by themselves.

In so many places, so many pre-existing cultural differences made it seem impossible to connect and help one another, despite the best intentions. What had he thought about that, I wondered. "And our differences? Did those not stand out to you?" I asked,

"Of course. We have differences. But that doesn't need to be divisive. Not when we share the bigger picture, right?"

"Of course not," I agreed, feeling in sync with him; Ali's optimism drew me in. But somehow his simple answer seemed too easy and too appealing all the same. Why couldn't life be that simple, I wondered, wanting to believe his words. Culture and customs didn't always have to complicate things, did they?

I glanced between Ali and his brother, trying to imagine what others saw as they looked at us. Here we were, a prime example of two very different cultures, meeting in the middle. Would they approve or disapprove of our get-together? How did the passing locals perceive our outings, the company we shared? I knew without a doubt what it looked like to a westerner--a date, a romance in progress.

Yet even knowing in my heart what *I* thought it was, I couldn't be sure if Ali had the same perception. For all that we were the same, there was still something different there, I thought, quickly getting caught up in my own emotions.

8

It simply wasn't black and white between Ali and I. And though we talked about all manner of topics, we never seemed to stray back to the original discussion of relationships, courting or dating. It felt like I was in the dark, in every sense of the word. Where was this going, I wondered to myself.

We'd been having these conversations over dinner for months now, plus a handful of weekend adventures to see the sights--yet it was almost surreal in the way they were labeled. Or weren't, rather. Dissecting it piece by piece: there was mutual interest between us--we both could feel the chemistry and enjoyed each other's company. And the outings themselves had an undeniably personal, even intimate feel to them. Only we weren't allowed to call them dates. Like an exercise in semantics--if it seemed like a date and felt like a date, so wasn't it a date, regardless of what you called it?

I was hard-pressed to understand what made this *not* a date. But it didn't really matter; titles and labels were simply that--only words.

Naturally, the lack of physical intimacy was clearly one sign that this wasn't a date. I had a tough time adjusting initially. Religion-wise, I understood it went against Ali's beliefs, but still, for me--a kiss or a hug didn't seem that controversial. Just a sign of affection. And most of the guys I'd ever dated always assumed hugging and kissing were the natural order of things, even as a typical way to greet someone, particularly if they're considered a good friend.

But other than that one point of contention, which was founded in religious belief rather than desire, I couldn't see how Ali and I weren't dating, regardless of what this time together was called.

I looked across the table at him, in the middle of a crowded restaurant, and I tried to fight the urge to bring it up. But I knew as I stared into his eyes that day, I wouldn't win. I was done fighting my curiosity on this topic. I needed to know where we stood.

"Tell me, Ali. What do you think about relationships?" I waited, watching his breathing increase. Khaled squirmed in his chair, drawing my eyes away for a second.

"Ali," I asked, watching him struggle with the innocent question. "Just generally about relationships. Or better yet, why does it matter what we call these little outings that we have? An answer to either question will do," I said, point blank.

Ali paused, choosing his words carefully. "It shouldn't matter, but it does. It's simply how things are done here. I imagine once a culture ignores its history, its practices, then surely one by one it erodes. Wouldn't that be a negative thing for society, or for a religion? If you simply pick and choose which elements to follow? And who makes that choice? Surely not someone with respect for their upbringing." Ali looked troubled by his answer but convinced all the same.

"But what's the difference, in your mind, between a 'date' and what we're doing?" I asked, not trying to start a fight, or trying to be right in any way; I asked out of curiosity and for the intelligent debate that would follow. And for the obvious desire to understand exactly where the trajectory of our 'friendship' was heading.

At worst, even if I didn't end up with any clear cut answers, in a strange way, these discussions always made me feel closer to him. Ali was so open minded about our differences, so well versed in conversation, there was nothing to lose by asking the question, perhaps except for a little pride.

"This compared to a date?" Ali clarified.

I nodded, feeling unnecessarily anxious I'd asked about it.

"Having never been on one, I can't say, but let's look at the bigger picture. Every culture, every religion has their own philosophy. I don't think I'd want to hypothesize whether one was better than another with regards to anyone other than myself. But for me, and this is my opinion, not that of my faith, I can't understand how dating, in the west, is anything other than lust. Surely, if there is so much physical contact that becomes the primary focus of your relationship--there is no deeper bond, no greater understanding created between both parties."

"And you obviously think this way is better--with a chaperone, and restrictions? Does that encourage a more honest relationship? Don't you think it sets people up for a lot of surprises if they do eventually get married?" I countered.

"Perhaps, but then again, isn't that part of the bond of marriage? Learning to love one another, faults and all? No one is perfect, surely that we can agree on. Aren't forgiveness and compassion, understanding and acceptance all elements that make up a healthy marriage?"

"You speak like you have experience," I laughed. "Yes, of course--all those things are part of a marriage. But why go into it with the deck stacked against you? Shouldn't you know someone as best as possible before committing your life to them?"

Ali grinned at me. He enjoyed our debates as much as I did. Khaled, on the other hand, now looked positively bored.

"Okay, then how do you factor in those who have an arranged marriage? Surely there is something to be said about the success of those relationships. Not formed by love, but by others for social or familial or some other type of gain, yet many of these couples manage to live together in harmony for their entire lives."

"Are you making a case for arranged marriages? Even in this day and age?" I asked, trying to put myself in those shoes, trying to imagine a wedding where I had not chosen the groom, and perhaps he had not chosen me. It seemed surreal, so outside my comfort zone, and my reality; it was almost impossible to imagine.

"Arranged marriages--absolutely. They are very popular in Islam. And successful, too. What makes you think otherwise?" Ali asked, curiously.

"Love, obviously. There is no love in an arranged marriage," I answered.

"Are you sure?"

"How can there be? The two people didn't choose each other, not freely, or independently."

"Perhaps not, but how well does all that choice fair out? Can someone not learn to love another? Does having love at the beginning mean it will carry on forever?"

I thought carefully before answering, knowing how valid Ali's points were. I'd had a choice, any man in the world, and - twice now - I'd not picked a love that lasted. And it wasn't just the marriages. In most of my relationships, the romance and love had died very quickly especially when it came to facing the real issues in the real world.

"It's..." I paused, wanting to be honest, but respectful all the same. "It's difficult for me to understand how it works, the type of faith and trust in your family to make such a monumental decision on your behalf. And, if I'm honest, the idea of marrying a stranger seems wrong on some level, despite the fact it might work in some cases."

"How wrong can they be when statistically, arranged marriages prove to be more successful and lasting than ones derived from a western type courtship?"

I nodded, still processing the idea of this. Yet, as I tried to think it through, I couldn't help but remember the way my friends and I had mocked and disrespected the very notion of an arranged marriage, years earlier. And now, here I was wondering honestly if that type of arrangement would have given me a longer marriage, and a lasting relationship of some sort.

"I imagine you have a theory as to why they're more successful?" I asked.

Ali smiled at me, taking the questions all in stride. "There is an old Arabic saying: 'the mirror of love is blind, it makes zucchini into okra.'

It means love blinds people. It blinds them to potential problems in the relationship."

"So, if you choose to marry because you're already in love with someone, it means you're also already blind to who they really are?"

"Yes, exactly. Whereas on the other hand, with an arranged marriage, they are not based on physical attraction or romantic notions but rather on critical evaluation of the compatibility of the couple. It's much more objective and pragmatic in a sense, all to the benefit of the couple later down the road."

"That's an interesting idea," I said, trying to think about it objectively myself. Even with the knowledge that it may be more successful, would I, even now, opt for an arranged marriage, instead of love? It was hard to say.

"Well, it is a theory. Who knows; it's my best guess though as to why those marriages often prove successful," Ali shrugged. "Have you ever been blinded by another man's charm?"

I laughed nervously. "Do you mean in my marriages?"

"Or any relationship? Or rather, do you think it can happen?"

"Definitely, it happens quite easily, I'd say. There is so much that gets in the way of objectivity--someone can easily be blinded by physical appearances, distracted by attraction, preoccupied with passions; with even just one of these, it'd be easy to overlook the bigger picture of compatibility. And that's such a main ingredient for success, but it's so easily brushed aside by a charming smile," I said, laughing at the teasing, intentional smile on Ali's face.

"It's an interesting question though, isn't it? What's the best route to a happy, lasting marriage?"

I thought for a minute, though I knew Ali meant it rhetorically. "Honesty," I said quietly. "I think if you're honest with each other and honest with yourself--no matter how you get to the altar, if it's based on honesty, then you should have a fighting chance."

Ali looked at me for a quick second before staring down at his plate. Khaled twitched off to the side, also preoccupied with his meal.

I looked at Ali, wondering what I had said that was wrong or had been misinterpreted. Surely there could be no argument against honesty? In that moment, I wished more than ever I could just reach over and touch his hand, connecting with him on a physical level. Though it was hard at first, not having any physical contact of any sort with him; at times like this, I craved it--just a quick touch of the hand, a simple, instinctual reassuring gesture. But I knew Khaled frowned upon it.

I wondered if this level of formal modesty would be the same in a more informal setting, say at the beach. And it wasn't long before I received my answer.

"Did you bring a towel?" asked Ali as I headed for his car. I spotted Khaled already waiting inside as usual.

I nodded to Ali, pointing to a tote bag for the beach, slung on my shoulder.

"Will we be going in the water? I mean, people swim in Aqaba, right?" I asked, my head teeming with the familiar images of beaches and turquoise waters from another life.

"Absolutely," agreed Ali. "Aqaba is known for its marine life too. With your diving experience, I'm sure you'll love it," said Ali.

"So, you'll come in with me?" I asked, thrilled by the idea of letting go a little and playing on the beach, like old times. As I looked over at Ali, unable to even touch his hand or hug him to say hello, part of me thought maybe a change of scenery would relax these restraints between us. The beach has a way about it--of loosening people up, of thawing out the stresses of daily life.

But, Ali just paused, avoiding my question as I got into the car.

"It Jordan's only coastal town, you know," said Ali as we made our way down the highway. "It's very popular as you might imagine, everyone heads here in the summer."

And as soon as we pulled into the seaside city, I understood why. While in my mind I had been imagining the beautiful blue waters of the Caribbean, I never expected to see something comparable here--but there it was. The gulf of Aqaba was a stunning aquamarine, complimented by a beautiful golden sand beach, both looking inviting and ready for our enjoyment.

People covered almost every inch of the landscape. My head spun as I tried to take in the mash-up of cultures and customs on display before me. There were plenty of Europeans, parading around in their bathing suits, splashing in the water, lounging in the sand; but there were also those from Jordan and other parts of the Middle East if I had to guess--dressed much more conservatively, showing little to no skin as they went about the same activities.

We picked a calm spot not far from the water's edge where I put down my tote.

"Do you mind if I go in?" I asked, looking over at Ali with a little more anxiety than I was used to. Suddenly, seeing all these women, half covered in modest attire, half dressed in bikinis, made me slightly unsure of how Ali would react if I went into the sea wearing just my bathing suit.

"By all means, we're at the beach--enjoy yourself," said Ali. But I caught Khaled's eyes turning away from me as I took off my top layer revealing my swimwear underneath.

But I was getting used to sometimes doing the Western thing (the wrong thing) from time to time, and receiving unsettled glances from strangers. My approach to life in Jordan was: be respectful, but also be myself. And as there were others enjoying the beach as I would have in the Caribbean, then so would I.

With a carefree laugh, I ran down the beach into the cool waters and waved at Ali, as he sat down on the sand, smiling happily and soaking in the rays. Most importantly, he brought me here and he was not offended that I wanted to swim and play. I just wished that he could join me, as a friend, or whatever he actually was, and let go – jump in the sea, in front of everyone – because there seemed to be something holding him back, and it was more than just his culture and religion.

Nevertheless, in this vein, our relationship maintained its course, with few bumps as long as we stayed off the topic of what indeed our relationship was. Yet, it was clearly something that remained on both of our minds as we sat down for another dinner, with Khaled beside us.

"Darla," said Ali, speaking quietly.

I looked over to him, trying to ignore Khaled. Something was different in Ali's voice. Concern, or worry? Was he anxious? That didn't seem right.

"What is it, Ali?" I asked.

"Darla, I know we come from different backgrounds. We come from different regions of the world, and different religions. But we are both one and the same in so many ways."

"Yes," I agreed warily, not sure where this was headed.

"I accept you for who you are," said Ali. His stare was intense, as if he were trying to convey something greater than just his words.

"Absolutely. I love who you are--every part of you adds to that. If I could, I'd change nothing," I added, trying to reassure him with my smile.

"Thank you, Darla. That means a lot." Ali looked down at his lap, playing with something under the table, his napkin, I guessed. He hesitated before speaking again. I'd never seen him anything but confident, yet today he seemed anxious.

"What is it? You can tell me," I said softly.

Ali looked up at me and smiled. "I've enjoyed these conversations between the two of us. Our time together has been treasured by me. You mean a great deal to me."

"And you to me," I added, feeling slightly nervous myself.

"I respect you, Darla. You know that, don't you?"

"Of course. And I respect you. Ali, is something the matter?" I asked, unable to help myself.

"No, actually. There's something I want to ask you, that's all."

"Please," I said, gesturing with my open palm for him to go ahead.

"Darla," he started, pushing a small traditional box in front of me. "Darla, will you do me the honor of marrying me?" asked Ali. "Be my wife."

I stared back at him, flabbergasted. Though we had enjoyed plenty of wonderful, open, honest, enjoyable conversations, discussing anything and everything, and though I was fairly certain he fancied me romantically, never had I considered the possibility of marrying Ali. Simply put--I assumed it was out of the question. Given our differences, wouldn't it be difficult for his family to accept me? Wouldn't public perception alone be enough to stop our love from ever blossoming?

"Ali," I started, my voice shaking. I didn't know what to say.

"I'm ready to marry you. I'd like to spend more time together, our lives together. I don't care that you're a western woman, that on paper we've got more differences than similarities--I'd very much like you to be my wife."

In my head, in that moment, I couldn't think of the words to say. A third marriage. Was I ready for that? Did I want that? Questions flashed through my head while others piled up, waiting their turn.

I closed my eyes, not bothering with social convention. I needed to pray, not out loud, but pray nonetheless. "Oh Lord," I prayed silently in my head.

I imagined Ali watched my still figure, curious no doubt as to what I was doing, but I didn't care. "Lord, what should I do? Ali wants to marry me!" My heart pounded as I thought the words, as others chased behind them with lightning speed. *Mrs. Ali al-Majali.*

"Darla?" a voice called me back to reality.

I blinked my way back to the present, my heart still racing from the adrenaline.

Could I do this? Was this what I wanted? It was hard to think rationally in the heat of the moment. But whether or not I would have made a different choice if I'd had forever to decide, I simply cannot say.

"Ali," I said quietly, slowly, looking at the man before me with new eyes. I asked myself: Did I love him? Did I want to spend my life with him?

I looked at his chiseled features, his beautiful caramel skin, with his warmth radiating out of him--he was so very different from everything I'd ever known. So much like me, yet so different. But none of that mattered in this instant, at that moment, for part of me, the idea of being his wife sounded like a dream. Being a Mrs. again, being part of a team, part of a partnership in every sense of the word.

I hadn't dared think of getting married again, that was never my intention. The relationship happened innocently enough, a chance encounter that fateful day in the shopping mall. But being a wife, being a Mrs.--my heart swelled at the very notion. Something about that title seemed so alluring to me.

In my core, I felt a sense of validation swell up, like somehow, being tied to another made me better in a way. It was like someone saying they loved you best of all, better than everyone else in the world--and saying it loud enough for the rest of the world to hear. The idea was like a drug; the promise of being a Mrs. was a boost to the self-esteem, enough to erase any residual pain and shame from my past divorce.

But I was smarter than I had been, learning something from my past mistakes. I could really make this work this time.

I stared at Ali, wanting to choose my words carefully, knowing that Khaled was still at our table, albeit doing his best to give us our space. "I very much enjoy our time together. And I would be honored to be your wife. But how do you see our future? Do you think this can really work?"

Ali beamed, his smile spreading up to his eyes with relief. "No difference is too great. We can make anything work if we truly believe in our love." He seemed convinced, as if everything was possible. But I wouldn't, couldn't fall into the same trap again. This time, I had to think about this. I had to block off the allure of marriage and ask some questions.

"I'm sure we can do anything, Ali. But tell me, how does it work here? I imagine it must be different in certain ways. Everything else about us is different than I would have anticipated. We've never even kissed and now you've proposed! Tell me, what have I not asked, what is there to understand that I might not be aware of?"

"Once you are my wife, we are married, like any other married couple. We can be together. In every sense," he explained.

"Where will we live?" I asked, not wanting to get carried away by the idea of us together, no chaperone, no supervision, no rules--just together, him and I.

"Here, in the city. I have a place--it will become our place, if you accept. It's not extravagant, but we can make it a home." Ali smiled as he painted a picture for me of our life together.

"And now--as an engaged couple, do the rules change?" I asked, wondering if they were serious about the no contact rule until marriage, no one-on-one time until then.

"No, nothing changes during the engagement period. Until the actual wedding, it is much the same as now. A chaperone until we are joined together. It is important to me that we honor my faith."

"Of course, Ali. I completely understand. I merely wanted to be on the same page as you," I explained.

"And? What do you think?" asked Ali, pushing the box towards me.

I'd completely forgotten about it, now front and center. Slowly I opened the lid of the intricate box, revealing a beautiful diamond ring inside. "It's gorgeous," I whispered.

"You like it?"

"I love it," I said quietly, feeling almost at a loss for words. My heart rate picked up again, beating faster inside my chest as I tried to process what I was about to do. Was I really going to put this on, say yes, and get married again?

I shifted my eyes back up to Ali and stared at him for a long moment. He looked back at me, letting me take my time with this.

"Yes," I answered. "I'll be your wife."

9

Ali and I were to marry in the early spring; just a small ceremony, mainly family and a few friends.

To mark the occasion, we threw a bridal shower, which consisted of one of the traditional events in the region called Laylat Al Henna. A few friends that I had met in the area, Deena, Layla, and Cynthia, along with Aila and my three best friends from home, Sharon, Thelma and Patricia, were all there to join in the occasion.

With intricate patterns and beautiful designs, it was a ceremony that involved tattooing the hands and feet with temporary henna ink. This event signified attractiveness, fortune and healthiness—and it was strikingly pretty and felt like a wonderful way to celebrate the culture of the country that was becoming my home.

After we adorned ourselves in the beautiful henna—giggling throughout as we were tickled during the drawing process, and also feeling like children playing with paints in kindergarten, or perhaps more like rebellious teenagers getting 'inked' with real tattoos—we then gathered at Deena's mansion. She had hired a private caterer and disc jockey to feed and entertain us. Just the women, all getting together, and dancing the night away with our freshly dried tattoos.

The next day, after a long shower to wash away the ink (and wash away our aches from being on our feet, dancing around), Aila and I went to our dress fitting together for some mother-daughter time.

"Mom—does this look okay?" asked Aila.

"You're beautiful," I said, turning to see how her dress looked for the occasion. Our first and last fitting, all at the same time. Thankfully, everything fit to perfection.

I smiled to myself at how easy going I'd been in planning this wedding—nothing like the drama and expectations I'd had with my wedding to Adam. This one really was shaping up to be so different from the other ones; in reality, my prior weddings seemed like a lifetime ago.

But my head still tried to explain it--why was it different? Why was *I* different? I looked down at the long-sleeved white dress I was wearing and then across at my lovely daughter. Her presence in my life was enough to explain the difference. Maybe now I finally understood what was important in life--her, me, Ali--it was those people that mattered, not an event; not a ceremony, followed by a party.

It was easy to explain away the difference by just Aila alone, but somehow it felt like it was more than that. I stared at my reflection, not really recognizing the woman looking back at me, all covered up. It was strange--I felt devoid of the giddy excitement I'd had expected to feel about getting married again, despite feeling the most ready I had ever been for the events ahead of us.

Maybe it was because I'd already had the "dream" wedding with the big reception; I didn't need it a second time, did I? Or maybe it was because I saw how much a wedding is truly just a day, compared to the ongoing relationship that is formed from it? Or maybe it was because other than my three best friends and Aila, there would be no one else from my side in attendance? Regardless, this time, it seemed less about the details of one day in my life and more about the love and relationship at the root of everything, for the rest of our lives.

"Thank you, honey, for coming. It means so much to me that you'd spend your spring break over here," I said, smiling at Aila.

"I wouldn't miss it. Besides--where else would I want to be with my mom about to be married? And it's not like I've ever been to Jordan before now. Two birds with one stone?" She smiled.

"Exactly. I'm serious though. It's nice to have someone here who knows me as me."

Aila stared at me, as if hearing a hidden meaning in my words, one that hadn't been intentional.

"What do you think of him?" I asked her, hoping to change the topic.

"He seems nice," she said politely.

"You two have gotten along pretty well, I think."

"Ya. Like I said, he seems nice. I'm not sure about everything, but from what I can tell..." She drifted off, letting her sentence hang in the air for a minute. "He's not exactly around every day. For better and for worse. Wait--you're supposed to be saying these sort of lines on the big day, not me," she teased before suddenly going quiet. She looked to the floor, nervously tapping fingers on the smooth fabric of her dress.

"What is it?" I asked, sensing she was holding back from me.

Aila paused, shaking her head slightly. "Are you happy here?" she asked me.

"Yes. I mean, the idea of staying anywhere terrifies me, but Ali makes me happy."

"I can see he does. But you will be staying here. And... well," started Aila, pausing again as if to pick the right words.

"Please, just tell me what's worrying you, sweetheart."

"This," she answered, picking up a scarf draped on the back of a chair, passing it to me. "It's not like you're trying to stay put in the U.S., you're talking about staying here—" Aila paused, regaining her composure. "Jordan is beautiful, Mom. And I'm happy you're happy. There just seems to be a lot of rules, a lot of restrictions. This isn't the Middle Ages." Aila huffed out a loud breath, as if the words had been pent up in her for a while.

"No, it's not the Middle Ages, you're right. It's just a different way of living."

"I see that. But I want to make sure you do, too. I want to make sure you know what you're getting into."

"I do. At least, I think I do," I answered honestly.

"Well, then explain to me--maybe I'm missing something, but why do you need to cover yourself every minute of every day? It seems, I don't know--extreme. I'm worried, Mom. That you can't... that you aren't being yourself."

"It's just the culture, that's all. I agree, it seems a bit over the top at times but it's how things are done here," I shrugged, as the fabric of the scarf slipped through my fingers. Of course, being covered all the time wasn't what I was used to, or what Aila was used to seeing, but there was simply no other way to explain it--one American woman wasn't going to change an entire culture, nor should she.

"Remember in South Korea, and in Haiti? Everywhere really--this isn't the first time we've seen another culture that seems different from our own. That's what makes it special, doesn't it? That's what we travel to discover--those unique and wonderful differences."

"I get that, but as much as we've lived by the local customs, it just seems you've taken this to another level. But you're not even Muslim, Mom. Are you? I mean, you haven't converted, have you? The same rules don't apply to you as they might do to others. Unless there's something you want to tell me?"

"No," I smiled shaking my head. "I haven't converted. Of course not."

"Has he asked you to?"

"Ali never would. He respects me. He respects my faith. And I respect his."

"But you've changed, Mom. Do you know that?"

I laughed softly, running my hand over my daughter's arm. "I love you, Aila. Thank you for caring about me. But people change when they're in a serious relationship. That's what happens. It's a give and take. Literally--I give part of myself to him, and I adopt part of him into my way of living. We become one, a team--right? He's bound to rub off on me," I added, trying to lighten the mood a little.

"Why are you doing it?" Aila asked quietly, the wind lost from her fighting spirit. She wasn't being rude, I could hear it in her voice; she was simply trying to ensure I had truly thought things through ahead of time. "You haven't known each other for very long at all. This seems pretty sudden, don't you think?"

I smiled again, unable to help from shrugging my shoulders ever so slightly. I glanced down to my ring as I spoke. "I love him. Isn't that reason enough?"

Aila looked sternly at me, unconvinced, "Yes. Just make sure you're sure. You may love him but I love you. I don't want you to get hurt, that's all I'm worried about."

I looked at my daughter, still smiling at her; it was a strange feeling having your little girl switch roles and try to be the one looking out for you.

"I love you too, honey. No matter what else happens in my life--what I'm wearing, who I'm married to, where I live--that'll never change, okay?"

She looked at me for a long minute before wrapping her arms around me in a big hug--so warm and genuine.

"Let's get you ready then, we'll make everything perfect," Aila whispered.

The week together flew by. And somehow, it was soon the morning of my wedding day. I found myself awake before sunrise, all by myself. It wasn't planned, but I'd always found the quiet moments to be centering, clarifying for my thoughts.

Looking out the window of my home, I was feeling a strange mix of emotions--nerves and anxiety filled me, coupled by a strange sense of resignation. Aila's words came back to me in those moments--why *was* I doing this?

But instead of answering for myself, a voice inside my head started arguing the bigger picture, throwing around generalities, instead of just focusing on Ali and I.

Surely love was the very best reason for getting married, was it not? And I felt that I did love Ali. But loving someone you had barely touched, had never kissed, had never been alone with? This was undoubtedly a very different kind of connection from any that I had ever experienced before. Love, but without any of the physical expressions customary in the West.

Still, there was an undeniable connection between us and it felt stronger and deeper than I would have ever imagined possible. But were we rushing into things? Was that what Aila had meant? I mulled over the question, knowing the minutes I had left as a single woman were rapidly counting down.

It was hard to imagine two middle aged people jumping the gun on something like marriage--we weren't teenagers, we weren't being pressured into anything, or fooling ourselves with unrealistic fantasies of what married life might be like. We were walking into this with our eyes wide open; it didn't matter that our courtship had been quick, did it?

I shook my head, answering my own question. I'd waited for so long before marrying Adam, and look where it got me. They hadn't been the happiest years of my life, and even after sticking it out, constructively working on it together, we'd still ended up divorced.

It wasn't like divorce just affected our relationship either--ours was hardly the first or only marriage to break down. The high rate of divorce confirmed that; there were plenty of people in the same boat.

So, maybe how long you know someone ahead of time has nothing to do with the success of your marriage.

I stared out the window, reveling in my epiphany, the words of my revelation ringing true for me. It wasn't like the advice back home was a recipe for a solid marriage. Couples can know each other for years, be intimate, live together but somehow even that kind of trial run still doesn't guarantee a happily ever after. And if that didn't maybe nothing could.

Surely, what Ali and I were doing, we had at least as good a chance as Adam and I had? People get married all over the world, and in lots of places they do so knowing each other even less than we did. My mind wandered back to my time in India, and even to a few of the friends I had met in Jordan. I'd met so many people over the years who hadn't even had the opportunity to get to know their future spouse as much as Ali and I had: arranged marriages rarely offered you this many 'dates' even if they're with a chaperone. Yet, their success rates were at least comparable to those in the West, maybe even higher, at least based on the experiences of my small circle of friends.

I guess, I thought to myself, there was no other conclusion: the embers of romance and love simply do not equate to an everlasting tie or bond between couples. It must be some other elusive quality that leads to a happy, lengthy marriage. And perhaps this time I'd found it. Though this was a sad reality, it rang true to me on so many levels.

One important feature that I did admire about a Muslim marriage was Contract. In the contract, it spelled out what each will contribute to the union and what happens in the event of a divorce. In our contract, Ali agreed to provide a fully furnished house, eight pieces of gold, and financial support for me. I agreed to give him unconditional love, wifely duties/support and a comfortable well maintained home. I even added a clause in the contract that stated that Ali would give me complete freedom of movement both in country and out. In theory, in this culture, if you leave and do not have your husband's permission, he could call the police to bring you back home to him. I also added one other clause—no woman shall be brought into the conjugal home without my consent.

In the event of divorce, Ali agreed to give me one of his four houses, a car and a monthly maintenance fee of so many dollars for a period of 15 years if I remain single.

That being said, getting divorced was the furthest thing from my mind—after the divorce from Adam, which I now accepted indeed had a chance of working out, even though our marriage failed. I sighed to myself, with a feeling of acceptance gradually settling over me. In my heart, this next step felt right, to walk down the aisle once again, and I told myself it was a different story, with hopefully a different ending than the one that Adam and I arrived at.

I looked over to the garment bag hanging on the back of the door--my wedding dress inside. Had I changed then, I wondered? Aila seemed to think so. Or was I simply getting older, getting wiser with my years?

Soon, I'd be a married woman--part of a couple, something bigger than myself. I was going to say 'I do' even though I knew Aila had her reservations; they weren't big enough to make me reconsider this new life--she liked Ali and they did get along. Besides she wasn't a child anymore; maybe it would have been different if that was the case. She was just worried about me. And in reality, probably every one back home was, too. Too fast, too different, did I really want to do this? I'm sure they all had the same reservations.

But maybe Ali and I weren't the real reason for these reservations and doubts before a marriage even leaves the starting blocks; maybe it was something broader? A clash of cultures, of the expectations of love and marriage. Perhaps in the West the romantic notions we have are simply unrealistic, even harmful to the people involved. They've proven to be as much in most cases--staying together forever is never easy. Does anyone get their death-do-they-part anymore?

I sighed, looking out as the sun slowly started to rise over the dusty horizon. Hardly the mindset and questions to have on your wedding day, I thought, shaking my head. I'd prove them wrong--maybe this marriage would be the one to last. There was only one way to find out.

Hours later, dressed in white in a modest wedding gown, with Aila by my side, I looked into Ali's eyes and said my wedding vows. Third times a charm, I thought to myself, praying the saying would hold true. As we walked away from the ceremony, I was struck by an unexpected pang of emptiness, like something was missing; but I shook it off as my new husband squeezed my hand for the first time.

Ali wanted me to experience a tradition most couples share: Dabke, where the bride and groom are carried on chairs, in the middle of the sea of guests, where they circle around us, dancing and singing.

Being lifted up, above everyone's heads in a giddy jig, scared I'd fall off my seat but seeing Ali beside me, taking this risk together. It was a joyous moment and I kept laughing and reaching out for him over the raucous crowd below us.

Needless to say, the rest of the day was a blur of excitement and activity. The ceremony had gone as planned and was in fact beautiful despite the lack of fussing on my part. And the huge party afterwards that went on long into the night was just as wonderful. It was a great day, and evening; a perfect lead in to our new life together.

Amidst the wonder and glory of the honeymoon period, our life together was wedded bliss. We enjoyed the time together alone, enjoyed our new home, and slowly, happily adjusted to our new life. Everything was good. In retrospect, perhaps I was foolish to assume it would stay that way.

The change started about six months after the wedding.

"Will you be home in time for dinner tonight?" I asked, as Ali finished up a phone call. He'd been juggling so much lately. Working late hours, and on the phone more than usual. It was as if he had a second job, a second life. But running a successful business, multiple businesses in his case, took a lot of time. I understood that and tried to be supportive rather than nagging.

Ali didn't answer me, holding his finger up to his mouth to silently shush me.

"Perfect, great. I'll see you then. Looking forward to it," he said, quickly ending the call. Despite his words, Ali looked stressed.

Even before the phone was hung up, I walked over to my husband and gently placed by hand on his face. "What is it, Ali? What are you worried about? You look like you've got the weight of the world on your poor shoulders."

Ali sweetly lifted my hand from my face, kissing the palm of it ever so gently. "Ahhh, my Darla. You do love me so. And I love you. But I do not deserve you."

"Of course you do," I smiled, blushing a little. "You love me and I love you. And we can be together now. Forever, right?"

"Wouldn't that be lovely?" said Ali, closing his eyes as my hands ran along his arm.

"It is lovely, yes. Now I didn't mean to interrupt, but what time will you be home tonight? It's Friday, so I thought maybe we could have dinner together, since you shouldn't have to work too late, right? I mean, doesn't Khaled usually handle things on the weekend?" I said, rambling a mile a minute, waiting for Ali to interrupt me, but he didn't.

He simply shook his head. "Not tonight. I've got work to do."

I stared at him, unable to hide my disbelief. "Again? You've been late three times this week. Is everything okay at the shop?"

Ali nodded briefly. "It's nothing for you to worry about. Do you miss me when I'm out late?"

"Every minute." I laughed, though there was more seriousness than sarcasm in my answer. "I don't like sharing you all the time, that's all. I guess I though now that we're married, I'd have you all to myself, all the time." I couldn't suppress my chuckle at this notion. "You might as well have a second wife—it's like you're married to the business some days."

Ali's eyes grew wide, though he said nothing. "You don't like it much, do you?"

"Which part?"

"Sharing me."

I shook my head. "I understand--work is work, but it just seems like you've got a lot going on lately. I guess the honeymoon period is over as they say."

"That's a terrible saying. I don't want it to ever be over with you. I love you, Darla."

"I know you do."

"I just wish---"

I paused, staring at Ali as he stumbled over his words, editing out whatever it was he didn't or couldn't say. "You can tell me, you know. If something isn't working, or if you're worried about something, you can tell me. I might be able to help. I'm pretty clever, you know." I grinned, teasingly.

Ali stared at me, nodding slowly, like he believed my words more than I intended. He smiled and leaned over and gave me a kiss. "I'll be back late. Don't wait up for me." He headed for the door right after.

"Ha," I laughed. "I don't usually sleep until I know you're back here safe and sound. How would you feel if the shoe were on the other foot?"

Ali paused, turning back towards me. Again, it was as if he took my off the cuff comment much more seriously than I'd meant for it. "I'd never allow it, Darla. It's just not like that here." He shook his head, as if trying to straighten out something inside. "We're alike on so many levels, but still so different."

"I know. That's what makes us such a wonderful pair. Just the two of us, working together."

Ali looked down to his feet. "Please, don't wait up. I'll be back as soon as I can."

True to his word, I shouldn't have stayed up late. I ate dinner alone, telling myself that everything was okay--he said he'd be home late, and so this was to be expected. But still something felt wrong.

I watched the clock on the wall, focused solely on the minute hand making its revolutions. Minutes ticked by. Hours. Where was my husband, I wondered, wringing my hands with worry as time ticked on. I dialed his phone, desperate to hear his voice. It was the third or fourth time I'd tried it. He'd never been out this late before. It was long past midnight, well into the morning hours.

There was no answer on the other end, though it rang and rang. I felt the desperation in my voice as I left him another message.

"Ali, please. Pick up the phone. Call me. It's late and I'm so worried. Tell me you're alright. Tell me you're safe."

I stayed up that night, and many more, pacing the floor of our little home. The ticking of the clock became my constant companion on those long desperate nights--it was as if time stood still, the clock moved so slowly. I prayed and hoped, hoped and prayed for Ali.

"Please, God," I said, kneeling down in the bedroom. It was overly formal, yet I was more than willing to get down on my knees and pray traditionally, just in case that helped get an answer from above. "Please, protect my poor husband. I don't mind where he is, or what he is doing, but please, please let him not be in any sort of trouble. Let him be safe somewhere. Let him come home to me."

I paced the floor again for another few hours before my legs gave out and I crashed on the couch.

I dialed his phone again--wishing so desperately that he would pick up. But he never did.

"Ali? Is that you?" I mumbled from the couch, hearing someone fumble with the lock on the door. I rubbed the sleep from my eyes, feeling like a mother waiting to catch a child getting in after curfew.

"Shhhh," whispered Ali. "You shouldn't have stayed up, Darla. You need your sleep. Come, let's get you to bed."

"Where were you?" I mumbled, not about to let it go. "I tried the shop but no one answered. And you didn't pick up your phone either. "

"It doesn't matter. I'm here now."

"But it does matter. Are you okay? What's going on?" I asked, my words slurring together from exhaustion.

"You're tired, sweetheart. We can talk in the morning."

And so I let it go, too tired to try and figure out what was really going on. I tried again in the morning to ask what had kept him out so late, but of course, there were no answers to be had over breakfast.

It was as if a switch had been thrown: the first six months had us settling into married life, adjusting to a new routine, where we spent our evenings and weekends together like any other married couple, but then something had changed. I could feel it, feel the relationship slipping away from us with every night he came home late, every weekend we spent apart, with no reasons why.

I wasn't looking to be attached at the hip, and I understood he had things that needed to be done, but this was different somehow. And I couldn't or didn't want to see where this was headed. I had to try and get things back on track between us, before it was too late.

"Ali?"

"Yes? How did you sleep? You look so peaceful lying next to me." Ali smiled, trying to smooth away the worry lines on his forehead.

"Fine. I know things are still hectic at the shop, but I just wanted to check that we were still on for our plans this weekend--the Dead Sea? We were supposed to go at the end of the month. And now that it's the end of the month," I paused, letting the half question hang in the air.

Ali's smile dropped; I could see the look in his eyes the moment he realized he'd have to disappoint me.

"Don't worry," I said, letting him off the hook. "How about next weekend, then?"

"Yes. Definitely, let's do it then."

"Do you need to write it down somewhere? I can put it in the calendar so we remember?" I said, trying to sound teasing. "It'll be the first weekend we've spent together in ages. What, do I only get every third or fourth weekend with you now?"

Ali smiled, though it seemed a little strained. "The Dead Sea is beautiful, just like you. We'll have a lovely time. You'll have to cover up though. I can't have a wife of mine luring other men with her beauty? Maybe we could pack a picnic even? What do you think?" he said, coming over to plant a kiss on my forehead.

I melted under his touch. No point staying upset with him, I rationalized. This was all about compromise, wasn't it? And understanding. I looked up at Ali with a smile, knowing, feeling the love that was in the air. Yes, I needed to be forgiving and understanding--for whatever reason, my husband was feeling thinly stretched at the moment and it was my job to be supportive rather than demanding.

"Next weekend will be lovely. I can't wait."

Indeed, it was a lovely trip to the Dead Sea. But the happy memory was soon overshadowed by the return to our normal routine: nights in alone, with Ali coming home later and later.

Until it got worse--there were nights when Ali simply didn't come home at all.

10

It was dark and oddly cold for Jordan as I lay silently in my bed, waiting for my husband to come home. Though I had no intention of sleeping, I found myself with my head on my pillow. The anxiety had taken its toll—my legs shaking and my breathing was erratic. I was beside myself with worry and grief. Was Ali okay? Would he come back to me again? Why didn't he call me? Surely he could have done at least that.

I wrung my hands trying to pretend my husband was just working late like he had done so many other nights before. But it was too late to accept that as the truth; I could feel that this was different. Even still, I tried to lull myself to sleep. Pictures of Ali raced through my head as soon as I shut my eyes—imagining the countless possible fates my dear poor husband might be facing. Dreaming was hopeless; nightmares more likely.

It was morning when he finally returned. I rubbed my eyes, willing myself awake as soon as I heard him drop his keys on the counter.

"Ali?" I mumbled. "Ali, is that you? Are you alright?" I moved as quickly as I could, anxious to see that he was indeed safe and really here; my body fighting back exhaustion every step of the way.

"Good morning, Darla," said Ali quietly. "Can I make you a coffee?" he offered politely, heading for the kitchen like nothing was wrong.

I froze in my tracks, staring at him as I tried to process the events of the last 12 hours. Here he was—fine, unharmed, unaffected by whatever mysterious circumstance had kept him out all night long and away from his phone. I waited for an answer from him, dumbfounded by his nonchalance. But there was no explanation forthcoming, no word of where he'd been all night.

"Ali, you're okay?" I asked, walking a few steps toward him. There was a distance between us that I tried to close but something held me back.

"Of course. Did you want a coffee?" he asked, as if this were just any other morning. "How did you sleep?"

I shook my head, but was unable to dispel my confusion. Did he really think there would be no discussion about this? That he could just disappear and then come back when he felt like it? Like a lost cat wandering off and then coming back whenever he pleased?

"Ali," I started slowly, trying to find the courage to ask the questions that had to be asked. It was in the back of my mind that there may be answers I didn't want to hear, but I knew I needed to know them regardless.

I couldn't let it go. Unlike the first time, where my relief had overwhelmed me, there was no way I could simply let this kind of dismissive behavior pass. I needed to know where he'd been, why he'd stayed out all night, and if he planned on doing it again. It was possible there was some reasonable explanation; though in my heart, and my mind, a million and one nefarious ones sprung forward instead.

Nevertheless, I prayed I was wrong. I hoped my husband had just fallen asleep at his desk, after a long day's work.

"Ali," I continued, trying to hold back my emotions.

"Yes," he said with a gentle smile.

"I was worried about you. You didn't come home last night."

Ali stared at me, I could see it in his eyes—would he try to deny a fact that we both knew to be true? He had to know I wasn't a fool, that anyone would notice if their husband went missing all night.

He simply lowered his eyes. "I'm so sorry, Darla. I hate that I made you worry." Ali closed the gap between us, taking my hand into his and kissed the top of it. "I shouldn't make such a beautiful woman worry about me."

I closed my eyes, comforted by his touch, though his words did nothing to reassure me. Focus, Darla, I told myself, pulling my hand back. "Ali, where were you?

Ali took a deep breath but didn't answer.

"I think I deserve to know," I said, feeling my cheeks burn at his silence.

But he said nothing. His eyes flickered from the floor to the coffee pot. "Come on, Darla. Let's move on from all this."

But I shook my head, determined not to shrug it off. This morning the question wasn't optional. "Ali, you're kidding me, right? I know you don't think you can just avoid this. The first night you stayed out, I can maybe forget, or try to forget, but two nights! I'm sure there's a third on the way. What is it, Ali? Who is it?" I asked, not wanting to admit to myself that there was someone else, but the words just came out.

He looked back to the floor, his feet shuffling on the tile. "I'm sorry, Darla. It's not fair to you."

"No, it's not. Whatever is going on, we can work it out. We can fix this, Ali. But you need to be honest with me. I love you and I want to be your wife, but you've got to talk to me. Tell me what's going on. Tell me where you've been."

Ali's eyes darted up to my face for a short second before returning to his feet. It was easy to see he didn't want to have this conversation, yet his hands were tied. Still, he said nothing, maybe hoping if he stayed strong, his silence would win over my resolve.

"If I didn't come home, what would you say? I'm sure you'd be worried too, but would you be able to just let it go?"

Ali looked up at me, his eyes now focused on mine.

"I did that the first time—could you have done the same?" I asked, but didn't wait for an answer. "Let me tell you—you'd be a fool to. You did it again last night, and I know you'll keep doing it, Ali. I don't want to believe that's the case, but I can feel it—it's a pattern. It's going to be a pattern. You staying out all night, me staying up with worry. You not answering my calls, me thinking you've been hit by a car or something terrible like that. You coming back home in the he morning like nothing's happened, me wondering if I'm over reacting, if I've dreamt the whole thing up."

I sighed, composing myself. Ali didn't even try to interject, so I continued on. "It's not right and it's not fair. You'd never stand for this if the situation were reversed. And no one should. Me included. Tell me, Ali. What is it? Where have you been?"

Ali sighed heavily, his face resigned. "Darla," he spoke softly. "Darla, I love you. You know that, right?"

"Yes. And I love you. We're in this together. You and me. Tell me, Ali. Let me in," I pleaded. "Tell me what I'm up against. Tell me what or who is taking you away from me."

Ali nodded and waited for what seemed like forever before speaking again. When he finally did, my palms were sweating from the suspense.

"My wife," he said quietly.

"Yes, I'm right here, waiting, Ali. I'm here for you."

"That's who I've been with."

I paused, looking at Ali, utterly bemused by his implausible response. "That doesn't make sense," I said matter-of-factly. "I don't understand. You weren't with me. So how could I have taken you away from—" I stopped, unable to make sense of his words. "I am your wife."

"Yes, you are. And I love you, Darla. You are one of them."

I closed my eyes, exhaustion from the sleepless night finally setting in. Surely I'd misheard him. The words my husband was saying didn't make any sense. "I'm sorry, can you say that again? I must have misheard you."

"I have been married before, Darla. Just like you, in a way."

"Okay," I said quietly, still trying to find the sense in his words. "And now *we're* married. You and I."

"Yes."

"So, what *do* you mean?"

"I've been married twice before. Just like you. Only I never got divorced."

I paused, trying to look my husband in the eyes so I could read between the lines, but he refused to meet my stare, focusing intently on the ground. "You were widowed then?" I asked, grasping for the thread that made everything fall into place, but I was reaching, too far it seemed.

I felt the answer tingling on the tip of my tongue, though I still couldn't see what I was headed towards when Ali shook his head. "No," he admitted. "I didn't want to tell you, Darla. I wasn't sure you could accept it, accept the life I could share with you."

"Ali, you still haven't said anything—you still haven't told me. Where were you last night? And the time before that?"

Ali stepped closer, holding my hands in his. "I was with my family, Darla."

"Khaled?" I said, shaking my head.

"No. My other family."

Suddenly, the walls of the room felt close and cloying, like they were coming in, crushing me. I coughed to clear my throat and find my voice again. "What are you saying? That you have children you never told me about? I can deal with that," I said, my brow still furrowed. If that was all that he was hiding from me, I could understand; we could figure this out. But my relief was premature.

"Yes. I have children. Many of them. They live with my wife," Ali paused, hesitating again. "Wives, actually."

I stared at Ali, letting his words swirl in the air. Even hearing them out loud, they made no sense. It took me a minute or two to try and process before I could say anything and even then it was a poor attempt at unraveling this surreal confusion more than anything else.

"I don't understand—wives? What's that supposed to mean? I'm your wife, you have one wife, and that's me. We got married six months ago. I was there, so were you. In fact, I believe it was your idea, so I know you remember. Tell me what you mean, Ali." My voice was calm as I rationally tried to think around his words, looking for any explanation other than the obvious.

"I will explain. Here, sit. I'll answer any questions you have, but please just know how much I truly love you."

"I'm listening," I said, trying to remain unemotional and detached; my mind hadn't caught up to reality—in fact, it seemed to be caught in this shroud of secrecy that was impenetrable in my dazed state. Or maybe it was simply a defense mechanism given the shocking revelation that Ali was about to deliver to me.

"I'm married, Darla. To you, yes. But also to two other women. It's not unheard of in Jordan; in fact it's quite traditional. I have families, children with them—they've been a part of my life for years, before I met you."

I stared at him, forcing myself to hear it out before I reacted, but pressure mounted inside of me; anger, humiliation, and the sheer crushing knowledge that my life in Jordan was over—this all hit me harder than any emotional blow in my entire life.

"You are my third wife," said Ali. "And I love you dearly, truly I do. And I know how happy we are together, how happy we can be together, Darla. I love you. I love our life together. It'll even be better now, now that you know. No more secrets, okay?" Ali smiled as if now that things were out in the open, the problem had been solved.

"You don't think this was important!? You felt you had the right to keep secrets from me, Ali—a secret like this?" I said, my anger simmering to the surface. My heart was pounding and I felt the heat rise up inside me. My emotions were threatening to bubble over uncontrollably at any second, but I needed to keep my composure; I needed answers. "Why didn't you tell me? Don't you think this is something I deserved to know? Before we got married?"

"I wasn't sure how you'd react. I wasn't sure you'd agree to be my wife," he said, looking down.

"Your third wife," I corrected.

Ali ignored my irritated tone. "But I thought once you saw how much I loved you, once I could convince you of my true love for you, you'd stay with me. We're married now. Regardless of everything else, we made vows to stay with each other forever. I take those seriously, Darla, and I know you do too."

My cheeks flushed, burning with anger. He couldn't be serious—trying to guilt me into staying with him. As his third wife! "You took those vows with me having already said them to other women! Women who you are still married to!" I shrieked. "You know that's not even legal in America? Bigamy—I know you know that. And you knew exactly how I would feel about this, but you went ahead and did it anyway!"

"I love you, Darla. I want to be with you. What other choice did I have?" Ali pleaded.

"To tell me the truth! I think I deserved it. Didn't I? How would you feel if the shoe were on the other foot, Ali? If I went missing all night and then you found out I had another husband? You'd be okay with that?"

"It could never happen. It doesn't work that way. You belong with me, Darla. I love you, but I would never share you. I couldn't." For the first time Ali looked flustered, though he hid it well. It was as if he'd never even thought about how it would feel, if the situation were reversed.

"That's right. You wouldn't share me, but I'm supposed to share you? Just like that? No questions asked? I can't believe this. You don't love me," I said, anger and emotion driving me on, unwilling to let me crumble until I'd defended and protected my heart.

"But I do, I do love you."

"Right. You love me, but not enough to be only with me. You need two other wives to keep you satisfied, is that it? In what world do you live in?!"

"Calm down, Darla. Here, it is very acceptable."

"And do those women know that their husbands have other wives before they get married, or am I the only one who is left completely in the dark?" I shot back at him.

"Lots of couples are in this position—lots of relationships are like this," Ali continued regardless.

"Couples? I'm not in a couple, Ali. I'm married to you and you're married to *them*. To two other women! I don't know what kind of relationship that gives us, but it's got a lot more people involved than a couple. I didn't sign up for this... How could you possibly think I'd ever be okay with this, Ali?"

"Slow down! Darla, think about it. Nothing has really changed between us. We still love each other, we can still be together—" he spoke with such conviction. Ali meant every word he said, but he was clueless if he thought that I believed a word of it.

"Of course we can still be together—if I'm willing to share you with the other women; if I'm okay to have a husband that gets passed around. What kind of life is that for me, Ali? Don't I deserve 100 percent, instead of 33 percent? Or if you get married a fourth time—25 percent?"

"Just open your mind and your heart. It's the exact same as we've always been. Honestly, nothing has changed." Ali took my hand, his voice pleading with me in desperation.

"Nothing has changed—for you. Now I know the truth, that changes everything."

"It doesn't have to though—you could embrace this lifestyle instead of running away from it. I love you. I care so much about you, Darla."

"If you truly loved me, it would only be me and no one else. I need no one else. Why do you?"

"It's not like that. Be fair, Darla."

"Be fair? Are you kidding me? I can't believe this, Ali. You lied to me. The whole time I've known you, it's been a lie."

"I never lied about how I felt."

"No, but you never mentioned that you'd be leaving me to sleep in someone else's bed either." I stared out the window, emotionally exhausted from the bombshell, physically exhausted from the late night. "The phone calls, the late hours, the weekends away on business—oh, God, I'm such a fool." I shook my head, knowing the writing had been on the walls all this time. But still, to suspect this? I shook my head, refusing to blame myself for this mess. How would anyone have suspected this deceit?

There was silence for a few minutes before Ali spoke again. His tone was casual, all trace of tension removed. "Do you still want to take that weekend break away? We can go this weekend, if you'd like? I know how much you like Aqaba."

I spun around on my heels, all my feelings flooding to my face. "That's it? You think, now that your big secret is out in the open, we're going to go back to normal? A little trip away will fix everything? Sure, why not invite everyone? Now that I know, don't I get to meet the whole family? Sorry, families?" I glared at him, my hands clenched in fists as my rage grew. "Don't you get it? This is a deal breaker for me, Ali. I'm not being over the top, I'm not being dramatic or unfair, or unrealistic. I think it's very realistic to think your husband is yours and yours alone when you get married. And if not, then you should get a warning in advance—not six months after saying 'I do'."

Ali stared back at me as I spoke, wisely not interrupting me.

"That's what I signed up for, Ali. That's what I expected. And you know it. I'm not doing this," my voice firm as I shook my head. "I won't play happy family and be the obedient third wife. There's just no way."

"Is this it then, Darla?" asked Ali, looking like he finally understood what was happening between us. Was it not patience then that fueled this latest silence, but resolve instead?

"I think, yes, this is it. Yes. I don't even know anymore if it ever was. How can it be real, when it wasn't? I never had you, never truly."

"Of course you did," Ali said softly, his voice melting right into me.

But it wasn't real. No matter how wonderful a part of him made me feel, he was whispering the same sweet words to his other wives as well. "Stop, Ali. You were silent when it served your purpose, and now—you've said enough."

For a moment, we just stood there. Nothing more to be said. Just taking the time for the reality to sink in.

As the sun rose in the distance, my thoughts were quick and decisive. "It seems it'll be no trouble for you to stay somewhere else for a few weeks until I get my things in order. I'm sure one of your families will be more than happy to have you back with them." I paused, hesitating for just the shortest of seconds. "I don't see any other way forward, Ali."

Ali walked over, taking my hand once more. "Darla, don't make any rash decisions. Stay, please. Stay with me. We can make this work. It's possible. I know it's possible."

It was torturous to hear him say this. I'd witnessed my marriage collapse in a matter of minutes and he wanted to pick up the pieces, but I couldn't. We were on different pages, and always had been. Tears ran down my face, tears that would continue in a steady steam for days. I shook my head. "Maybe for you. But not me, Ali. I can't. I won't," I said quietly. There was no fight left in me at that moment, but my resolve was strong; I was willing to compromise on a lot of things to make our relationship work, our marriage work, but this wasn't one of them. For me, a marriage is a bond between two people. That was never going to change. Ever.

The weeks that followed were rocky. I wept and wept for my lost marriage, for the life that I thought I had but never did. I was beside myself with despair before any other emotions came out. Then anger grew alongside my disappointment. I was livid both with Ali and myself.

"How could I not see it?" I asked Aila, feeling almost embarrassed having missed my husband's double, triple life he was leading.

"It's not your fault. Don't blame yourself. You've done nothing wrong. You trusted him, you loved him—that wasn't wrong, Mom. You're allowed to do that." Aila spoke softly, trying her best to comfort me from across an ocean.

"I just want to crawl under a rock and hide. I can't believe he thought I'd be okay with it."

"Is he still calling you and coming by the house?" she asked.

"Every day. Honestly, he thinks there's some way to win me back, I think. Some combination of words that he can say that will make me stay." More tears flowed as I spoke—despite the fact that it was my decision, it was tough for me seeing Ali. He was still pleading with me to stay and declaring his love for me every step of the way. The whole situation left me heartbroken.

Yet, there was nothing Ali could do to pacify me. I knew in my heart of hearts that I could never accept this type of life for myself.

"Have you made any decisions yet?" Aila asked.

I sighed, as feelings of failure mixed with my resignation. "Soon. I can't stay here, I can't stay in Jordan."

"Will you come back here, or go somewhere else?" she asked.

"I'm not sure. I feel," I paused, "lost." I sighed. "I just know I'm leaving here. And I can tell you it'll be to someplace that doesn't have such a strict dress code!"

Aila laughed on the other end of the phone.

"It's true! I'm sick and tired of wrapping my head and covering my body! What am I hiding, and who I am hiding it from?"

"That's what I was saying to you six months ago," chided my daughter, narrowly avoiding the words I told you so.

"And you were right! For two years, I've smothered my skin! Never allowed to show anything except my face. Not even my hands!" I felt disgusted by my own compliance with the dress code than with the tradition itself.

"Your hands will be happy to be set free," said Aila,

"Every part of me will be! No more clothes in the heat of the day! No more coverings for every inch!" I shook my head at my own actions, part of me thankful for the tragic twist of fate that was taking me away from Jordan, as it would also allow me to reclaim my independence and follow the customs I was more akin to. "I know that's the way here but apparently there are lots of customs that just don't suit me," I said, trying to make light of the situation.

"Think about it, but don't rush, okay? He's not living there anymore, and I'm sure he doesn't need you to hurry out," said Aila, always the voice of reason.

"I won't. I better not keep you any longer, though. Thanks for checking up on me, sweetheart. Love you."

"Love you, too. I'm here. Call anytime."

I smiled as I hung up the phone but the charade of being strong and 'fine' was impossible to keep up. I'd been pretending for Aila, knowing how much she worried about me. But once our call was over, I fell back onto my bed, feeling at my lowest point.

I closed my eyes and did what I always do whenever I hit bottom—I prayed.

It was then, as I prayed for guidance, for strength, for answers, that I realized what I'd forgotten all those months ago on my wedding day: I hadn't bothered to invite Him to the wedding.

My mind crumbled even further with my realization, plunging even lower into self-doubt and disappointment. It was like the act of praying in such despair brought all my past mistakes to the forefront—I remembered the last time I'd felt so confused, praying just like this. It was about Ali, about marrying a man so different from myself in every way. I prayed then for guidance and only now, two years later, did I realize that I never gave God a chance to answer my prayer!

And so, amidst my hours of prayer, I quickly and humbly asked God to forgive me for not waiting on His answer and for not inviting Him to my wedding. And I asked him for a sign of how I should proceed to extricate myself from this mess...

After pondering for weeks, the signs became clear—I'd been craving something different, yet something familiar at the same time. Somewhere foreign but not new.

I sat in bed and closed my eyes, letting my mind wander through its memories of every adventure I'd been on. After a short time, they settled on a wonderful meal Aila and I had shared, the evening she had been accepted into university—a wonderful plate of rice and kimchi, with a comforting cup of ginseng tea. My head wouldn't move past it—and soon I began to crave that Asian lifestyle.

The food, the customs, and the openness and friendliness of the people made it so inviting. Just the change that I needed.

And so, I made arrangements to return to South Korea.

11

It was cathartic to return to South Korea. Being back in a country that I sincerely loved, and it loved me back, felt wonderful. Though the move was designed to create a fresh start, it was impossible to fully rid myself of the heartache that I tried to leave behind in Jordan. Yet, as I walked up to my favorite corner cafe, I managed to put my troubles with Ali into the back of my mind. I reminded myself that I wasn't running from my humiliation, from my regret, from my failed marriage, but instead, I was coming back to visit an old friend.

"What can I get for you?" asked the kind-eyed waiter as I sat down at a table by the window.

I glanced at the menu to be polite but I knew what I wanted, what I craved.

"Gejang, rice and kimchi, please." I'd missed these flavors from my travels—there was something oddly comforting about the taste of marinated crabs in soy sauce, and the traditional fermented spicy cabbage dish. I laughed to myself remembering Aila's first impression of the Korean cuisine—it sounded so adventurous, she was more than happy to try it. And once she gave it a try, she loved it as much I did.

Our time here seemed like a lifetime ago. I was a different woman now. It was an entire marriage ago.

Had I changed then? Really changed? I wondered, as I felt different in my mindset and my soul, but then again, I'd also felt that way when we'd first arrived in India. And clearly even if I'd learned something from my first and second attempts at marriage, it apparently wasn't enough to avoid the many pitfalls that could befall a bride (or groom).

I closed my eyes, trying to cleanse myself from the guilt and the blame of everything that had happened in Jordan. I repeated the same lines Aila told me time and time again—it's not your fault; you did nothing wrong; you should be able to trust your husband.

Still, I was riddled with guilt and humiliation that I didn't see the reality that was part and parcel of who my husband really was.

I sucked in a deep breath and shook it off; I was stronger than this, stronger than Ali's weaknesses. His lies wouldn't break me or my spirit. At the very least, I would walk away from this having learned something. I wouldn't give up on trusting other people, but I would keep my eyes open, knowing what people are capable of.

I stared out of the café's window, watching the world go by before my eyes—people passing me on their way to somewhere, going about their business in a multitude of arrangements—some by themselves, others with friends, those in a couple, married or not, simply holding hands as they strolled along the sidewalk. It was easy to imagine their relationships as I stared at them, casting my assumptions based purely on how they presented themselves to the world. Of course, in light of everything, I was also postulating what little secrets they might be keeping from each other as well.

"Here it is," said my server, setting the food down before me.

"Thank you."

As I took in the comforting smells, I tried to forget the lasting negativity that was still lingering in the air above my head. Learn from this, I chanted, trying to focus on something constructive.

It was a routine that I repeated time and time again in my first few weeks and months in South Korea—a warm meal at my favorite eatery, coupled with some serious time for reflection over a cup of fresh ginseng tea.

I thought long and hard as I watched the people around me, and pondered about my marriage—my marriages. What worked, and what didn't. Why they'd failed and how or if I could have saved them in any way. Had I contributed to their demise or merely been a victim of circumstances—irreconcilable differences, as so many divorces state as the reason for dissolution?

I tried to ignore the issues with my first marriage as best I could, casting it aside due to my young age at the time and the incredibly short length of it, yet memories of Adam and Ali demanded my attention.

Had I married these men for the right reasons, I wondered, thinking back to my prior mindsets. I'd married Adam, partially out of obligation—his persistence had paid off, and I'd given in to his demands. Of course I'd loved him on some level, but was I ever *in love* with him, I wasn't sure of that.

Ali though, I had been in love with him; the rawness of the emotions and pain of the split that were ever present were testament to that love that we'd kindled between us. Yet, would I have married him if there hadn't been such religious and cultural pressure to do so? If we'd been able to be alone and even have some sort of physical relationship without it? Even after weeks of reflection, I wasn't sure.

I did know though that I never would have gotten to know Ali had I known about his circumstances—that he was already married with two wives and two families. No matter what my feelings were for him, that would have always stopped me in my tracks.

I stared at the couples strolling by, wondering what makes them decide to be together, to stay together, and get married, or if not, why they'd hadn't. Was it ever a clear cut decision? Would anyone else's reasons make any more sense when considered logically? Would I ever know why my marriages had failed or have the answers I was seeking?

I sighed to myself as I drank my ginseng tea. This self-study and analysis couldn't be just a one off occurrence—I knew if I really wanted to explore my choices and situation, it would take more effort than this. Thankfully though, the negative thoughts and suspicions about others were dwindling over time, but the need to take something away from the experience with Ali lingered on much longer.

I went to the cafe regularly—weekly—forcing myself to reflect upon my past relationships. And eventually, I saw things for what they were and I felt more at ease with how things had turned out. As I considered my previous paths to Mrs and back again, I realized that there had been multiple different routes to take and possibly an infinite number of outcomes, but no matter what: I was still me, Mrs or not. And it was good to be here, and it was good to be me. I swore never to lose sight of that again.

"How are you doing over there, Mom?" asked Aila, still worried about me.

"I'm okay, I think. South Korea's always good for me."

"I know you're fine there, but that's not what I meant. How are you doing about everything else?"

I sighed deeply, knowing what she was getting at. "I think I'm okay. I can't explain it," I started. "I guess it feels maybe marriage just wasn't meant to be. Maybe marriage isn't for me."

"Don't say that, you don't know that," chided Aila.

"I'm okay with it, really. Three marriages down, I think it's a good bet. And I'm fine, I can deal with that, honestly."

"Really?"

"Yes. I think I'm on an adventure, like the ultimate journey to discover and learn all that I can about marriage—I might not have been successful, but I think I learned a lot about what not to do," I laughed, though my thoughts were serious.

"Tell me then, what have you learned?"

"It's not a list I've compiled, Aila. It's not written out in bullet points. More of a study."

"Okay, where are you at then?"

"Well, I'm in a better place overall. I genuinely think this is a good thing, that I feel compelled to dig deeper into the whole concept of the institution of marriage. And really, I feel like I can say with certainty that marriage is not something that can be guaranteed—there are a lot of variables. Two people, who can have a world of different ideas and other differences between them. And many other factors in-between. It's not a science, it's an art. And a lot of it just... depends."

"Maybe those ones just weren't the right ones. You haven't told me about how you're studying this, but I think, just like with everything, there are different kinds of marriages, Mom," said Aila. "Maybe you didn't have the right kind, that's all. What you had with Ali was different from what you had with Dad, right?"

I couldn't help but laugh a little. "Very much so. At least it was just your father and I in that marriage! But yes, they were both different."

"What went wrong there, with Dad?" Aila asked quietly.

I thought over Adam and mine's relationship quickly, having reflected on it many times over the years and again quite recently. It was hard to put into words whether or not there was simply enough love in the marriage. It was certainly more balanced and an equal partnership compared to my relationship with Ali, but still, there was this under current between us, of certain gender stereotypes and assumptions, a certain level of control and preference that he tried to exert over me; whether it was staying home to take care of the house, or sticking to his schedule for our intimate times, Adam's needs and opinions still seemed to trump mine every time.

"Honey, I have a few ideas, but really, I don't think it's fair to analyze that relationship with you. You love both your father and I, and I respect that. Just because it didn't work out between us, doesn't mean I don't want it to work out between you and him."

"I know that, Mom," said Aila.

"I know you do. So, without getting into specifics, let's just say it was a partnership that was unbalanced—I think that summarizes the type of marriage we had. But, Ali on the other hand—that was a marriage that was rife with complications from the start, even before I found out about the double life he was leading. I'm not sure how much of a role the different cultures, different religions played into it, but I know if he'd been honest, I never would have married him. How would it have worked if he hadn't had other wives? I'm not sure. I think the bigger question would be, how might it have played out if he hadn't needed or wanted other wives, and was content with just me, just one wife." I nodded resolutely. "But I suppose that would mean he was a different man than he was, right? And the game isn't to figure out a way to change my ex-husbands, to mold them into the perfect beings, but to look at the relationship critically, to see where and what went wrong."

Aila paused, waiting to make sure I'd finished before adding her two cents worth. "Wow—you do sound like you're in a good place, Mom. A better place than I expected. So you're still open to relationships then? To marriages? Even after everything?"

I laughed. "Relationships, yes. But I'm not sure I should ever get involved in a marriage again. I can't even imagine what that would look like. I suppose that's just it though—it'll look different and sound different, and so I'll want to believe it'll be different. But I'm not sure I'll ever be confident enough to go through with another wedding, all for the sake of being Mrs. Just the thought of it not working out again..." I shuddered on the phone, imagining the heartache.

"Oh, Mom. It might not be like that, you don't know. But I think it's a good idea not to rush into anything, anyhow."

I smiled, glad we were pretty much on the same page. "But what about you? I hope I haven't scarred you for life!"

"Nope. Not a chance. I think you're doing amazing. You've been a great role model, honestly. Taking care of yourself, standing up for yourself, for what you need, what you want—that's really important, and an important part in any relationship."

"Well, it's certainly a key part of it. If both sides are getting what they need while the other is still content, then it might just work out, but if you're not being true to yourself," I shrugged, "I don't see how it can last. Not in the type of marriage I want. I was never interested in a utilitarian type marriage."

"What do you mean?"

"Like some of the ones we saw in India; and there were some in Jordan, too. It's more like two people live together and work for a common goal of the family but they're not really doing it together, at least not how we usually think of a partnership or teamwork. What I mean is there tends to be an absence of mutual involvement or passion in the marriage and it's usually held together by social, family and financial considerations. Those pressures can be very real, Aila. Times have changed, but not everywhere in the world. "

"Like you mean with arranged marriages? Is that a utilitarian marriage?"

"In certain cases, yes. But I don't think it needs to be just those. It's more like a different approach to marriage, one more devoid of love and passion from what I've seen—it doesn't fit my personality, but I guess it works for some people. Again, I think it really depends on what you're trying to get out of it, what you need from it."

"I think I'm with you on that one. If I ever get married, I'm definitely looking for more out of it than just someone to share responsibilities with, or getting married just for the sake of being a Mrs," added Aila.

"Good plan, sweetheart. I'll do what I can to support you—and you won't have any pressure from me to get married, though I'll stand by your side if you meet the right person and make that choice."

I smiled after we ended our call. I had a feeling that Aila had watched me make decisions for so long that when her time came, she'd fare better than I had. I prayed that she would.

I'd been in South Korea for a year and a half—with plenty of time to process what had happened with Ali and move on with my life. I was stronger, and in a much better place; I was finally getting used to being single and, in a way, enjoying my personal study of the institution of marriage.

One day I was looking into the concept of intrinsic marriages, when the phone rang. My eyes raced through what they'd just read before I answered it. I sighed as I reached for the phone, knowing this type of marriage wasn't my cup of tea either. Although an intrinsic marriage has a high degree of emotional and sexual involvement, and it's considered more fulfilling, there is a tendency to avoid activities resulting in separation. And I needed my independence, my autonomy.

"Hello?" I said, forcing myself back to reality.

"Darla?"

"Jung Lee! How are you?" I asked. It had been a few days since I'd seen my neighbor.

"I'm well, Thank you. What are you doing tomorrow for dinner? I'm having a few people over and I wanted to invite you, too."

"A dinner party? That sounds great. I'd love to come."

"There's actually someone I want you to meet."

"Oh?"

"He's American, just like you. And he's here alone just like you, too."

I laughed. "Jung Lee, are you trying to set me up?"

"Would I do that?" my neighbor giggled. "Six o'clock. I'll see you then."

I tried not to think of any ulterior motives and opted to just enjoy myself as I got to know a few of the other guests at Jung Lee's. A small group of us sat on the floor around the table, nibbling on all of the delicious side dishes ahead of the dinner. We snacked and chatted for a few minutes before the doorbell rang again; I could hear an American accent from afar.

"Oh, Darla," called Jung Lee as she entered the room. "I want you to meet a very good friend of the family," she said, motioning with her hand toward the tall man beside her. "This is Wallace Armstrong. He is a university professor, just like you, here in Korea. He teaches theology."

I smiled at him, feel slightly awkward and put on the spot, though I vowed not to let it show.

"Wallace—how nice to meet you. Where are you from originally?"

"Nice to meet you too, Darla. I'm from Memphis, Tennessee."

Wallace smiled at me with a nod before eyeing the spot on the floor next to me. "May I?"

I smiled, despite myself, strangely comforted by his accent. It was easy on the ears.

"Yes, of course you may," I answered coyly, not wanting to engage him too much. The last thing I needed was someone interested in something more than just a casual conversation over dinner. But something in Wallace's eyes told me he had a future mapped out for us from the moment he sat down.

"How long have you been here?" he asked. "How do you find South Korea?"

"This is my second stretch here, actually. I love it—I've been here almost four years total. And you?"

Wallace smiled broadly. "Four years as well. Back-to-back though. I settled here right after my divorce. Are you a traveler then at heart, or did circumstances bring you here, like me?"

The questions continued to come, and the conversation flowed—with Wallace carrying much of the burden for the evening. We continued to exchange formalities as we ate our food, and much to my chagrin, Jung Lee had been right—on paper, we clearly did have a lot in common.

The evening flew by and before we knew it, it was time to exchange goodbyes. "Thank you for having me, Jung Lee. It was a lovely evening. And good night to you, Wallace. It was nice to meet you." I added with a nod in his direction.

However, as I stood to leave, I noticed that Wallace too was getting up. I felt my eyes close in a long blink, as I silently wished it was just a coincidence but I knew it wasn't.

"Oh, Darla, before you go," Wallace said, gently reaching out for my arm to stop me.

I turned around at his touch, forcing a smile on my face. "Yes?"

"I really enjoyed getting to know you tonight. I'd love to keep talking with you—we have so much in common. Perhaps I could call you sometime and get together."

I nodded silently, not wanting to offend him, nor encourage him either.

"Could I have your number?" he asked.

My eyes flashed over to Jung Lee who was watching from the corner of her eye. She smiled at me before quickly looking away.

I looked back at Wallace, and hesitated for a moment, a wave of reluctance coming over me. I wasn't interested in meeting anyone new; I wasn't looking to start a new relationship either—least of all with a very talkative, American man. But under Jung Lee's watchful eye, I didn't want to be rude. So, I smiled at Wallace. And gave him my number.

12

Wallace wasted no time—before the week was out, he'd called to set up lunch.

"Saturday afternoon? I can do that," I agreed, trying to convince myself I wasn't being foolish. We were just going out for lunch. No strings attached. Nothing else had to happen. This didn't mean we were dating. It was just a casual get-together. Two Americans in South Korea; that was all.

"It's a date then," said Wallace. I could practically hear him smiling on the other end of the phone.

I sighed, feeling my anxiety increase another notch at his eagerness. "Just to be clear, I'm not really looking to get romantically involved with anyone right now. If that's okay, then we can still go. If it's not though, just let me know. I really don't want to lead you on in any way. I'd hate for you to get the wrong idea. So, just as friends?"

"Sure," Wallace agreed. "Whatever you need. We can be friends. We can be more than friends. Why don't we just see where it goes, okay?"

"Just friends then?" I reiterated, knowing that no matter what he wanted, this was what I needed.

"Let's start there."

There was a tone to his voice that I recognized—patience, diligence—something akin to determination. Whatever Wallace's true motives were, he was happy to bide his time until I came on board with them. His awkward confidence was both familiar and frustrating.

But I'd said my bit—if he wanted to play a long game, a waiting game, that was his choice as much as it was mine to follow my heart, wherever it led. Even if that meant not in his direction.

Despite my reservations, a friendship between Wallace and myself was formed over several bowls of kimchi, over the course of several lunch 'dates'. Our common backgrounds in a foreign land brought us closer together than I ever would have imagined. But like I predicted, it wasn't true love—at least not for me. And although we saw each other regularly, I was constantly reminded of the unbalanced nature of our relationship. Regardless of the romantic factor, Wallace was always keen for us to be together, to get together much more often than I was. I could take it or leave it, whereas if he had his way, we'd have been inseparable.

"Thanks for coming over for dinner. It was a nice night," I said, looking at the empty mugs on the coffee table. A yawn escaped as I stretched my arms out. Getting together after a full day's work hadn't been my idea but it turned out well. Wallace's company was surprisingly welcome.

"It was nice, wasn't it? So, I was thinking you might come with me tomorrow? I've got tickets to go see that performance at the university? You know, the play they're putting on? And we could grab dinner first?"

My eyes flickered over to the couch, where Wallace was sitting awkwardly. It was still a strange sight, seeing him here—how had he become such a fixture in my life in just a matter of a few weeks?

"That sounds more like a date, Wallace. Dinner and a show?" I questioned. Our little outings had started innocently enough but, over time, these romantic undertones were not lost on me. Nor was his persistence at advancing our relationship.

"It doesn't have to be. But yes, it could be, if you'd like? If you're interested or ready for that, I can be too."

"Have you dated anyone else since your divorce, Wallace?" I asked point blank. "Or am I the first?"

"Wait, are we dating now?" he said, with mock shock.

"You know what I mean. Am I the first person you've tried to date since your divorce?"

"Well, yes. I think so. It's hard, I'm sure you know that. And I wasn't looking for just anybody. I'm not much for the dating scene, in case you couldn't tell. But I like you a lot. You're funny, mature, sensible and you've seen the world, literally and figuratively."

"But I've told you I'm not ready. Don't you think you're wasting your time on me? Shouldn't you be at least keeping your options open? Doing things with other people so you can find Mrs. Right?"

"What if that person is you? I think it could be."

I laughed. "I think you're serious, Wallace."

"I am. Completely."

"Then I think you're crazy, I can't be any clearer. I'm not available for that kind of relationship and don't plan on changing my mind any time soon."

"Well, for someone who isn't interested, we've sure spent a lot of time together."

My eyes snapped up to his; I could feel my irritation building. "Mixed messages, Wallace. Do you want to stop spending time together, is that what you're saying?"

I looked at the man before me, knowing that thought had never entered his mind. He probably couldn't even hear the double meaning in his words. It was hard not to feel a little bad for him—so socially awkward, it seemed like reading people wasn't his strong suit.

"Of course not. I was trying to say that I think you like me more than you know, and maybe that'd be even more if you let yourself like me."

I closed my eyes, exhaling loudly before looking over to the full moon outside the window. It was late. We'd had dinner hours ago and I was way too tired for this kind of conversation. I glanced at my watch, and yawned again.

"Aren't you tired?"

"Never with you."

I groaned at his over-the-top lovey-dovey comments. And for what I was about to do.

I hated telling someone that they had to leave, but Wallace never seemed to know when it was time to go, and didn't seem to take a hint that the night was coming to an end. "Wallace, I think I need to call it a night. I'm exhausted."

"Are you sure? I could make us some coffee, that might help."

I shook my head knowing I was going to have to spell it out. "No, I think sleep is the only answer for me. Here let me walk you out."

"Okay," he reluctantly agreed. "And I'll give you a call tomorrow. I heard the play is really good, so let me know if you want to go. I suppose if you don't, I can always give the tickets away."

"No, we can go," I agreed, feeling a certain degree of pressure from his words. "But you should be able to go by yourself. You don't always have to go with me, or with someone else. You'll survive if it was just you, I promise."

"But it's so much nicer going together, isn't it?"

I sighed, my eyelids closing for a long blink. "Let me walk you out. Good night, Wallace."

Invitations from Wallace became commonplace—every weekend there was something to do and every faculty event meant we'd attend together.

"Come on, Darla. You've got to go with me. Who else can I take?" he asked teasingly.

I smiled though I knew there was a lot more seriousness to his question than he wanted to let on. After having gotten to know him, it was hard to hide the fact that he didn't have many friends here in South Korea. A handful at best.

"Fine, I'll go," I agreed, not really minding. Wallace was growing on me. Not that I wanted to do things together every waking minute of the day like he did, but I didn't mind his company; in many ways, I sort of liked it. It was nice to have a friend, even if he was constantly pushing for something more. Still, I couldn't agree to every offer, as there were just too many.

Yet, despite his overbearing tendencies, there was something intriguing about him. He was so different from the other men I'd known; worlds apart from the more confident charms of Ali and Adam. Instead, there was something sweet and innocent almost about Wallace's social awkwardness. Even if he wanted to be smooth and charismatic, it was like he was completely inept at wooing me on any level. He couldn't fake something if he tried, whether that was just his guileless style, or the fact he wouldn't have known how to act like that in the first place.

"Faculty nights like this are so nice, aren't they?" said Wallace, who hung close to me, as usual.

"Absolutely."

"They give everyone a good opportunity to get to know each other. Visiting professors, I mean."

I nodded, laughing slightly.

"What is it?" Wallace asked.

"It just sounds funny coming from the guy who hasn't left my side all night, that's all. It sure doesn't seem like you're interested in mingling with the new faces here." I smiled.

Wallace, undoubtedly, was a clinger. I'd learned that fast and it normally drove me up the wall but here, right now, all I could do was laugh.

"I'm sure I've told you—meeting new people isn't really my thing," he admitted. "Not on this sort of level. Sung Lee's dinner party—I can handle that, but this—" he said, pointing to the medium-sized room filled with aging professors, "You know I'm way out of my comfort zone."

"But you just said what a good thing it was." I laughed.

"I did, for someone else especially. But at least I can appreciate the benefits for others even if I can't really enjoy them on my own."

"Wallace," said a tall man, walking over towards us.

"Nice to see you, Mr. Kim," Wallace answered politely.

"Are you having a nice time? You've been here for years now, but still, it seems like just yesterday that you arrived. You're a real asset, Wallace. "

Wallace nodded silently, awkwardly. "Thanks. Um, have you met Darla?"

"A pleasure," I answered, politely.

"Likewise."

"Darla, Mr. Kim is the head of our department," explained Wallace.

"Indeed. And unfortunately, I'm here on official business. Have you any plans for this weekend, Wallace? The reason I ask is I need someone to look over the latest research paper for the department before we submit it for publication. We need someone to go through it, ASAP."

I turned to watch Wallace, my mind already jumping ahead to our plans for the weekend—we'd made arrangements to visit some tourist attractions in the country. The schedule was tight; there was simply no room to squeeze in a review of an academic paper.

Wallace met my eyes before sheepishly turning back to Mr. Kim. "I can do that, sir. No problem."

"Perfect. I'll send the file through later tonight. Thanks, Wallace. I knew we could count on you."

I felt my eyes turn from a stare into a glare as Mr. Kim walked away.

"I know, I know I should have said no."

"Where's your backbone, Wallace?" I asked. "I don't mind, but we did have plans. And I know you remember them."

"Of course I do. It's just..." He paused, trying to think up an excuse, I guess.

"Never mind. We can do it the following weekend. That is, unless you agree last minute to do something else."

I sighed, putting the incident behind me almost as soon as it had happened. It wasn't the first time, nor would it be the last time I called him on his spineless behavior. Still, I had lowered the bar substantially. I could handle no backbone, so long as there were no secret wives or lives floating around. Not that we were a couple; not officially at least.

As I looked back to Wallace, there was a softening there; a slow melting towards each other. Maybe Wallace had been right—that it was only a matter of time until we grew into something more than friends.

And sure enough, a few months after that, my heart gave in to his advances as our relationship moved to the next level.

"What's this?" I asked, opening the bag that Wallace had handed to me. I was suspicious after Ali when men came bearing unexpected gifts. I didn't get the same vibe from Wallace though, that he was plotting to bombard me with gifts as a cover for his lies. Still, my curiosity was piqued as I opened the bag.

"It's for you. I hope you'll wear it," he said, smiling brightly.

My hands grasped onto a lovely, soft cotton t-shirt, and pulled it out with ease. "Ooooo," I said, feeling the gentle blue fabric beneath my fingers. "It's lovely. Definitely, I'll wear it. What good taste you have, Wallace," I said, as my eyes flickered over to him. "Shall I wear it tomorrow for our trip downtown?" I asked.

Wallace's eyes lit up. "Yes. Perfect. Where are we meeting again?"

"By that little café on the corner. You know the one we were at last week?" I said, my own mind pulling up the image of it with ease.

"That's right. I'll be there. Now, I've got a few errands left to run this afternoon—are you sure I can't talk you into coming with me? It'll be fun."

"Oh, Wallace," I said, practically shoving him out of my office. He was determined to have us be attached at the hip, though I had been more than clear that I needed some independence, I needed some space.

The next day, I sat at the cafe, at my favorite seat in the window, drinking ginseng tea as I watched the world go by. I looked down at my new t-shirt—it looked nice; it really had been a kind gesture.

I was staring off into the crowds and didn't notice when Wallace walked in. My eyes squinted as he came into focus, trying to process what they were seeing. Oh God.

"What are you wearing?" I started and then stopped myself, as I knew the answer; I looked at his blue t-shirt and recognized it. He'd bought himself the very same one as he'd given me. A matching pair.

"I see," I said, forcing myself to remain lighthearted. "Oh no. Let me tell you, Mr. Armstrong," I said teasingly, "I will not start dressing as twins."

"Darla, don't be silly. No one will think we're twins."

"You know exactly what I mean—there's no way we're walking around like a matching set. It's a bit much," I said, setting down some coins to pay for my bill.

As we stepped outside into the street, I tried to pretend that no one else would notice that we were dressed in identical shirts, but I knew it wasn't true. I couldn't help feeling embarrassed and couldn't wait for a quick wardrobe change to fix the situation.

Thankfully, being downtown, I had no trouble spotting a small little clothes shop to duck into.

"Stay here," I instructed Wallace not five minutes after we left the café.

He looked at me, dumbfounded, as I headed into the store shaking my head. My eyes ran over the racks and shelves of clothes before me—it didn't need to be a nice shirt, any shirt would do, I reminded myself. Wasting no time, I picked out a shirt and bought it, quickly slipping it on and tearing off the tag, while tucking the blue one that matched Wallace's into my purse.

"I don't understand?" said Wallace, still utterly confused. He eyed my new shirt, as if he were unable to process what I'd just done.

"I got a new shirt," I explained, matter-of-factly.

"But you were wearing the one I gave you. It looked lovely. Not that this one doesn't," he said fumbling over his words.

"Yes, I like the blue shirt, Wallace. But I can't wear it when you're wearing the same one. We can't dress the same, do you understand that?" I explained again, shaking my head. "Wallace, we're not a couple like that. But even if we were, that's not something I've ever done, nor something I'm ever going to do," I said shaking my head at the thought of that sort of shameless fashion camaraderie.

Wallace looked at me, trying to make sense of my words. I could see it in his face that he utterly didn't understand my logic. He didn't see anything silly about dressing in matching outfits, in public.

I sighed to myself, not wanting to offend him any further. It wasn't about him understanding the big picture, so much as understanding that we weren't going to be a matching set, now or ever.

"Okay, Darla. Are we ready to keep going?" asked Wallace, shaking it off.

"Definitely," I agreed with a smile, looking down at my – unique and independent – new shirt.

Regardless of our many differences, we truly shared more things in common than set us apart. Our relationship continued in a positive direction and we grew closer together, with only the occasional side-step to avoid another fiasco like the issue with the t-shirt. But I still considered us friends, rather than anything else.

Yet, one morning, a warm and sultry summer morning, a thick layer of humidity hung in the city air; I heard a soft voice whispering in my ear: "Darla."

I rolled over in bed, knowing the voice and the only person who should be lying next to me. I opened my eyes, meeting Wallace's. "Hi," I mumbled, wiping sleep from my eyes. "Morning already?"

"I let you sleep in," he said teasingly.

"How late is it?"

"Just past ten."

I rubbed my eyes, slowly adjusting to the light steaming in through the window.

"You had a long night." Wallace smiled.

I groaned, not wanting to think of the night before. It was a hard reality to deal with—having been raised a good Christian, here I was now sleeping with a man who I wasn't married to, nor did I have any intention of marrying.

The pressure and guilt mounted on me after the fact; it was as if in the cold light of day, I somehow remembered my upbringing more, or perhaps it was just trying to rectify my lifestyle, my choices with my faith. And it didn't matter that I knew what Wallace was going to say next.

"Darla, we're perfect for each other. Let's get married. Marry me, Darla. Make me the happiest man."

I closed my eyes and shook my head. "I can't," I whispered, like I had every other time he'd asked me the same question over the last two years. Wallace was a lot of things, including persistent.

"You know it makes sense—I want to do things right and I know that's what you want too," he said arguing on behalf of my conscience, and coming at me from any point of view that might make me cave,

But I didn't. I wouldn't. No matter how much my heart caved with guilt, how great the pressure built up inside me—I could resist his offer of marriage. I had to. Though I was healing more with each day, I didn't feel ready to walk down to the altar again. I didn't know if I ever would. I'd experienced before and after marriage on several occasions, and it wasn't something that I wanted to repeat, especially if it's not with the right person. Still, the pressure and guilt were very real; so real, they almost drove me to crumble and say yes.

"It would make everything right between us. It's what we're meant to do," he insisted. "If we love each other, if we're together like this, doesn't that mean we should get married?"

"I know on paper it seems that way."

"You said so yourself—you said that what we're doing is wrong, that what we're doing goes against your Christian upbringing. Those are your words, not mine. So let's rectify that. Let's make it right."

I shook my head, refusing to get caught up in the mind games of this mess. Yes, I had feelings for Wallace, and I think I might have even loved him, more than a friend loves another friend. Yes, we were together and as intimate as a married couple. But getting married again just wasn't in the cards for me.

"It is wrong," I said quietly, knowing in my heart that was how I felt whenever I had any sort of objectivity. "But I can't marry you."

I might not have been able to articulate the precise reasons why I couldn't, but I had at least an understanding of the broader picture:

marriage is an institution and like all institutions it has and needs guidelines. But that's where I always got stuck. These guidelines were my trouble area, my Achilles' heel. I never really knew what those guidelines were, nor could I ever find out. In a way, they were even more elusive than finding true love, as I'd at least managed to convince myself I'd found that a few times.

What this all amounted to was that Wallace would not be having me as his wife. I knew that would be more wrong, and two wrongs don't make a right (and certainly not a Mrs. Right).

As I stared out of the window of my favorite café, I decided this was the end of my time in South Korea. My favorite country had served its purpose; it had taken care of me. It allowed me time to heal, to become whole again. This respite had given me the chance to relax and reflect.

But I could feel it in the air, in my bones—I was stronger than I had been, I had rebounded back to my old self, although hopefully a little wiser. And now, it was time to say thank you again to Korea, and bid my farewell.

Of course, when I told Wallace he was confused and distraught. "You can't leave, Darla. I beg you – stay. Stay with me. Stay for me. Stay because you love it here as much as I do. Pick any reason, but just stay."

I shook my head, feeling the tears pooling in my eyes. Although I would never, could never marry Wallace, I loved him. He'd been a good companion, despite our differences, and it was difficult but still it was time to say goodbye.

"I can't stay here forever. I've never been one to stay in one place, Wallace, I've told you that."

"But this is different—I'm not asking you to stay somewhere you don't like; you love it here as much as I do. And I could give you everything your heart desires. Marry me, Darla. I've said it before, and I'll keep saying it for as long as I have the chance to. Be my wife. I'll give you the world, if you stay with me. I love you so much, Darla. We're meant to be together."

Tears escaped, trickling down my cheek as I shook my head once more. "Wallace, it'll never work. I don't know why but marriage just doesn't fit with me."

"Don't say that, Darla. It's different with us. Be my wife, my love."

"And I don't want to hurt you, Wallace. We've been over this and you know I can't. I won't change my mind. I won't go down this path again. My heart can't take it."

While that wasn't the only reason, it certainly was one of them. And, as I looked at Wallace even now, on the verge of leaving, I knew he would never be able to satisfy me in any way. We were too different, our needs too far apart from each other. What he wanted and what I needed weren't even in the same ball park. While we might have been compatible in lots of ways, we'd always have too many differences to make this work as a marriage.

"I'll keep in touch, I promise," I whispered, leaning in to give him a kiss on the cheek. "Good bye."

I wiped away the tears that were streaming down Wallace's cheek before turning around and heading for the door.

Goodbyes were never easy. Even though this time I wasn't saying goodbye to a husband, or ex-husband, there was no denying that it felt like I left a part of my heart in South Korea.

Still, I was strong enough to leave, and it was time. Time to move on to the next place: Palestine.

13

I felt it in my soul as I took in my new surroundings. I was in a completely different place. Somewhere in my life and in the world that I'd never been before. Yes, Palestine was a different way of living, different from anywhere I'd seen; but I was also mentally and spiritually in a different place, within myself.

It was as if a switch had been shifted inside me. Not turned off—oh, I certainly was still interested in men, and part of me, infuriatingly so, still attracted to the romantic notion of being a Mrs., once again. But, at the same time, I didn't *need* it the way I once had. Perhaps I'd finally learned my lesson—even though it had been the hard way.

Funnily enough, after my first marriage, and then my union with Adam, and then Ali—even after everything I'd seen and done, it might have been Wallace who showed me in the end, that I truly didn't need to have a husband. Being with someone just for the sake of being a Mrs. was quite simply not worth it.

Maybe it took seeing Mr. Wrong, and having all the signs clearly saying, practically screaming at me that he wasn't Mr. Right (at least, not for me). Maybe I needed someone in my life whom was worth dating, worth being with, but who blatantly wasn't compatible with me as a long term, life partner. And maybe, after everything, the message had finally stuck.

Being Mrs. shouldn't define you as a person, especially if being with that Mr. forsakes who you truly are and what you truly want.

In the safety of my little home, I still closed my eyes at the sound of the missiles flying through the air. This wasn't the first time I'd heard them, nor would it be the last. It was a way of life in Palestine that I'd sadly become used to, all too quickly. Still, they bothered me; I hated hearing the projectiles overhead, knowing that this land, my temporary home was under attack. The people of Palestine had been so kind to me; I enjoyed getting to know them all. But with every week that passed, and it seemed there was another missile being shot, yet the world kept turning, like it was just another day. A war wasn't on their doorstep, like it was mine. And this certainly kept what matters in life in perspective. So, with this outlook, I embraced the time I had. Every minute of it.

On this particular weekend, I stretched as I got out of bed early. I loved my weekends, time for myself, a day to soak in the local culture and community on a level outside of school.

I headed into town, throwing my pocket dictionary into my handbag. My Arabic was so horrible I never left home without it. Saturdays were always busy, and I was headed to the center of it all—the market. Full of fresh grown vegetables and nice selected fruit, I wandered through the stalls, taking it all in. There was an energy here that I enjoyed; a hum almost, a happiness of living in the moment.

"I'll take these," I said, picking out a handful of ripe oranges.

"Beautiful. Let me get you a bag," said the market vendor. "Busy weekend?" he asked, making conversation.

"Not really. Though I was planning on crossing over to see a few more of the sights."

The vendor eyed me warily. "Into Israel?"

I nodded.

"Are you from here?" he asked, trying to figure me out, my situation that is.

"I'm teaching in Palestine. I live here, yes."

"You've been through the check points then? Get used to them."

I nodded, not really sure how best to answer him. Of course, I knew of the Israeli checkpoints and I'd been through several, but having stayed primarily in Palestine; I had yet to experience the full extent of the ominous militarized checkpoint.

But by the end of my first month, that had changed. I knew them all too well. And I despised them. Being questioned and interrogated each and every time I crossed over into Israel—it was a tiresome, annoying practice. Without taking a political stance on the issue, simply from a practical point of view; the checkpoints were an omnipresent force, a controlling, monitoring entity unto themselves. It was such a task to simply go in and out of Palestine. I couldn't imagine living like that long term.

Without a doubt, life in Palestine was a reality check for me. Living under this sort of near constant state of tension, from the regular air strikes that I hated so much to the ever-present checkpoints, it put my life into even more focused perspective. Regardless of the challenges in my personal relationships, regardless of my struggles to stay a Mrs.; my life on this earth, overall, was so blessed. I'd grown up away from any conflict of this magnitude, and I was able to travel the world and raise my daughter, free from this sort of constant tension as well. In a way, with the heightened sense of conflict, where life and death very well could hang in the balance for so many; it became easy to put aside my own feelings of remorse or confusion regarding my personal challenges. In the big scheme of things, which was now easier to see, I'd had it so good.

"Tell us, Miss—tell us about your travels," a young boy asked. As I packed up my things, a handful of students stayed behind, like always, to quiz me about my many adventures.

"Where's your favorite place?"

"What's the weirdest food you've tried?"

"What do the kids in America do for fun?"

I smiled at the children, their questions fast and unrelenting. "Let me finish clearing up before I sit down. You're my third class of the day—and I didn't get a chance to tidy up after the other two."

"Do you have three classes every day, Miss?"

"I do. Every day. It is lovely though—to share, to teach, for so many to learn—I wouldn't have it any other way," I answered, smiling back at them.

"I wish we could see the world," said one little girl quietly.

"Of course you can. When you're older," I said, patting her on the shoulder.

She shook her head, her eyes welling up with tears. "No. It's not like that."

"How so?" I asked.

The little girl didn't answer, only shaking her head in response. But one of the older students chimed in. "It's a... passport issue."

I felt my face scrunch up in confusion. "Can you not get one?"

"Some can. I mean, they do offer them, but they're issued by the Palestine Authority, because they don't recognize Palestine as a state," he explained.

"But that doesn't work?" I asked, sensing there was still more to this.

"Again, maybe, but it's pretty useless. It doesn't get you in many places—we always need to apply for visas, and even then, they don't always grant them. And how do we get anywhere anyway when we're not allowed in the main airport?"

"Not allowed?"

The boy shook his head. "They need to grant us special papers just to fly out of Ben Gurion."

"And they don't grant you those papers," I said, guessing where this was going.

He nodded.

"Well, there has to be some Palestinians who travel—how do they do it?"

"Depending on your family, you might be able to get a temporary Jordanian passport and fly out of there," he shrugged.

The little girl looked down at her desk; her situation becoming clearer by the second.

"So, for most of us, we're just not able to travel because we aren't allowed to have a passport," the boy explained.

I nodded as I took in the information, though it came as a bit of a shock to me—a world without a passport—my entire life would have been so different.

While I tried to console my student, I knew in my heart there were no words to make this better. I'd told her about a life that could only be a dream for her. It wasn't like there was an easy solution to her problems. It wasn't as if the Middle East conflicts were going to resolve themselves anytime soon—after decades of unrest, decades of uncertainty. Despite what I wanted to say, I couldn't very well offer blanket reassurances that everything was going to be okay, because these children knew as well as I did that this was something that wasn't going to change in the near future.

As I tried to comfort the girl, I looked over at the handful of students before me. To live a life restricted geographically, to be contained in the same region, a small space relatively speaking, for your entire life—it was hard to fathom. I couldn't and didn't want to imagine a life without my passport, without the option of the world at my fingertips; all the people I'd met and places I'd seen. Certainly, we in the west take so many of these things for granted.

"Miss, please tell us more about your travels—what is it like out there?" the little girl asked again, wiping away the last of her tears.

I smiled again at her, happy to share my memories with her. At the end of the day, she wasn't asking me to solve her problems, or the problems of her region—she was simply asking me to share my experiences. And so I did.

My weekdays in Palestine were an easy routine—students in the day, followed by an informal social hour after my last class. I enjoyed my time in the country and loved teaching the students. The people here were simple and kind.

And I enjoyed the pace of life here—such a different energy than South Korea. In a strange way, it seemed calmer, despite the political conflict. And I needed that. Though I hadn't wanted to marry Wallace, it had been hard to leave him behind; on so many levels, I enjoyed the time we spent together. But just like every new adventure, my heart took what it needed from the environment and healed itself.

Ultimately, my days in Palestine came to an end sooner than I would have liked. I hated to go, but it was simply so unstable, and unsafe, at that particular time, that in my heart I knew it was the right choice for me.

I stared at my passport as I stood in line at the airport—so many options before me, every destination was truly at my fingertips. I couldn't help but feel overwhelmingly humbled and grateful, as my options were so great and varied compared to my Palestinian friends—all because of where I'd been born.

Everything was put in perspective—regardless of the ups and downs of my marriages, my life was always safe and within my own control. And perhaps those riches were what I needed to focus on instead of concerning myself with getting involved with another partner.

I looked up at the departures board and smiled—my flight back home was on time. And there was someone waiting for me who I was very excited to see.

"Aila!" I cried, running towards my now grown baby. "I've missed you!"

"Mom, I've missed you, too. You look well."

I smiled, wrapping my arms around her. "So do you. Here, let me get a good look." It was tough to have gone so long not having seen her. It was good to be back together—quality time before my next adventure.

"Three months?" asked Aila. "I'm so excited!"

"Three. And I don't want to intrude, so don't change your schedule for me."

"Mom, I never get to see you, compared to before. And it's not like I'm going to be visiting you on the weekends in Central Africa!"

"I know, I know," I said, giving her another quick hug. "It's so good to see you. So what's new? Get me up to speed on everything. Has anything happened with that guy you were telling me about? Javier?" I bit my lip as soon as I'd brought it up. I didn't want to create the same pressures for Aila that had been there for me.

"Maybe," she smiled coyly. "Come on, let's get out of the airport, there's so much to get caught up on."

"How's school?" I asked in the car, impatient to hear everything.

"Good, good. I can't believe I'm a junior already. Time flies, doesn't it?"

I nodded knowing all to I well how quickly life was passing us by. My baby girl was now practically all grown up. And it had happened before my very eyes. Now she was studying medicine at an Ivy League school on a soccer scholarship.

"Did I tell you Javier's from Bolivia?" Aila asked, already blushing as she spoke of her first boyfriend.

As it happened, Aila only socialized with the foreign students—maybe this had something to do with the fact that she'd never attended a school in the USA, due to our travels.

"You did. And he plays basketball, is that right?"

"Yes. And he's so good at it. And at everything. He's amazing, Mom. Just so incredible. He's in medical school, too. We've even talked about opening a medical clinic in Bolivia... one day."

I watched my daughter as she gushed over this new boy in her life. "Is he staying in one of the dorms, too?"

Aila shook her head. "Off campus. But don't worry—I'm not changing anything—I love the dorm life, so I'm staying there for another year for sure."

I smiled, unable to hide my relief. For whatever reason, it made me feel better knowing she was on campus in one of the dorms instead of off by herself, or in a house with a group of friends.

"I love it here, Mom. Traveling is amazing and I'd never change how we did it, but I love being settled for a while. It feels like home. Is that weird to say?"

"Of course not. Home is where the heart is, right? I guess what I mean is you've always been American, even if we never spent a lot of time here. But we will be, for the next three months!" I smiled.

"Road trip!" cried Aila, rolling down her window.

"California here we come!" I cried back.

We had a busy summer planned—making the most of Aila's time off on summer break. They were three glorious months of adventure together. We enjoyed our road trip in California, driving up the Pacific Coast Highway, soaking in the salt air and sunshine. And we even had time to take a cruise in the Caribbean...

Unexpectedly, Aila's fateful trip aboard another cruise ship a few years later changed her life forever. During an internship, she went on a Caribbean cruise with a few of her girlfriends. While she still had strong feelings for Javier, she wasn't looking to meet anyone new. But, life had other plans as Aila met a man by the name of Winston Rodgers. She swears it was love at first sight for them both. Winston was an electrical engineer for the cruise line, which meant on his working days he lived on the ship. As a result, Aila's friends did not see much of her because she spent most of her waking hours by Winston's side.

Winston was from a small island in the Caribbean, St. Kitts. He was really interested and attracted to Aila, and she felt the same way. But, she also knew that she'd soon be returning to dry land, and to Javier.

After the cruise, Aila was happy but confused. She promised Winston that she would keep in touch, and she did. They would Skype, email or call each other every day. She was slowly losing interest in Javier and yet didn't know what to do as her heart was torn in two directions.

"Mommy, I am in a real life dilemma!" Aila said as she came to me for advice. She told me about her cruise and how she loved the beautiful caves in Barbados, the beautiful countryside in St. Lucia, the colorful buildings in Curacao and the friendly people in St. Martin... but more than anything, she loved Winston. She loved the way he seemed to understand her without really knowing her. She loved the idea that he actually paid attention when she talked, unlike Javier who always pretended there was a language barrier between them.

Once Aila had laid her cards on the table, I told her the dilemma could only be resolved by following your heart. I had been influenced by external pressures in some of my decisions, but I knew that the times when I listened to my heart, I never regretted it. My heart had never steered me wrong, in fact it guided me through my marriages and my life, to the point where I am today.

And so, Aila eventually told Javier of her interest in Winston. Javier suggested couples therapy and Aila gave it a chance, but it only convinced her of what her heart already knew: she did not want to be with Javier anymore; she belonged with Winston.

Thankfully, my many attempts at marriage didn't sway Aila's views on the subject. Aila became a Mrs. – she and Winston got married. I remember watching as she headed down the same aisle I had so many times before, praying to God she would find happiness and a partner who loved her and whom she could love forevermore.

After tying the knot, they both worked on the same cruise ship; Winston as an engineer and Aila as a doctor. And after two years at sea, Aila discovered she was pregnant. So, they both left the ship and moved to St. Kitts, where they are still happily married with two children; my beautiful grandchildren.

According to Aila and Winston, their marriage is successful because they have excellent communication and a deep love and concern for one another.

She'd found a recipe for success that worked for her. Admittedly, she was of a different generation—there weren't the same kind of pressures for girls her age, no one forcing them to get married, or guilting them into becoming a Mrs. before they were intimate with someone. Of course, those had been factors that I'd faced, and pressures that I'd felt. But it was more than that—it wasn't the allure of a wedding, of being a Mrs. that attracted her. And for all of these reasons, and many more; I was proud of Aila and hopeful for her future with Winston.

While, to this day, I am still on my search for the reasons why other people get married. Nevertheless, I have decided that I was not created to settle down and be the typical wife.

I now believe that I'm most likely better off with a man who is compatible with me on all levels, and one who loves to travel the world just as much as I do. A male companion and not a husband.

Partly I've realized that my doubts and questions about marriage are due to my background of being raised as a Christian. I was always told that it's a good thing to be married. But they never ever tell you how to be married and stay married. If they did, I must have missed that lesson.

Instead, I learned many life lessons. And the key to it all, I feel, is my realization that marriage does not keep love alive. It's love that keeps a marriage alive.

Rachael

1

I stared at the computer screen on my desk, my eyes widening to the words in the email. Of course I'd read it before, but it was only now just finally starting to set in. I'd gotten the job; they wanted me. And this weekend I'd finally be out of this house, this city, this state.

I was being dramatic—It wasn't all bad, but I was more than ready to leave and start my new life.

"Rachael, honey, come on down for dinner!" my mom called from the kitchen.

"Coming!" I looked around at the packed bags, the suitcases full to the brim—it was really happening. After months of applying, the job of my dreams was mine: in a matter of days, I'd officially be a computer programmer at one of the big tech companies in San Diego. California here I come!

I bound down the stairs, clinging to thoughts of my future to get through the next hour. It was quiet around the dinner table, but the silence spoke volumes.

"Would you like to say grace?" My mother turned to my father, knowing full well that he took it upon himself to pray before every meal. I bit my lip and I bowed my head, anxious for the meal to get underway. This was their last chance to fill my head with their concerns and objections—and as much as I loved them both, I wasn't looking forward to this at all.

"God Almighty, bless our baby girl as she ventures into the world, forging her own way. Give her the strength to follow the path you have set out for her and keep her safe from the temptations of this life. In your name we pray, Amen."

"Amen."

I looked around the table, between my two parents: this was the last thing they wanted for me and I knew it. Still, it was what I needed.

"I'll be home for Christmas," I said, pushing the chicken around on my plate.

"Mmm-hum," said my mother, refusing to make eye contact with me.

I looped my curly red hair around my finger, twirling it as the silence lingered.

"Have you found a church there, yet?" asked my father. "I believe they still have those in California, you know."

"Not yet. I'm still here, remember? But I'm sure I will in no time. I'm just moving. I'm not about to change who I am, Daddy." I looked up at him, meaning every word. This was an adventure most definitely, but even though I craved the distance away from them, there were parts of me that would never change—my faith being one of them.

My father knew this already. So right now he was being ridiculous, obviously. But I didn't really expect anything less: growing up in a strict Christian home, if there was anything that was not left to chance it was our faith.

"Oh, my baby," moaned my mother on the other side of me. "It's such a big world out there."

"I know. That's kind of why I'm going—to be a part of it. I can't stay here in Mississippi forever."

"You can," countered my mom. "We did. And look at us—happily married all these years later. We have a life here. A good life, Rachael. And you could too, if you wanted."

I shook my head, knowing it was futile to argue with them, but I couldn't help myself. Maybe if they understood, maybe if they knew how much I'd thought this through; I wanted to believe that would make a difference.

"But I'm not happy here. I'm not happy with how things are."

My father looked sternly at me. "Now don't go talking about things you shouldn't be talking about, Princess."

"That's it—that's it right there: I know I'll always be your little princess, but it's not us versus them. White versus black. I don't see the world that way."

"Neither do we, honey, you know that." My mother stared at me sternly.

I turned my head between my parents, doubt cast on my face.

"Come now," she said, her tone chiding me. "We've never been anything other than fair, no matter who is involved. We don't care what's on the outside, it's what's on the inside. Isn't that what we've always taught you?"

I chewed the inside of my cheek, not wanting to answer. But I did. She was telling the truth, albeit a simplified version if it. Still, they'd never been blatantly racist. "Yes. That's what you taught me. But I can see it, see it in your faces when I bring home my friends," I countered, still wanting them to finally understand.

"Your friends are all very nice, Rachael. We've opened our doors to all of them, haven't we?" asked my mother.

"Yes, but--"

"But what?" said my dad.

"But there's a difference between the way you look at my friends from high school and the way you treat my friends from around here. Don't try to tell me I'm wrong."

"You're not. It's just the ones from school don't have the same upbringing we're used to. We only want what's best for you, Princess. We don't want the neighbors getting the wrong impression—that you'll associate with just anyone." My dad's eyes never wavered in their conviction. He meant every word—that somehow the opinion of the neighbors in this upper class neighborhood mattered. And he believed whole-heartedly that they'd look down on us, well, just me really, for socializing with my black friends from school.

"It's not right," I said, knowing this wasn't an argument I was going to win.

It was hard because even though I knew that my parents were good people, and that they were products of their upbringing, things had to change. The racism, both overt and underhanded, needed to stop. "So the fact that all my closest friends are black has nothing to do with it? It's just that they're not from the right families, is that what you're saying?" I asked, not afraid to finally call him on it.

My parents exchanged a glance between one another. I knew this bothered them, how I had predominantly black friends. I knew it and they knew it. But no one ever wanted to put all their cards on the table and call it for what it was.

"They run in a different circle from us, that's all. Our kind needs to stick together," explained my mother quietly.

"Our kind, meaning white?"

"That's not what your mother meant."

"Our kind—we're from a higher class, that's all I meant," she explained.

"So, just to clarify—so long as my friends are rich, you'd be happier?"

My mother sighed, shaking her head in frustration.

"Princess..." cautioned my father. "Don't speak to your mother that way."

"Sorry." I took a deep breath, knowing in my heart there was no good way for this to end. We were from different eras; and my parents simply didn't want to adjust their views of the world to match the times.

And unfortunately, they weren't the only ones around here. It just made me that much more impatient to leave town. I was long done with the racism and ignorance—it would have no place in my life, if I could help it.

"You can still change your mind, you know. There's no reason to go so far away," said my mother, changing her tone completely.

"This is what I want to do," I said, standing firm.

"I know you think it is, but it's hard out there, Rachael. It's not going to be like high school where everyone loves you and fawns over you."

"Dad, it wasn't like that in high school," I said, letting the lie spill off my tongue. In all honesty, high school was very, very good to me. Lots of friends, and more than my fair share of admirers. Of course I enjoyed the attention, but it wasn't my whole world; I would have been fine if it hadn't been like that.

"You think so? Ha. Well, the real world can't sustain that kind of admiration. You might have been special in high school and you will always be special to us and The Lord, but it ends at some point." My father's sharp tongue pierced through me, but I vowed not to let it show.

I sighed, looking at my parents, trying not to get into an even bigger fight on my last night at home. They loved me. They were only trying to help—protect me and make sure I didn't get hurt with unrealistic expectations. They were just doing what they thought was right.

So, I nodded but didn't dare say anything else in the huge long awkward silence that followed, only punctuated by the scrapes of knives and forks on china.

"What time's your flight tomorrow?" asked my mom.

"First thing."

My mother nodded before wiping a tear away from her eye. "We'll miss you, Princess."

"I'll miss you too, Mom."

In a matter of a few hours, my plane had touched down; my new life had officially begun. And California didn't disappoint. It was everything I imagined and so much more. Being on my own for the first time and being able to finally make my own choices without the constant scrutiny of my parents—and their outdated beliefs—it was amazing.

But their advice and insights hadn't all been untrue. Making friends wasn't as easy as it had been in high school—there just wasn't the breeding ground for friendships in a work environment. I met plenty of nice people, but everyone had their own things going on. So did I, technically—taking care of my own place, and myself; it was an adjustment, but one I was enjoying.

Nevertheless, when Saturday night rolled around, there were no calls asking me to go out, though I had met at least several potential friends in my first few weeks in a new city. I grabbed a slice of takeout pizza, and put my feet up on the small coffee table. I flipped through the channels on the TV, looking for something to catch my attention. Halfway through, I saw it, or him rather—the sight of the man on the small screen made me stop in an instant. I couldn't take my eyes off him; I panned up and down his tall frame, taking in his rippled features, and firm body. He looked like a fantasy come true—handsome beyond belief. His exquisite face caught my attention, and the rest of the package was just as dreamy.

"God will guide us—each and every one of us. If only you let Him into your life, you will feel the grace and power of his presence. No longer will you face the world alone as he will be with you—to support, to help, to guide, to listen." The words came from the beautiful man, who spoke with a raw intensity, a passion, as rare as it was sincere.

I listened to his service that day—my attention captivated. He spoke about God, inspiring and motivating his viewers to become connected or get reconnected with their faith. His words rang true, striking a chord with my engrained beliefs. But unlike my experiences in Mississippi, here was a charismatic preacher who was closer to my age, from my modern world. This was not the sort of preacher my father would connect with, but his encouraging words certainly resonated with me. He was charismatic, charming, and easy on the eyes—and I found myself attracted to every part of him as a human being.

Our Saturdays together became a regular date—I tuned into his TV show every weekend, staring at the screen, hanging onto every word that came out of his mouth.

"We are in this fight together—against evil, against corruption, against temptation. Do not forsake the Lord for he loves you for who you are. He only asks that you be true to Him and yourself. And you can do that—we all can do that. For the Lord asks of us only that which we can give. Can you hear Him calling you? He's asking you to love Him. And in loving Him, turn around and share that love with others. We are all God's creatures—and if we truly love Him, how can we not love each other?"

I watched the man before me—Pastor John Atkinson—admiring his words and features concurrently. I stared at his face, his high cheekbones, his smooth black skin, his deep brown eyes. If he'd been before me, in the flesh, I'd be so swept away by his looks that I would have missed his words completely. I'd never felt this way before at church back home—and I doubted every pastor in California would have this effect on me. John was special. He made me feel special, and feel connected to a higher cause at the same time. How strange to have such strong feelings for a man whom I'd never even met in real life. Yet, somewhere deep down, I knew we would meet one day. I could feel it.

"Hey, Tricia—come see him!"

"See who?"

"The man I'm going to marry."

"What? Where is he?"

"Right there," I said, pointing to the screen. "You see him?"

Tricia stared at the screen for a minute watching the Pastor speak to his audience before she burst out laughing.

"What?"

"He's on TV! He's preaching on TV. How are you going to meet him, let alone marry him?" she asked.

"Oh, I'll figure it out. Give me some time."

"You sound awfully convinced."

"Listen to your Lord God—He is here for you—to show you the way. For everyone has something to offer, something to give. And for those of you who can give financially, know that every penny you can share goes to help those in need. As you know, part of our mission is to love one another as brothers and sisters in Christ. We're reaching out as we do every week to those in need—helping wherever, however we can, to ease their suffering as Jesus helped those around him."

"He talks a good show," agreed Tricia. "So, do you give money to this guy too then?"

"Every week."

"But have you spoken to him? Like ever?"

"It's only a matter of time. God will make it happen—I can feel it—it must be his plan."

Weeks and months passed and I tuned in every Saturday to see my future husband, donating money as I could.

"Tricia, come in here—he's on again!"

"Who?" called Tricia from the kitchen of my small apartment.

"My black prince, of course."

"What's he saying today?" asked Tricia, sauntering in with a coffee. "Turn it up."

I grabbed the remote control, more than happy to increase the volume. My prince's voice was like velvet—soft and supple, so easy on the ears. On the small screen before us, he paced along the stage, microphone in hand.

"Have you met him yet?" she asked, sitting down beside me.

"Not yet. But it'll happen. I know it will."

"How so? Tell me, how are you going to meet him?" asked Tricia.

"My plan—positive affirmations."

"Are you serious? How does that work?"

"It's true, Tricia. I have been speaking my positive affirmations and I am going to speak that Pastor John Atkinson right into my life." I explained, forever grateful that Tricia was so accepting of anything I said. There were no questions, no interrogation—I said it was going to happen and she accepted my word.

"Now, I know what you're thinking," said Pastor John on the TV screen. "You're thinking you don't have enough for yourself, how could you possibly have enough to give. But if you have a roof over your head, if you have food on your table, if you have heat in your home, you have more than many."

I felt myself nodding at the screen.

"God calls upon us to help out those in need—it is our duty as a community to stretch out our hand, to help our brothers and sisters. If you're a regular contributor to our ministry to the poor, then we thank you—we appreciate your help. And if you're still waiting to make that donation, then make today that day!"

"Did you hear his voice? It's wonderful, isn't it? I could listen to that voice all day."

"Um-hum," agreed Tricia, not nearly as affected by the Pastor as I was. Although, technically, that was probably a good thing—I wanted John all to myself.

"For those of you not in our audience today but who would like to be... stay tuned for details. We'll be taking our show on the road! We're heading down to San Diego to host a revival!"

Tricia and I froze and turned towards each other in the next second. "Did he just say he's coming to San Diego?" I whispered.

"He did!"

"Positive affirmations, what did I tell you! Come on Tricia, pack your bags, we have a revival to attend."

"We're really going?"

"Of course! But first we need to go shopping!"

It took more than a few trips to pick out the perfect outfit and shoes for the occasion. I'd always been a tad spoiled when it came to fashion, so for such an important occasion I may have gone overboard in picking out the perfect designer outfit. Still, it didn't matter how long that part took – I only had one shot to make a great first impression with John.

"I plan to wake up the minds of all those closed minded family and friends of mine. Can you imagine my parents' faces when they see my black prince?" I said, day dreaming every moment since hearing about the revival.

Tricia laughed, shaking her head.

"Oh, their faces when I show up with a beautiful black man on my arm! Everyone in town will be floored—they won't know where to look or what to make of it!"

"You'll have to parade up and down the street with him, showing him off."

"You know I will. It'll be incredible."

Tricia and I laughed at the thought, laughed until we cried.

The day of the revival came up quickly. Tricia and I were there early, ready to snatch the front row seats as soon as they opened the doors.

And there we sat, watching the man we'd seen on my TV screen week after week, except now he was only a few feet away, preaching the Lord's word before our very eyes. But we would soon be closer, much closer. When the show was over, John stepped down from the stage and began shaking hands with his congregation. It was now or never. Finally we would meet and I would feel the warmth of his touch for the first time.

With an outstretched hand swallowing my delicate palm, he smiled charmingly at me. "Rachael. What a lovely name. A pleasure to meet you. Call me John."

I blushed, my cheeks turning a bright red, almost matching my hair at his words. John shook my hand with a gentle but firm grip; he held it a little longer than usual. My heart raced from the electricity between us.

"Are you from here, Rachael?"

"I am now. But I'm actually from Mississippi originally."

"And how do you like it out here?"

"Love it. It's liberating—maybe it's the area or just being independent, but it feels as if I'm in charge of my own destiny. It seems like I'm able to hear God a lot clearer now."

John laughed. "Sounds like you have a plan. I like that."

I smiled back at him, feeling myself blush again.

"Isn't that what you always say—listen for God—he'll show you the way?"

"It is," said John, smiling widely. "You watch my service regularly then?"

"Every weekend actually. You've been my date every Saturday night for the past few months, ever since I moved out here."

"Wow—we're dating already! Had I known, I would have shown up with flowers."

I giggled, feeling a little silly for my choice of words. Still, he seemed to find the humor in them. "Well, I suppose I can forgive you—but next time..." I said, letting my words trail off.

"Next time," he agreed with a smile. "I like the sound of that. Tell me more about yourself, Rachael—you're a breath of fresh air around here."

I shrugged. "Not much to tell." I felt oddly nervous and giddy at the same time. It was a weird sensation meeting someone in person who I'd been fantasizing over for so many months.

"Well, for our next date; if I came to your work, where would it be?" he asked.

I shook my head. "Well, security's pretty strict there—I work at a tech company. But I'm also a jazz singer, which is much more entertaining."

"Wow—I'm impressed."

"If that impresses you, I should take you sky diving with me." I laughed.

"Now, I know you're teasing."

"I am. But I want to go! Imagine seeing the world from high up—just you and the clouds—I like to think it's as close to heaven as I can get. While I'm still alive, that is."

John laughed and gently touched my arm.

"Well," I said, seeing the line of people milling about behind me, waiting to capture the Pastor's attention, as I fended off internal butterflies, I concluded it was time to wrap up. "I suppose I shouldn't keep you from your flock."

"I suppose not. But..."

"Yes?"

John paused for a moment before continuing. "It's been a real pleasure meeting you, Rachael. Do stay in touch."

"Oh?" I smiled. "I bet you say that to all the girls," I teased.

"Actually, I don't. Is it too forward of me to ask for your number, or your email, or something like that?"

I felt myself blushing again, as I quickly took a pen out of my purse. "Here," I said, handing him over a piece of scrap paper with my email and phone number written on it.

"Let me give you mine as well," he said, taking the pen from my hand. His fingers lingered on mine, and my heart pounded unevenly.

"I'll be in touch. Is it too soon if I call you next week?"

I smiled. "That would be great."

And that was our beginning.

2

I closed my eyes as I looked across the dimly lit bar, taking a big gulp before belting out the last note of the song. I always hit it, but tonight I was nervous. I'd been half joking at the Revival when I mentioned John should come listen to me sing; but here we were—at his insistence.

"So, when are you performing next? I'd love to come," he said on the phone. True to his word, he called me within days and the conversations flowed between us.

"Ha. Well, we'll see. What about something more conventional?"

"We could do conventional. Does that mean sky diving is out of the question?" John laughed.

"Well, um, I think-" I paused, not sure if he was serious or not, or how I wanted to play it.

"I'm kidding, Rachael. About the skydiving anyway."

I exhaled in relief. Not that I wasn't up for sky diving, but talk about an adrenaline filled first date. And first dates usually have plenty of nerves, without the butterflies of jumping out of a plane.

"Oh, okay. That's good because sky diving is definitely more of a second date kind of thing, for me," I teased.

John laughed easily. "A sense of humor—I like that. But just so you know, I was serious about wanting to hear you perform. You can't just say something like that and not show off your skills."

"I certainly can," I laughed. "Besides, you don't really want to hear me. When was the last time you were even in a jazz club?"

"Ummm," John paused.

"Exactly," I said, feeling a little smug. But then it hit me—saying no and not letting him into my life wasn't exactly the route I wanted to take. It certainly wasn't the road to becoming a Mrs., to becoming the wife of this wonderful man, the wife of a pastor, my beautiful dark prince.

Ugh, I sighed to myself—talk about getting carried away. Sure, I'd watched him from afar for months, but in reality we'd only just met. We hadn't even had a real first date yet, and here I was planning our wedding. Nothing like piling on the pressure, Rachael!

"John," I said, starting again, "of course you can come, but wouldn't you rather get something to eat, or go for coffee? Something where we can talk, rather than where you watch me sing?" I shook my head, knowing that while I adore singing, this would certainly not be in my top ten for a date, especially a first date.

"Well, I don't imagine you'll perform the whole night, will you?"

"No," I conceded.

"And you've seen my work, week after week, apparently." His voice had a teasing edge to it. Though he was still on the surface making his case, there was an unmistakable light and friendly tone underneath. He was playing with me; well, I could play too. Especially if the saying held true about playing together and staying together.

"Well, I have, that's true. As far as I'm concerned we've been dating for months now. But honestly, it's not exactly the same thing. You're not really performing. You're not putting on an act. You share yourself with the world, with your followers."

"True enough. But then, I imagine, singing is who you are, a part of you, isn't it?" I could hear a little laugh coming from the other end of the phone. He wasn't gloating, but of course he'd just won the argument.

I paused, chewing my lip. There was no denying his point—I'd always loved singing; it had been a part of my life for as long as I could remember. I sighed, already picturing my nerves on that night. On any date with John I would have been nervous, but this would add an extra level to the whole evening.

"Please," he said quietly, his silky smooth voice easily crushing my hesitation.

It felt like I was putty in his hands. I was mesmerized by him, even when it was just his voice, even more so now that my dreams of meeting him were finally a reality after weeks, months of watching him, getting to know him from afar. How was it possible that these, my wildest dreams, had come true? I could barely believe that this was all real, that we were actually here, now, chatting away, making plans together. I think I would have probably agreed to anything he suggested at that moment.

"Okay," I said.

"Okay I can come, or okay singing is a part of you?"

"Both. I sing from my soul and yes, if you're really interested, you're welcome to come to hear me sing."

John laughed warmly. "This is a good thing, trust me. Doesn't it sound like the perfect way to get to know the real you? Watching you do something you love?"

I hesitated again, not totally sold on what I'd just agreed to.

"Oh don't worry, Rachael. It'll be great. Besides, you know I'm right," he teased. "Afterwards, if you're up for it, let me take you out for drinks. The best of both worlds. Does that sound good?"

I smiled to myself, unable to help but do the math—if I was going to perform, and then we were going out afterwards too—this was no quick outing, we'd have at least a few hours together.

My cheeks flushed with excitement. "Okay," I agreed. "That sounds great. Friday?" I smiled, my hand wrapped tightly around the phone, my insides warming at the words coming out of his mouth. It was like a dream, a fantasy, my black prince was real and we were actually going on a date together. It was as if everything was somehow, someway going in the right direction. How has this happened, I wondered, feeling like

I needed to pinch myself. My real world was about to become one with my dreams. Me and John—oh, please let him fall in love with me as I'd already fallen in love with him! And please God, let him be as wonderful in person as he had been the other day, and as great as he was every week during his broadcasts!

The week went so slowly leading up to our date but it was worth it. Looking out at him now, I met his eyes as I exhaled the last of my breath, finishing the song with as much attitude as it deserved. It felt like he was the only one I was singing for.

My knight in shining armor, my beautiful black pastor, a person so truly good it almost hurt being with him!

John walked up to the stage, extending a hand to help me down the few stairs to reach the ground floor. "Wow--you're amazing!" He put his arm around me, guiding me towards our table.

A rush of energy flooded my system; I tingled from his touch. "Thanks," I said, sheepishly, feeling the blush take over my face. I inhaled deeply, savoring the warm, woodsy scent that rippled off of him. He smelled as good as he looked, and he looked incredible.

"Rachael?"

I shook my head, pulling myself back to the present. "Sorry, what?" I laughed. Getting caught up in a guy was not a usual occurrence, much less when he was right in front of me.

John smirked, staring at me, watching my every move as if he could read all about me from every little shift in my weight. Of course, as a result of the intense starring, I shifted around even more.

"What? What is it?" I asked, looking down at myself, to make sure there was nothing out of place. There wasn't.

"I'm just watching you, enjoying you, that's all."

"No, that's not all. You're staring like you're trying to figure me out." I shook my long hair out, savoring the extreme release of having finished the performance. Well, maybe John had been right—I'd been so stressed and nervous about the performance, that now, it was like a weight had been lifted off my shoulder, and I was blissfully looking forward to the rest of our night together, instead of feeling stressed throughout it. And it kind of turned out great, actually. "What is it? You are trying to read me, aren't you?"

"You think so?" John laughed.

"Yes, I do, actually." I laughed back. "Now either tell me what you're looking at, or stop staring. It's not polite, you know."

John laughed again, shaking his head. "I can stop if you'd like. If you'd be more comfortable."

"Yes. Please do," I said, letting out another sigh of relief.

John laughed again. Louder though, like he was genuinely amused.

"What?"

"You."

"Me what? What are you laughing at? This is getting out of hand, you know."

"You're funny. That's all."

I reached for my drink on the table, carefully taking a sip to see if he would elaborate on his own. Of course he didn't.

"How so? I mean, I don't mind being funny, but I'd rather you were laughing with me than at me, and since I'm not laughing-" I said, letting my thought dangle unfinished.

"Okay, fair enough. I can stop."

"Good. Now do I at least get to know what about me you were laughing at? I think that's only fair, seeing as how you really shouldn't be laughing at someone before you really get to know them," I said, mock scolding him.

"Fair point again. You're a sharp one, aren't you?"

"I try."

"Well, I was laughing because it seemed funny that you'd stand up on stage and sing so beautifully for us all, but then, it was as if the minute you came down, I wasn't allowed to admire your beauty anymore."

"Oh," I said. "Well, then, I guess, if there was ever going to be a good excuse that might just be it. Still, try to admire my beauty from afar. I'd much rather not be ogled at close range." I laughed, hoping John could hear the sarcasm in my voice.

He laughed again, shaking his head.

"See—laughing with me. Much better than at me."

"Definitely. So tell me, what is it about singing? Have you always done it? You seem like such a natural on stage."

"I wish," I said, looking back up to the stage where the next group of performers were now getting set up. "I've dabbled here and there, but this jazz thing is only recent."

"Wow—you're brilliant at it. Absolutely incredible."

I looked down at my drink, feeling strangely awkward.

"Don't play shy—I don't buy it. You certainly didn't give off that impression the last time we met."

I turned my face up so I could look at him square on. Nothing gave me more confidence than being challenged. The friction, though minimal and largely playful, was arousing in a primal sort of way.

I stared him down, any trace of shyness effectively removed. "The last time we met was at a conference, a religious revival. Here, now—" I said, pointing back behind me towards the stage, "That was me—my turn in the limelight. I can take it. I just don't have to have it all the time. No one likes to be on, to be the center of attention every given moment."

"Of course not. I apologize. And just to be clear, you nailed it tonight. You commanded the stage like a pro. The audience was eating out of your hands—I know I was."

"Thank you," I said, refusing the urge to look away, to look at anything other than his piercing eyes which seemed to see right through me. The blush in my cheeks deepened at his words.

I was never this nervous with guys; at least I hadn't been in high school. What was wrong with me now, I wondered. But I knew what it was, the only thing it could be—John was different from the others. Unlike my friends at school, and the boys I used to talk with there; this was a man who I'd made plans with. Sure, he didn't know about those plans yet, but I'd cast him as my future husband long ago!

What other role could there be for someone so interesting and intriguing, distinguished and faithful, someone this perfect. He was in a league all of his own and I knew it.

"Tell me about your family—what are they like?" John asked, scooping up a piece of pie into his mouth. Our evening had progressed to coffee at a small little cafe.

"Wonderful. They're kind, caring, generous. They're good people," I said, happily glossing over their shortcomings. I took a sip of coffee, savoring our time together.

"Wow—not a lot of people can say that. Were you guys close? How did they handle your move out here?"

"Ya, we were. And I guess they handled it as well as any parents could. They weren't thrilled with the idea of it, but they knew it was important to me. They miss me of course, but then they respect my decision to try and see what life out here might be like for me. And your family?" I asked, equally intrigued.

"I've been blessed in that area as well. My parents loved me very much and helped me become the father I am today."

"Oh," I said, trying my best to hide my shock. Had I misread the signs? Was this not actually a date then? My eyes closed in a long blink as I tried to limit my expectations and reassess our evening so far. Maybe I'd read this all wrong. Maybe this was simply part of his pastoral outreach or something, I thought, scrambling to make sense of his actions, his words.

"Yes, I hope that didn't catch you off guard. I've got four children actually. Four sons. Grown up for the most part now. I was married before," John explained.

"And, not anymore?" I said, trying my best not to sound like I was prying.

"No. Not for years now. I'm divorced."

"Oh, that's good."

John smiled awkwardly.

"No, I don't mean that's good, it's just, I'm glad you're not still married." I said, back tracking as best I could.

Thankfully, John laughed, "Well, that would be awkward, wouldn't it? What can I say—having a long lasting marriage is a challenge in its own right, wouldn't you agree?"

"Absolutely. But it's still a goal of mine. I want to grow old with somebody. I want to sit on a rocking chair, looking up at the night sky, admiring the crazy world we live in until we're old and gray. Nothing sounds more wonderful to me."

"Nor me. A long lasting marriage, till death do us part. It's always the goal, isn't it?"

"Well, of all my goals, that's the one I'm most determined to meet."

"What makes it rise to the top like that? I'm assuming you have other goals, so why does this one take precedent?"

"I've just always wanted to be a wife, to be a partner, to be part of a team—just us against the world. And I saw that growing up. My parents have been married for forever. And they're still in love, still happy.

"Wow, not just a passing whim, you know what you want, don't you."

"Ya, I do. I've seen it; I want it for myself, that kind of marriage that lasts forever," I said candidly.

John nodded, seemingly reassessing me, if I was reading him right,

"Did you not see that in me?" I teased, trying to lighten things up again.

"I'm not sure," he said hesitantly. "I don't think I did. But I like it. You've got conviction. And a goal. Now you just need a partner."

I looked into John's eyes and laughed awkwardly. No matter how great the night had gone, joking about someone being Mr. Right, or a future husband on a first date was never going to be a good move.

"Well, I'll have to keep my eyes open. Let me know if you see any potential candidates, will you?"

"Absolutely. What are you looking for?" he asked softly, his voice somehow seductive even though his words were perfectly suitable for the cafe.

"Someone with a good heart. I need someone honest, someone kind and caring. Someone ready to be on that team with me, so we can support each other. Oh, wait, was I supposed to say something easy like 'tall, dark and handsome?'"

John laughed, though it did nothing to dispel the tension in the air between us. He leaned in closer over the table, and took my hand, gently rubbing circles on the back of it. My body tensed with excitement, my nerves on edge from his touch. Suddenly it was as if this open cafe was nowhere near private enough for the intensity between us.

"I like what you said—about finding that partner, starting a life together. You two against the world."

"Thanks," I whispered.

He nodded. "Hopefully you won't have to be looking much longer."

My mouth opened slightly, though no words came out; I had no idea what to say to that.

Suddenly, John's phone buzzed, interrupting the moment, and effectively slicing through the tension between us. Reluctantly he picked it up, giving it a casual glance before putting it back in his pocket.

He sighed, rubbing his temples.

"Is everything all right?"

"It is. Just one of my sons. But I've got to call it a night it seems."

"Oh," I said, disappointed.

"I wish I could stay longer—I've had a really nice time tonight, getting to know you."

"Me too. You're exactly like I'd thought you be, but even better, if that's even possible."

John laughed. "I'd like to see you again. Would you be up for that?"

"Definitely. I'd like that too."

Over the next few months, John and I saw each other with increasing regularity. We were seeing each other exclusively, and somehow my dreams had merged even more with reality and we were fast becoming the team that I so desired. It was us against the world—even if that world was our families.

"How's our little princess?"

I smiled, hearing my mom's voice on the other end of the phone.

"I'm good, Mom. Real good."

"You taking care of yourself all the way out there in California?"

"You know I am. You taught me well."

"I can't wait to see you, sweetie! I can't believe you're coming home next week!"

"I'm looking forward to my visit too. I miss you guys."

"Oh, it's not the same around here. We miss you too, princess. And is John still coming?"

I laughed awkwardly. "He is. He's looking forward to meeting you guys,"

"Us too. My baby, dating a pastor! Who would have ever guessed. I'm so happy for you, honey. It's such a relief to see you in a serious relationship, and with such a good man. Oh, we can't wait to meet him. Your father especially."

I chewed my lip, knowing that my father's enthusiasm might very well be short-lived. "Um, Mom, about that."

"About what?

"About John."

"What is it? You just said he was coming. Is he vegetarian or something? You sound like there's something you need to get off your chest."

"More like I want to give you a heads up."

"About what?"

I sighed. This didn't need to be said, but if I didn't give them a warning of sorts it would probably take them the whole visit to get used to the idea. "Mom, just so you know, John's black."

There was silence on the other end of the line.

"It's not a big deal. You know it isn't. He's a wonderful man, Mom, a good person. I know you'll get along well with him if you give him a chance."

"Of course, princess. Of course. I'm sure he's lovely. And well, we'll get to see for ourselves, won't we."

"Yes, you will. He's amazing. Just you wait and see."

"Don't worry. I can figure it out, but now..." Mom said, drifting off.

But I knew what she was getting at. "Dad?"

"Yes. How do you want me to handle your father?"

"Put him on. I'll talk to him."

My mom exhaled in relief. "Let me get him. And next week—I'm so excited to see you!"

"Me too," I said, but before the words were out, the phone was being passed on.

"Rachael?"

"Hi Daddy. Did you get any of that?"

"Nope. What are you and your mother talking about that involves me?"

I inhaled deeply, mustering up some courage. "I'm coming home next week, right?"

"Uh-hum."

"With John."

"That's right. We get to meet this fella you've been seeing so much of."

"Right. Well, I just wanted you to know how important he is to me, Dad."

"I gathered that much. You're bringing him halfway across the country to meet us."

"I am, and I want you and Mom to be nice to him. I want to marry him someday."

"We'll be nice, we always are."

"Yes but..."

"But what?"

I paused for a second, silently praying this would go over better than I anticipated. "Dad, John's black."

I heard the same silence that had been there after telling my mom. Only this time it was for much longer.

"Dad?"

"Honey, are you serious?"

"Of course I am. And it doesn't matter. Not in this day and age. It's not a big deal, but I figured you might be surprised if you didn't know ahead of time, that's all."

My father groaned, like this small detail somehow overrode all the other wonderful qualities John had.

"How are we supposed to spin this? What will the neighbors say? What will the family think? It's just..." he sighed, sounding like he was beside himself with the news.

"It's nothing. He's a wonderful man, a man of faith, of God. He's hardworking and kind, he treats me well and he loves me, Dad. And I love him. Please don't make an issue out of this. You've got some time before we come to get it together. Okay? Promise me everything will be good by the time we get there."

"It will, it will. We'll figure something out, right? You're my baby—we love you no matter what."

"Thanks, Dad. Because I love him too. And I want him to feel welcome in our family."

My father sighed again. "We'll do what we can."

And they did. For the time we were there, everyone was on their best behavior; all worry and concern regarding what other people might think was temporarily cast aside.

In a matter of months, John and I had gone from being virtual strangers to being a solid team—spending every free second with each other, helping and supporting, and enjoying ourselves. Our life was bliss. The relationship we'd built together was everything I'd dreamed of and more. I waited eagerly, anxiously, praying he'd lock in our future together with a ring.

And then it happened. On a gorgeous afternoon walk along the ocean. John bent down on one knee. His hand ducked into his pocket and slowly pulled out a small, square box.

My heart raced, fluttering in anticipation. There were of course a handful of options for what might be in that box—and though I'd hoped and prayed for this moment, and being on bended knee suggested only one thing, I didn't want to get my hopes up. Logically, it was still too early, too soon for this to be happening. I was ready, but I never expected John to be as quickly as I had.

But he had; this was really happening. The smile on his face, the sparkle in his eyes—John was doing this. Right now.

He reached out, taking my left hand in his free hand. Slowly, with almost an overly exaggerated speed, he let go of me and opened the box.

"Rachael—my love," said John, "Will you marry me?"

Tears pooled in my eyes before I could get an answer out. I wiped them back with my free hand as John had taken my left hand again and held it tight.

"Yes. A million times yes! Of course I'll marry you," I squealed with delight.

3

The sun was setting on Honolulu as I stared into John's eyes. They were as warm and welcoming as they'd been that first day I'd met him, 21 months ago. So captivating, I didn't want to look away; in them, I saw everything I'd been dreaming of since I was a little girl: a partner, a family, a future.

"I love you," I said, holding his hand as we walked towards the pavilion up ahead, brilliantly decorated in sparkling lights.

John smiled and kissed me on the forehead. "I love you, too. And I thank God every day for bringing you into my life."

"So do I. Oh, John, I can't believe how fast this has happened. You've made me the luckiest girl. I love you so much," I gushed, unable to even try to be composed. My head was spinning; I was living in a dreamy romantic whirlwind. In fact, the entire day had been dream-like—our big, beautiful wedding in Hawaii, surrounded by all of our family and friends. It had gone off without a hitch. And we were ready to finish out the celebration with a reception to remember. Everything about the day had been luxurious and over the top, and the reception was no different, but it was exactly as I'd pictured it. From the sparkling lights overhead, to the beautiful tiered cake, to the lush white flowers and decorations that covered every surface—straight from the pages of a bridal magazine. Every detail, every facet; the whole day was simply incredible. No expense had been spared.

"How did we afford all of this again?" I asked, already knowing the answer, but not believing it.

"Your parents contributed some, and the rest was savings," John shrugged.

"Your savings, you mean."

"Well, I have been working much longer than you, but as of today, they're your savings too. We're in this together—what's mine is yours, what's yours is mine."

"Okay. That still seems surreal," I said, mumbling to myself. Of all of John's wonderful qualities that I'd fallen in love with, his financial assets had never been on the list. Of course, I wasn't against marrying someone who lived comfortably or, in John's case, more than comfortably, but it wasn't a deal breaker for me. I had a job—and I was happy to work. But finding out he had multiple cars, multiple property investments, small businesses, even land, and reams of savings for a rainy day—it was almost too much to take in.

"How did you get to this level?" I asked him early on in our relationship, after taking a drive in one of his fancier cars.

"God's will, on some level." John laughed. "He provides for me, and I accept it."

"That seems over simplified," I countered. "Seriously—how did you amass so much?"

John shrugged. "It hasn't come overnight. There's no secret—I work hard and am compensated for my efforts. Over time, that adds up."

I nodded, sensing that was as much of an answer as I was going to get.

It wasn't really a hard burden to shoulder. After all, extra money would be easy to get accustomed to, though I'd fallen for John long before I'd known anything about his wealth. He was the perfect match for me: funny, clever, faithful, and most important—he loved me. And I loved him.

"It's been quite the day, hasn't it? Just the reception left to go," said John, taking one last look at the pink and orange hues on the horizon before we headed into the pavilion.

I smiled at him, enjoying the blissful state we were in. Everything seemed possible when we were together.

"Ready?" I asked.

He nodded and led us into our reception. As we walked under the glimmering canopy of lights, I could feel all eyes turn towards us. All except a small table near the front—who looked away as soon as we entered. I barely heard the announcer present us to the room; I was so focused on the group of four men and their dates. John's children—his four grown sons. They were the only group who paid us no attention whatsoever.

I sighed to myself and tried to plaster a fake smile on my face for everyone else. It was hard to remember, being so happy personally, that not everyone viewed our marriage as a blessing.

"Do you think the boys will come around?" I asked, hesitantly. I didn't want to bring it up. I never did. But there was no getting away from the fact that John's four sons weren't a fan of mine. Not one of them liked me. No exaggeration—they were dead set against me becoming part of their family and had said as much to my face. They'd even threatened to boycott the wedding. Thankfully, for John's sake, they'd come around in the end—I suspect none of them could bring themselves to turn down a free trip to Hawaii, courtesy of their father.

"In time. I'm sure they will, sweetheart. They're just being protective," said John, as we made our way through the crowds of people, ready to hug and kiss us, celebrating our special day.

I nodded, knowing full well that his words were meant to be reassuring; they were in no way a real assessment of the situation. His sons eyed us as we made our way to the head table, staring intently, their eyes full of resigned annoyance.

"Give them time," whispered John in my ear.

I turned back towards my new husband and let myself get lost in his eyes. He was all that mattered. I would worry about his sons tomorrow, or the next day, or the day after that. We'd have forever to figure out my relationship with his sons. And maybe he was right, maybe in time they would come around.

But despite my optimism at the wedding, that familial resolve never happened. Though I moved into John's spacious family home, and had taken on more and more responsibilities helping with his ministry work; his sons still doubted my motives. They couldn't or *wouldn't* see that he was everything to me.

"You're always here, aren't you?" said one of John's sons as he entered the main living area of our house.

I looked up from my desk, my lips tight in frustration. "I live here, Sam. So yes, you could say I'm here quite a lot."

Sam, on the other hand, didn't live here anymore; none of John's sons did. Yet they still came and went like they owned the place. I tried to stay out of the line of fire, as John loved having them stop by.

"Don't you even have a job anymore?" Sam spat, opening the fridge and searching for something to drink.

I inhaled deeply, knowing this was par for the course. Still, the words were hurtful; his sons could be so rude. It was as if they thought they could scare me away.

"That's not exactly correct. I'm sure you know, seeing as how you keep up to date on every little thing your dad does, but he asked me to come onboard with his ministry. And that's the reason I'm working from home now; that's the reason I left my job—at his request. He thinks I can be of help to his work, and that it is God will—so it was an easy decision to make. And that's what I'm doing—I'm working for him, with him."

"Sure. Like you know anything about his work."

"I know enough," I countered. "He asked me to get things organized for the next big revival—the one coming up at the end of the month. So, to answer your question: yes, I do have a job. In fact, I'm trying to work right now."

Sam stared at me, curling his lip in disdain. "This wasn't your calling. Can't even figure out your own career—have to get in on my dad's. You're something else, Rachael."

My lips flattened into a straight line as I tried to quell my annoyance. "Actually, I do have my own ambitions, thank you. But believe it or not, your father seemed genuinely interested in getting my help. And as his wife, as his partner—I am more than happy to step up."

"Sure, sure. Keep telling yourself that. Not one of us believes your little story though. But the more you say it, maybe someday, someone finally will." Sam shook his head, his face distorted with disgust. "Just after his money, our money."

I looked back towards my computer screen, ignoring Sam and trying to refocus my attention on anything but him. It didn't matter what he believed, what any of them believed—I truly loved John for who he was. He was the most honest, faithful, hard-working, respectful man I'd ever met. And together we were working to make the world a better place.

But all of John's sons were the same—determined and relentless. Sam wouldn't let it go.

"I don't like it. Got your little finger in every pot. Squirming your way into every piece of his life. Cashing out as much as you can from him." Sam stared at me, as if waiting for me to defend myself again, but there was no point. There was nothing I could say or do to change their minds—and there probably never would be. So I bit my lip, and didn't say another word.

Thankfully, ignoring him did the trick—after another minute, Sam turned away from me and moved on. It was for the best, I told myself, not really wanting to believe it. I needed, I wanted, a resolution, but there was none to be had—John's sons had made it clear they weren't interested in getting along, and they'd stuck to their decision firmly. Instead, they were only interested in staying on good terms with their father. If anything, they were the ones determined to keep their fingers in all of his many pots—their noses were poked in every aspect of John's business.

Later that day, I broached the subject with John. "Sam came by the house again today," I said, as John and I headed to the couch with our coffee after dinner.

"Oh, that's nice," said John, looking up from the TV screen. "Are you getting on better?"

"Ha," I said, no trace of laughter in my voice. "They're out to get me, John. They don't believe a word I say. And they don't treat me with any respect, in my own house."

"It's hard for them, that's all. Once they get to know you, they'll love you as much as I do."

"No, they won't. Because they've already made up their minds—that I'm after your money, that I'm a gold digger."

"But you're not and I told them as much."

I sighed as I sat down on the couch beside him. "Well, I'm glad you know that."

"I do. Now how are you doing otherwise, sweetheart?"

I exhaled loudly, as if I could rid myself of their negativity. I wouldn't let them come between us. Then they'd win—because, as with every wedge, over time that distance would simply get bigger and bigger until it caused an irreparable fissure in our relationship. I wouldn't let it get to that point. Not if I could help it.

"Great, actually. Everything with the revival is coming together and things around here are super," I said.

I smiled at my husband, feeling a genuine sense of happiness behind my words. If dealing with his sons was my cross to bear then I was very lucky—it was a manageable challenge, albeit one that required patience and a thick skin. "It's nice to have you home this week. When do you head out again?" I closed my eyes, hoping, praying, I had misread his schedule and we somehow had a full week together.

"Friday."

"Right." I forced a smile, trying not to show my disappointment. He'd only been back a few days. And it was always that way—there was always another trip, another revival to attend. A sigh escaped, too loud to be undetected.

"Sweetheart, what is it?" asked John, taking my hand. He grabbed the remote with the other and turned off the TV.

I shook my head, not wanting to complain. "Nothing, really."

"Rachael—let me help you, let God help you. We're in this together, right? Partners? Honest with each other above all else?"

"But there's nothing you can do, so there's no need to get into it," I countered.

"That may be true. But at least let me know. If we're not honest with each other, things won't work, you know that. Open and honest, all our cards on the table. Right?"

I sighed again, blinking back the surprise tears that were threatening to spill over. "Okay. You're right. It's just," I paused. "I miss you, that's all. It seems you're always either coming or going. If it isn't a meeting, it's another trip, or another service. Or something else calling you out of town." I looked down as I wrung my hands together anxiously. "But I'm just being petty, aren't I? I knew what I signed up for."

"No, you're allowed to have your feelings. There are no wrong feelings. And it's good you told me. We can fix it."

I looked up into his eyes; my skepticism plain to read.

"Well, we can at least make it better," adjusted John.

"How?" I asked, disbelief edging into the tone of my words.

"Well, if you want to be together more, why don't you come with me to these things? You're such a help working from here, I'm sure you'd be just as helpful on the road. And I bet you'd enjoy yourself!"

I nodded, trying to think it over objectively. It would certainly give us more time together. Even still, I could feel in my heart that wouldn't solve everything I was feeling.

"But that's not what you wanted to hear?" he asked.

I shook my head. "Don't get me wrong—I'd love to come more often, and you know I'm committed to you, to your mission—but," I paused, not really knowing where I was going. It was as if something was wrong inside me, but I was still trying to articulate it, even to myself. Sam's words, his accusations from earlier rang out in my mind. "I think, maybe, it's a two part issue—I miss you—that's the first part, and for sure, going on the road with you would address that, but the second part I think is bigger than that. Something else is missing—missing from me."

"Missing? Like what?"

I shook my head, not sure if I fully understood as I rambled from the top of my head, trying to make sense of my emotions as I spoke. "My connection to the world, or something like that. I think I need to do something for me, have something that is my own."

John shook his head. "I don't understand. Aren't you satisfied with working with my ministry? My success is our success. You know that right?

"Of course I do."

Well then, what exactly are you talking about? Like a hobby?"

"That kind of thing, but maybe more than that, like a pet project. Maybe a business venture or something. Maybe just my own job, separate from everything else. A way for me to feel like I have my own purpose, or my own responsibilities. Does any of this make sense?"

John nodded, stroking my hand. "God has a purpose for all of us. And if you're listening to His calling, and this is where He's guiding you—then let's do it. Who are we to question Him?"

"I still want to help out with your ministry and keep doing what we're doing, but I think..."

"Say no more, sweetheart. I support you, whatever you want to do."

I kissed John, feeling surprisingly better—maybe that was all it was—I just needed an outlet, an avenue for me to flex my own independence and ambition.

And within the next few months, everything had been arranged. Juggling my commitments to John's ministry, with my new found goal; I set up a brand new women's boutique in town, and opened my doors. I'd also added a few more trips to my schedule to increase mine and John's quality time together, but I didn't go to them all. Things were certainly getting better.

Yet, on the home front, some things were not improving. Just as I poured out my morning coffee, I groaned as I saw the tall familiar figure walk through the front door. Tom—John's eldest son. Stopping by like clockwork, even though his father wasn't home. Although it was only one-sided, I continued to try, for John's sake, to be pleasant towards the sons, to welcome them into our home, despite their open disdain for me.

"Good morning, Tom. It looks like a lovely day out, doesn't it? Your father's already left," I said, taking a sip from my coffee. "Would you like a cup?" I asked, still seated at the table.

Tom said nothing in reply; he walked straight towards me, stepping right up into my space. "Dad?" he called out, staring straight into my eyes, loud enough to be heard all over the house.

"I told you he's not here," I said, shaking my head. I gripped the hot mug of coffee and stood up from my chair, trying to create some space between us.

Whether Tom was trying to be intimidating or not, there was no denying the threatening vibe coming off him. "What do you think you're doing, Rachael?" asked Tom, taking a step towards me, closing the little gap I had managed to create.

"What do you mean?" I looked around at the breakfast table, at the kitchen behind me—nothing was out of place, I hadn't been caught doing anything! Not that I ever did anything worthy of an accusation like this. My body tensed, nerves on edge; there was no trigger I could think of to explain his outburst. "What's going on?" I asked again.

"You. That's what's going on. It's always about you."

"What? I don't understand, Tom. Where is this coming from?" I asked, bewildered.

"It wasn't enough that you wanted to get your claws into his land, into his money, his cars, into his business—you've got to blow even more of it on *your* little business," he sneered.

My back straightened up in defense. "My business? What does it have to do with you?" I asked, as politely as I could manage.

"Everything."

"I highly doubt that. Look, your father's left already, if you want to catch him, he's working—"

"I don't need to catch him. I was looking for you."

"Then what can I do for you?" I said, my voice getting more confident with every word.

"You can stop stealing our money. Stop stripping his savings to run that little shop of yours. I know you already took what you needed to open it. How much money did you steal to do that? A fashion shop? A clothing store? Ridiculous. You'd have better luck heading to Vegas and putting it all on red. It's not going to work out. And it's not right."

"Stop it, Tom. You don't know a thing about my business."

"I know we're not going to let you just take our money. You can't steal from our father; you can't steal it away from the family." He towered over me, his face twisted in anger and frustration.

"I hate to break your bubble, Tom, hate to mess up your story, but not a penny of your father's money went into my boutique. All mine. All my own start-up funds. Happy now?"

Tom stared at me, doubt and relief mixing his face. "You're lying," he said, hedging his bets.

I shook my head, staring right back at him. I'd had more than enough of their attitude, their accusations, the whole lot of them. "Not a cent."

Tom scowled at me, pacing the room like a fierce predator. "I don't know if I believe you. But for your sake, you better hope that's true."

"If you're done throwing out wild accusations, I'm about to head out," I said, walking him towards the door. "Are you staying or going?" I asked.

Tom left without another word. But his words hung in the air, fueling my worries and anxieties about handling John's sons.

I picked up the phone. There wasn't much I could say, but even just to hear John's voice that would make it better.

"Hello?"

"John," I sighed.

"Rachael? What is it? Are you okay? What's wrong." John's words came fast, his concern genuine.

"I'm okay. Just wanted to hear your voice, that all." I couldn't tell him about Tom. I didn't want to. It would only drive that wedge between us. Like they'd planned, I'm sure.

"Are you sure?"

"Ya." I sighed. "How did the meeting go this morning?" I asked, anything to distract myself.

"Good. They'd follow me anywhere, you know." John laughed.

"You're worth following, that's why."

"I hope they think so. We need them to keep believing if we want to grow any bigger."

"They will. Of course they will. What's not to love about you?"

John laughed on the other end. "I'm glad you called—I forgot to ask you something this morning."

"What?"

"Well, do you have to be at the shop tonight? Are there thing you need to get ready for next week?"

"There's always things to be done. I can't believe how fast that opening has come around. But, no, I don't have to be there tonight. Not if you need me for something."

"I was just thinking, I could take you out for dinner. Things at work are going to get busier soon—I've got another trip in a few days."

"Right, and I'm not coming on that one because of the shop opening,"

"So..." said John, pausing for effect, "Should we go out tonight? Splurge a little? We deserve it, after all this hard work."

I laughed. "I thought pastors were supposed to be paupers. No vow of poverty, I guess?"

"Not here. Not in my ministry. God takes care of us—always has, always will," John laughed with me.

"Let's do it," I said, smiling at the thought of reconnecting with my husband. It was so easy, with him always travelling, and now with me caught up in my little boutique, to feel like two ships passing in the night.

"I'll be home soon."

"Great," I said feeling better by the second.

We deserved it, and it was a wonderful night – a beautiful dinner at one of the top restaurants in town. John had good taste, there was no doubt about that. I didn't mention Tom and didn't let his sons spoil our night by giving them a second thought.

And so, life went on—John's ministry grew, and we worked hard—individually and together. Before we knew it, months and years had rolled by; like all marriages, some of these times were better than others. Still, we were on the same team—playing for the same goal. Both of us helping, supporting the other—a living example of good Christian values. Or so I thought.

4

I stared at the calendar on the wall in John's office, flipping over to the next page. A new month—this one marked our fourteenth wedding anniversary, amongst the familiar revivals and services that happened again and again without fail.

We had a good life—idyllic, in so many ways. We'd been truly blessed and I knew it. How many other pastors could afford such a grand home, such luxuries on a regular basis? But somehow we did.

John provided for us, year after year. He worked so hard, just like he was today--meeting after meeting, shoring up donations for his ministry, making contacts, getting together with his followers. He'd turned into quite the celebrity, so much more so than when we'd first met and I'd felt like I was the only person in the world watching him on that TV screen, like he was talking only to me.

Of course, we weren't the same couple now as we'd been back then. Time had taken its toll, like it does with so many couples. But we loved each other; and we did our best to make it work. After all, as my mom used to say, getting married is the easy part, staying married is the hard part. And there was nothing else that I was committed to more than this marriage.

My eyes wandered the office space as I thought about our 14 years together. With the exception of my shop, I'd dedicated my entire life to my husband—committed to his ministry, to his calling. I'd been a good wife; the best I could be.

Little trinkets dotted the shelves from our trips and adventures, a few photos hung on the wall. Papers cluttered the desk top, piling on and around his computer. I poked on the surface, innocently bemused—it was fun to see his office up close; he never let me in here.

"I don't want you to clean up after me," he always said. "You've got the whole house to maintain. Surely, you don't need to look after in here too. I can have one room to myself? Besides, there's just so much paperwork..." He'd pointed to the stacks on the desk. "Let me have this space, sweetheart." John looked at me, his eyes serious.

And I'd agreed, though his reasoning never really made sense to me.

There were other odds and ends littered throughout the messy room—everything a man could want, John had it all. It was a mix between a traditional den and a man cave—both business and pleasure were represented in here in a healthy balance, just like John strived to maintain. But looking over his toys—I sighed to myself. It would be impossible to get him something for our anniversary that he didn't already have.

"I guess the only thing left is space," I said to myself, looking at the clutter and mess around the room. "He'll be so surprised if I tidy this all up, get it so you can actually see things on the desk again."

I rolled up my selves and readied myself to sort out the mess. I looked at the clock on the desk—he'd be gone for a few more hours; more than enough time to surprise him with a clean office.

First, the desk. I grabbed a stack of papers from the top and headed towards the oversized leather chair off to the side of the room, rushing to flip through page by page. There was no way to sort it without going through every piece—I needed to understand what things were if I was going to put them away, or reorganize them at all.

At first glance, most were bank statements and investment records. Both our personal ones and ones for the church. Maybe this wouldn't be too hard after all, I thought to myself, rummaging through the tall stack.

And it wasn't. Until I reached the halfway point.

I stared at the document in my hand, puzzled by the numbers.

Much like the other papers I'd seen this morning, this looked to be a financial record of sorts—a bank statement.

But not for a bank we ever used. Not personally, or professionally.

My eyes scanned the names and numbers, first trying to make sense of the account: whose was this and why had I never heard about it?

There in the top left corner was John's name. And only his—this wasn't part of a joint account with me, nor part of the church's accounts. It was his and his alone.

My eyes panned down to the balance at the bottom, where they came to an abrupt stop, unable to look away. It was a figure higher than I'd ever seen on a statement; certainly higher than our personal finances, at least the ones I knew about.

Where had all this money come from and why hadn't he told me about it?

Quickly, I rifled through what was left of the stack of paper, looking for the same bank symbol on anything else. I found another three pages—all with balances within the same range. All transactions were listed, but there seemed to be only deposits being made, at least on these print-outs. My eyes narrowed in on the most recent statement—and the deposit dates. All made on Monday mornings. And all in cash.

How many explanations could there be, I wondered, for these hefty balances, topped up on Mondays?

But I knew the explanation, even though it was virtually unthinkable. And I knew it because I knew John's routines, in and out. Monday, he always went to the back to deposit donations from the collection plate the day before. In the church account—supposedly.

I flipped through the pile of paper again, looking for the familiar logo of the bank where the church's finances were kept. Logically, there should be deposits being made every Monday morning, as that's where the collection plate was meant to be saved.

If there were deposits in both accounts, then it was possible there was some other explanation.

I found the church record, and quickly ran my eyes over the recent transactions, looking for that expected pattern of the Monday deposits. Nothing. Surprisingly, there was actually very little going on in the account overall. Just a few hundred dollars—nothing substantial. Nothing like the sum in the mystery bank account.

So, that was it then, I thought, still staring at the papers, hoping for a clue. I'd been looking at them for over an hour now, crunching the numbers, trying to figure out a connection; an explanation for the mystery account with the enormous balance. Anything other than the obvious, devastating conclusion that John was involved in shady conduct—because that simply couldn't be possible. Not for my John. Not for my famous pastor.

But for as much as I wanted to deny it, the evidence spoke it clearly: the stack of papers in my hands was formidably thick; documenting the last five years. It had been going on at least that long. Maybe longer—I just couldn't seem to find the records from before that.

"Knock knock," said John as he walked into the house. "Where are you?" he asked, making his way down the hallway. I could hear his footsteps, hear his approach towards the office. He paused outside before entering the room, eyes wide with shock, or maybe it was fear. What had once been my ultimate goal in surprising him now seemed like a bad joke.

I looked at John, trying to rectify the image I had of him, practically carved in stone with the revelations I'd discovered today. It was unsettling; I'd been so certain of his character—but the man standing before me was a stranger in every sense of the word. Who had I married? Who had I been sharing my bed with? What had happened to my picture perfect marriage? What had I done to my life?

I felt the tension increase, mounting steadily. Still, as much as I was ready to burst, part of me wanted to hold out that there *was* still a reasonable explanation. If not—my mind filled in the gap instantly—the loneliness, the tears, the disappointment, the failure, the shame. Me telling my parents, telling friends, packing up my things. Moving out.

Of course, there was no explanation for a secret bank account with tens of thousands of dollars. There could be no good reason not to tell me about it at least. Either way, this wasn't going to be a good conversation. No matter what he said, this day was going to end poorly—either with me reluctantly giving a second chance to a man who didn't deserve it or with the collapse of our marriage. Lose-lose.

"What have you been up to?" John asked, his eyes surveying the stack of papers in my hand, and another pile on the floor. The room was a state—file cabinets open, bank books out, financial records all over the floor.

"Cleaning actually. I think we need to have a talk, John," I said, feeling nervous and teary, already thinking miles ahead to the inevitable outcome. I spoke slowly, carefully. Every fiber of my being itched to yell and scream, but I wanted to give him a chance. I needed to—for me.

Maybe there was an explanation. Not likely, but maybe, just maybe. I wasn't above praying for a miracle, even if it served only the two of us.

As our eyes locked, both of us doing our best to read the other, the air around us shifted from that of a comfortable married couple to one of suspicion, where each side is assessing and trying to read the other. Did he know what I'd found? Could he guess? Were my assumptions right then?

Whether it was the look on my face, or the tightly clenched fists gripping the stacks of paper, I could see it in my husband's eyes—he could see it—he knew something was up. The next instant I saw the shift in him, easily read by the change in his demeanor—he had no intention of getting into it with me. He wasn't going to make this easy; he had no plan of playing ball.

"Forget it, Rachael. I don't have time for any drama today."

"I'm not kidding. I have some questions that need answers."

John scoffed, ignoring my words. My body recoiled in defense, stung by his casual dismissal, as he cast me aside with barely a second glance. "John, I'm your wife."

"Right. You've been my wife for the past ten years. I'm over it and so are you." He looked away from me, heading back towards the door.

"Fourteen."

"Fourteen what?"

"Years. We've been married for fourteen years. How many of those have you been lying to me?"

John turned around, surveying me; his eyes cold, detached.

"Stay," I said, anger ebbing behind my calm exterior.

"No reason to. You've got nothing I need to hear."

I could feel myself losing it, as his words sunk in. "How can you say that? This is a marriage and it takes work—communication, commitment... And honesty. We need to talk about this."

"This is my office. My things. I don't need to explain myself to you. Not now. Not ever."

"Yes, you do. Things that involve you, involve me—we're supposed to be on the same team."

"I've got nothing to say to you. It ain't your business," John spat back.

"Well, then you better listen. Here. Tell me what this is?" I said throwing down the stack of bank statements on the desk. "I know you know what it is. Because it's your name on them, not mine."

John barely glanced at the pile of papers. "No idea."

"No idea? Don't play me, John. You know I'm not dumb."

John just grinned, a smug, arrogant smile. "Sure," he said, his voice laced with the condescending tone of someone who thought himself superior. "You found those papers when?" he laughed to himself. "And they've been here in the open for how long?"

I gritted my teeth, more irritated by the second.

Fine. If he wasn't going to talk about it, then I'd just put my cards on the table. Maybe once the words were out there, he'd have to address them. I shook my head, knowing this wasn't going to end well regardless. Someone who could embezzle funds from a church, steal from the poor, was beyond help. And if he wasn't trying to defend his actions, then there was no other conclusion—he was guilty of exactly what I suspected—stealing from his flock, from the collection plate.

"How could you do it, John? How could you lie and cheat and steal from your own people? You're meant to be their leader. They look up to you."

"I can do whatever the hell I want. I don't answer to you, I don't answer to anyone, except my God. And I'm guessing he's fine with it—he's sure never complained. So who the hell are you to get involved in my business?"

"I am your wife, damn it! Do you hear me—your wife! And I want to believe that this didn't just happen, that this hasn't been happening for years! What the hell is your side of this story? I know what I think, based on what I found, but tell me, please—tell me what really is going on," I pleaded.

"Nothing to say. It is what it is." John stared out the window, unfazed by my half-crazed eyes.

"Then let me see if I got it right—you stole from your followers, from the church? All the donations, all the collections—how can you justify it to yourself? Every penny went into a personal account of yours! Sound about right? Every single penny."

John said nothing, he just looked over in my direction and glared.

"How long has it been going on for? The whole time I've known you? The whole time you've been doing the ministry?"

John laughed, shaking his head, smug and superior. "You have no idea. You got lucky—but you don't know what you're talking about. And I got nothing to say about it. You hear me?"

"Nothing to say? To me? I am your wife. Do you hear me? I've been your wife for 14 years. I'm owed this much—I deserve to know what the story is. Tell me there's an explanation. Tell me it's not true, that you didn't lie and cheat and steal from your ministry."

"I won't tell you anything, because it's none of your business. My ministry, my worry. Now get the hell out of my office."

I ignored his words, stepping towards him, as my anger seeped towards the surface. "You robbed them! Literally. Stealing from your own flock, how could you, John?"

"You don't know what you're talking about. So don't waste your breath on things you don't understand." John was cold and calculating.

"Don't understand? How about this—explain it," I said, shoving the financial records towards him. "Whose account is this?"

John said nothing, fanning through the paperwork.

"Yours. This is *your* account, John; only it's not your money."

"Shut up. If it's in my account, looks like it is my money."

"But it shouldn't be. They didn't give it to you. They gave that money to the church. To be used by the church."

"I am the church," John spat.

"No, you're not. You're not the be-all and end-all, John. You're not above the law. You're just a man pretending to be a preacher. Pretending so you can make a quick buck."

"Whatever you say."

I shook my head, as my hands twitched in frustration. "This is proof. Everything I have right here," I said, the stack of papers in hand.

"You've got nothing."

"You're going to stop this. Stop it right now, or I swear to God I'm going to expose you for who you truly are." My voice rose with every word; my anger fueling me. I was yelling by the end of it.

John just laughed.

"Stop it. Stop it, John," I yelled. "I swear to a god I'll tell them all what you've done. It won't be pretty, I can promise you that."

Suddenly, John stopped. And then he took a step closer to me, and another one, until he was towering over, glaring down on me.

"You can't intimidate me," I said looking up at him. "I'll tell your followers what a lying prophet you really are. I know who you are and what you are doing. And I've got proof. Real proof."

"Don't you dare. You're crazy, bitch."

"I am not crazy—you are crazy. And I'm done being silent. Consider this your warning—I'm breaking my silence. I know the truth. And others are going to know about it too."

"Shut your mouth. No one will listen to you."

"They will because I'm your wife. Say what you want, but I'm in your circle too deep. And now I know that you're a fraud. I know the truth about everything."

"There's no one to tell. You can't call the whole congregation, stupid," John yelled.

I stared at my charismatic minister, my husband who looked back at me with hate in his eyes, so charming and wonderful on the outside that no one noticed he was robbing them blind.

"I don't have to call everyone. But I will call the elders," I said, stepping back from him, and reaching out for the phone. "I don't care about everyone else, but the elders of the church need to know. I swear I am breaking my silence," I cried out, the receiver shaking in my hand.

John grabbed the phone, yanking it from me. My arm trembled as tears ran down my face.

"If you don't stop," yelled John, inches from my face. "Do you hear me?"

"No," I said, willing myself to be brave. "No, I won't."

"Don't push me. If you don't stop," he yelled, his threat dangling in the air.

Though I had seen enough now to know John wasn't the man I thought he was, I couldn't just let this go. This was bigger than just me and him. Bigger than our marriage, or our future together. Even if I wanted to let it go, I knew in my heart I couldn't. I couldn't let this man control me, just like he'd controlled every one of his followers

"Fuck you," I said, spitting out the words.

John stepped even closer, now right in my face. "Fuck you, bitch," he snarled.

I felt myself sink down under his words, losing all my strength. This wasn't me, this wasn't him—how had we come to this point?

I looked up at him, cowering in shock as my husband leaned over me.

"You don't know shit about me. Who do you think you are? You're nobody. You try this shit—yelling and screaming about me being a fake—you better worry about yourself. Beware—God, my God, instructs me, and I listen. You will be destroyed."

I shook my head, unable to get any words out of my mouth. My hands shook, but otherwise, my body locked down, freezing in place.

"See—you're nothing. You're just a silly ass bitch."

"John..."

"Shut up. I don't need to listen to this. You've got nothing on me—all I have to do is tell my followers, it'll be too easy."

He grinned, his smile pure evil, as he towered over me. But still, I fought back. "What could you tell them? They'll believe me, John. I'm telling the truth. I've got no reason to lie."

He laughed, as he shook his head. "The truth? The truth according to me is your ass is crazy. And I've see it with my own eyes—you've been overtaken by the devil."

I sucked in a sharp breath, my face draining of all color. I could see it in his eyes—he believed he was telling the truth. He would brand me possessed, scorned, crazy; he'd do whatever it took to discredit me to everyone we knew, everyone he knew.

I was immediately consumed by flashbacks of the past 14 years that we'd spent together, all the people we'd met, all the friends we'd made. How many of them would believe him, I wondered, already knowing the sad answer. All of them. "Don't you dare. I've done nothing wrong—you're the one who's defrauded everyone. You're the criminal—a sinner masquerading as a saint."

"Don't worry—I'll have them all pray for you. And they will. My followers will believe me, not your bullshit."

"No, they'll know when I show them the proof; they can't deny the evidence. They'll be shocked and horrified, just like I am. I was holding out that there was some reason, some explanation."

"Ha. Like I care what you think, or anyone thinks. This *is* my money. I earned it. Catering to all those people, giving them hope, praying for them."

"That's your job! And they are donating to the church, not to you."

"I am the church! And they need me. They look up to me. They revere me but you—you're nothing but a waste of space."

"I am your wife. Don't you dare say—"

"Shut up, bitch. You used to know your place."

"It won't work."

"Oh yes it will. You see we live by the code: we all fall down, we all sin, but then, we all are forgiven. So even if they ever believed you, which they won't, I'll be forgiven.

My eyes widened in shock—I knew theses followers—they were friends of mine. And he was telling the truth—they'd forgive him. Silly, stupid people—they'd move past this 'mistake'.

"Telling on me will be like trying to push the wave back into the ocean – it's not going to work. Not by any means. Ain't no weapon formed against me that will prosper. God's got my back. Don't you know the rules, bitch?"

I looked down at the papers in my hand, the smoking gun, for lack of a better word. He was right. None of it mattered. His followers were devout, blindly believing him, following him, just like I had. There would be no way to convince the vast majority of them, and even if I could convince a few, what good would that do? Even they would probably not believe me once John had a chance to talk to them.

I finally stared at my husband, looking for a trace of humanity, of compassion, of good in his eyes—anything that might save our marriage, not that I really wanted to stay married to him. But there was nothing but cold, lifeless, cruel eyes glaring back at me.

And then I smiled. It was funny, in a tragic way, I thought to myself, glancing over to the framed photos of us; our holidays, our memories, our marriage. I'd come in here to do something nice for John, something sweet—and this is where I ended up. Our marriage broken beyond repair, the truth finally exposed, my life essentially in tatters.

Without wasting another second with this man, I dropped the papers on the desk and slowly left the office, edging past, leaving John to finish the tidying. My work here was done.

As I reached the door, a photo on the wall caught my eye – a grinning snap of John and his sons. I huffed to myself, knowing they'd probably be overjoyed with the news. The 'Mrs.' was finally driven away—not by them, but by their father. And she was leaving for good.

5

Everything changed so quickly. We'd gone from being just another married couple, going about our daily routines, to suddenly two opposing forces, pitted against each other. Our marriage had completely fallen apart in an instant.

I couldn't even look at my husband anymore. The sheen was long gone off the apple, but now, it was as if my eyes were fully open to how he truly was: rotten to the core. A man who preached one truth while living a lie; a man so hypocritical it pained me to think I had ever fallen for his act, or ever helped and promoted his 'mission'. In fact, it sickened me to think of his deceitful ways, and that I had profited in any way from them. This wasn't who I was, of that much I was sure.

I said nothing of his deceptions though, to anyone. I had decisions to make and I wanted to make them for myself. If I couldn't trust my husband, the one person I had put all my faith and trust into, who could I trust? The bigger issue of course was how could I even trust myself. After all, my own judgement had been so wrong, so mistaken about his character. What did it say about me, that I'd been sucked in completely by him and this too-good-to-be-true life?

Of course, I wasn't the only one falling under his spell; he had that effect on everyone from the church who worshipped the ground he walked on – especially his personal secretary Lillie Wilson. In fact, I often wondered if she was keeping more than his books. There were many late nights and revivals that always ended with those two being seen together, sharing a laugh and a lingering hand on a shoulder or arm. The rumors had started spreading like wildfire about Lillie and John, and usually, where there's smoke there is indeed fire.

In the beginning, I just thought people were gossiping out of jealousy, like they were wishing an affair on my marriage, or at least the rumor of one to make waves between John and I. As a result, I had stopped going to most of his revivals because I had enough of seeing and listening to him behind the pulpit. So, when John had an invitation to hold a two week revival in India, I told him that I would stay behind, hold down the fort, and opted not to join them.

Nevertheless, one day I had a notion to surprise him. I had our travel agent arrange tickets for me to fly to New Delhi. He had called me from the hotel the night before, so I knew exactly where I was going after I left the airport. And when I arrived, I told the hotel's front desk clerk that I had accidently locked my key in the room and needed to get in. No questions asked, the clerk handed me the key to Room 187.

With a sneaky smile on my face, I inserted the key and opened the door; to my surprise, I found Lillie lying there, wearing a black chemise. She was propped up in bed watching television and John was sitting at the desk on his laptop, wearing only his briefs. They both jumped up and looked at me with shock and shame. That's when I knew the rumors were no longer that... it was the God's honest truth. He was cheating on me.

From that moment on, I started to believe everything I heard about John – all of his supposed affairs with several women in the church, and even his secret love affair with one of his deacons. Prior to this day, I did not want to believe that was possible, because that would mean either John was gay or bisexual. But, the smoke and the fire became too hard to ignore. Just like the money, the cars, and trips – all paid for with the tithes of all of the innocent people who believed and worshipped John – I couldn't ignore it for a second longer.

Feelings of regret washed over me, as tears ran down my face. There had to be a way to fix this, to make things better, even in the face of insurmountable problems; but the guilt was overwhelming. All those people, all their money, in his pockets.

I walked the halls of our house, shirking away from the sheer size of our mansion, now knowing how this wealth, this privilege, had been gained at the expense of others. My stomach churned at the falsity of the world around me—how could this have happened? How could he do this? How did I not notice? How long had it been going on—the whole time I'd known John? And were his sons in the know on everything, or merely profiting from the situation unaware of their father's lies?

Questions flooded by mind as I paced, shielding my eyes from the grandiose style of our life. Every part of it a reminder of what he'd done. It screamed to the criminal nature of my husband, now that I saw it, not to the success and accomplishments we'd worked so hard for. Everything around me was tainted, ruined by this revelation—there was nothing left here for me; there was no safe place to look, no comfort to be found in any corner. Stealing from parishioners was nothing to be proud of, and though I'd been only a passive participant at best, an uneasy feeling had taken root in me. Now I wanted nothing to do with him or my own life, as if guilt and shame had replaced the air throughout our house.

I sunk into a chair, trying to think things through. I knew I couldn't stay here, stay married to John. No part of me thought about salvaging my marriage. Were these irreconcilable differences? Easily. Fraud, too even—In no uncertain terms, John was not the man he claimed to be. Another batch of tears fell, as reality set in more and more. My life as I knew it was over. Everything I'd worked so hard for, fought for, and loved would be gone—if it ever existed in the first place, such was the size and scope of his sham. Every piece of my life was affected.

The realization that I'd failed, chosen the wrong 'soulmate', and that my marriage was over, beyond repair, was crushing. I took my vows seriously; I wanted nothing more than a life-long marriage with my partner. I still wanted that, I'd worked hard for that—but not with John.

Not with the man he truly was, who was nothing like the John I fell in love with. This wasn't who I married. This wasn't what I signed up for.

I shuddered at the thought, at the mere idea, of staying in a relationship with someone so despicable. There was no hesitation in my decision—I couldn't stay here. Not with him. Not in this house built on lies and deception. It was time for me to go.

But even knowing I was on my way out, the guilt didn't subside. I might be removing myself from the equation, but this was about more than just me. The stealing, the lies, the deception. It needed to stop.

I stared down at the form in front of me, my pen tapping nervously against the desk; *Internal Revenue Service* printed in bold in the top corner. I looked over my shoulder, though I knew I was home alone. Even still, my palms were hot, my fingers shaking as I started to fill it in. I had to do something to end this, right this wrong.

This life, this lie, was wrong on so many levels. I wasn't going to be a part of it, and I wasn't going to sit back and watch it go on any longer. Not if I could help it.

It was a quiet afternoon, but a long one, my ears listening for every creak of the floor boards, every sound unaccounted for. I'd been on eggshells for hours, digging through files, to find out what I could. And I'd done it—I'd found every little detail they'd been after. I'd made a case, and a strong one at that.

Still, it felt surreal as I put the envelope in the mail, sending proof to the IRS of John's crimes. It was antiquated almost. Surely in this day and age, there'd be a free tax evasion hotline you could call? My mind flipped through these inconsequential thoughts, desperately attempting to cope with what I was doing. You're doing the right thing, I told myself again and again. And I was; I knew that was true. But it still felt so contrary to me, making my stomach compulsively twist and knot. I may not have loved my husband any longer, but to do this—to bring in the government, to report him—it was taking things to another level.

There was no sense of sweet revenge, only a pit in my stomach as I watched the envelope disappear into the mail box. This was a line I was crossing and regardless of whether John ever found out it was me; I'd always know what I'd done.

Of course, he'd made his choices, horrible, unforgivable ones, preying on innocents and believers for his own personal gain; but even knowing without a doubt of his guilt, I felt sick for turning him in.

I peeled back the curtains at the front window, my eyes glued on the dark sedans pulling into our driveway.

"Who the hell is that?" yelled John from upstairs. "What have you done? Who did you call?" A slew of cursing followed as he made the same educated guess that I just had. We both saw the dark suits. And then came the knock at the door.

"Don't," yelled John, anxiety thick in his voice. "Don't touch that door," he said, flying down the stairs. "I'll get it. What the hell have you done, you bitch?"

I turned to look at him as he hit the bottom of the stairs. I shook my head. "Nothing, I did nothing."

"Right. And they're coming now because it's just a coincidence? Don't think so. You reported me? Is that it? You thought that would be a good idea? You better not be counting on getting any of my money. If they take me down, they're taking you down with me. You really are a bitch. A lying, scheming bitch." The words flowed with ease from his mouth, pouring out with such venom, it was impossible to believe this was the same man I had loved, who had claimed to love me too. The same man I respected and followed, the same man pretending to be a role model and Pastor for others to look up to.

"Who did you call?" he said, leaning down close to me.

"It wasn't me, I swear," I said, backing up away from him. John had never hit me, but that didn't make him any less intimidating.

Another knock from outside.

John's eyes flared, his hands twitching by his side. And then he walked to the door.

"Can I help you?" he asked calmly, no hint of the stress just a second before.

"IRS. Are you John Atkinson?" asked one of the men in suits.

"Yes. What's this about?"

"According to the filed paperwork, you are the head of a local church, is that right?" asked the government official, looking at his notepad.

"I am, yes."

"Well then, we have some questions for you."

I watched from afar as the IRS interviewed my husband, while other men in dark suits removed boxes and boxes of paperwork from the office. They wasted no time, efficient, organized, focused.

Then suddenly one of the men shifted his gaze. My heart raced as he walked over to me. My eyes shifted down, my fingers twitching as I realized that reporting my husband *anonymously* might not have been the smartest move.

"And how do you fit into this?" asked the man.

"I'm sorry? Into what?" I asked.

The IRS man raised an eyebrow in annoyance while a colleague of his stepped forward, walking right up to me. They exchanged a glance and a nod. And then the questions fired out.

"What was your role in the church?"

"Were you involved in the bookkeeping?"

"How long have you been married?"

"Do you work outside the church?"

"Do you contribute to the household?"

"Is there anything you'd like to tell us?"

"Where did you think your husband was getting the money from? You must have had some idea."

"If you knew about it and did nothing, you're just as guilty."

They threw out the questions in rapid fire, giving me no time to think of an answer, not that I had any.

It wasn't an official interrogation, and I had nothing to hide, but even still, I was terrified. This wasn't supposed to be happening to me; it was as if I was living someone else's life. I was a good person, an honest person—I was never part of this scam, I wasn't in on it, only guilty by association. Nevertheless, it sure seemed like in their eyes, maybe in everybody's eyes once they found out, that I was just as guilty as John.

The IRS was in our home for hours, questioning us both, searching for documents and records and seizing everything that might even remotely be of interest. John looked worse for wear by the end of it, though he kept his cool in front of them; I'm not sure I even managed that, I was so stressed by it all.

I wiped away the tears rolling down my cheeks as I watched them pull away from the house.

"We'll be back. Count on it," they'd promised before they left.

They needn't have bothered—we both knew this was only the beginning.

My eyes flickered towards John, who was sat on his chair, his head between his hands. Stress emanated off of him. He'd been confident, arrogant even throughout the day—exuding an undeserved air of self-righteousness. But now that his audience had left, and there was certainly no reason to hide it from me anymore, it was as if the gravity of the situation, of reality, had finally hit him.

I sighed, knowing he had only got what was coming to him. But I'd been roped into it too; somehow I was still part of it, even though I had nothing to do with his theft.

Their words echoed in my heads—if I had known and did nothing, I was guilty too—true or not, I hated that anyone might think that I was involved in this duplicity. I wouldn't, I couldn't, be part of this any longer.

"Where are you going?" asked John, looking up from his chair as I headed for the bedroom.

"I can't stay here anymore. I shouldn't be here."

I heard his footsteps follow me as I opened the door to our room. I sighed, bracing myself.

In keeping with his show for the IRS, our argument from this morning had been abruptly cut short. John had behaved himself, acting every bit of his image as the calm, cool Pastor, never raising his voice and certainly not confronting his wife. But now, with no one else in the house, I knew we'd pick up where we left off this morning.

"Rachael, I'm talking to you. Where are you going? Don't make me repeat myself." John spoke in hushed tones, the calm whisper all the more terrifying.

I shook my head as I rustled through the drawers, "I don't know. Away. Not here."

He paused for a second, his lip curled in disgust. "You're bailing on me? Now? Good. I'm done with you anyway. You're a drain on me, sucking the energy, the money out from me. Get the hell out of here then—go!"

My spine twinged with rage. He wanted to flip the tables? Pretend he was kicking me out, not that I was leaving? A small part of my brain tried to remind me it didn't matter what he said or thought, but my defenses were triggered. "Get out? You think you can just kick me out? After 14 years? No. I don't think so." I inhaled deeply, steadying my temper. "I'm done with this, John. I'm done with you." I shook my head and turned my back on him. "You may have bought this house, but it was *our* home for over a decade. I am leaving, but I'll be back for my things. You owe me that much."

"I don't owe you anything. Don't be thinking you can come crawling back, whenever you feel like it."

"I won't. I don't want anything to do with whatever kind of scam you've been running. I don't want to get caught up in your illegal affairs, in whatever the IRS is investigating. This is your mess, not mine."

John shook his head, rage brewing beneath the surface. "You shut your mouth. I ain't done nothing illegal."

I raised my eyebrows incredulously. "Really? Is that really what you think?"

"Well, I'll tell you, I don't give a damn what *you* think! Now get out." John turned and slammed the door of the bedroom shut behind him, another door slammed somewhere down the hallway.

A fresh set of tears spilled out as I stared to where my husband had just stood. Our marriage was over. Though I'd made up my decision to leave, to remove myself from this house, to end our marriage, it still stung knowing John felt the same way. What was the point of any of this? How on earth was I supposed to move on?

He didn't want to fight for me, for our marriage—he was done with me. I slumped down onto the bed, as the sting of his rejection hit. It hurt more than it should have.

I didn't want to be in this marriage, I didn't respect him, but his words hurt all the same. I didn't deserve them. I'd done nothing to merit his contempt, especially considering his own actions and choices. Didn't he owe me an apology? Hadn't he wronged me? Lied to me? How had it all gone so wrong?

The consequences of the night before felt heavy all around me as I awoke the next morning, in an unfamiliar bed, an unfamiliar room. I wasn't sure who I wanted to tell, or who I should lean on, so I found myself alone, at a hotel for the time being. It wasn't a long term solution, but I couldn't seem to think past the hour, certainly not past a day. And I was barely sleeping at that. Tossing and turning all night, it was as if my mind needed to process everything, to go over every little conversation, every bit of information I could remember. I must have missed something; I should have seen it sooner.

I tried to close my eyes again, curling back up into a ball on the bed. But sleep eluded me once more. It was as if my world had closed in on me, collapsed all around me—I was suffocating under the stress, under the change—everything felt so foreign, so wrong. I shook my head but it didn't help. I couldn't move past it. How had we ended up this way—I repeated the question time and time again, over and over, hour after hour. It was like part of me believed that if I could figure out what had happened, there'd be some kind of closure.

I prayed for that closure as it was the only way out of this mess that I could see. Had I been blind for my entire marriage? With too many questions bombarding my head, repetitively, hauntingly, I tossed back the covers, knowing I would be getting no more sleep.

Pulling back the blinds, I stared out of the hotel window, ignoring the rumblings of my stomach. If it wasn't one thing, then it was another.

I hadn't eaten properly in days. Maybe it had been weeks now, I wasn't sure. Not since I'd found out about John.

Nothing felt right, nothing was the same; the only thing that held any appeal was hiding out in this little space. It was like hiding under a rock. Maybe if I didn't tell anyone, it hadn't really happened. Maybe if I stayed here long enough, my own life would somehow come back to me, or at least the one I thought I had.

More tears fell—I'd never even had that life back then, so it was all but impossible to have it now.

I was sucked under once more, my feelings overwhelming me. It was like I was swimming but there was no way out. And I was running out of energy to stay above water.

No answer. No solution. No escape. I was sinking in my own misery.

Well, there was one final escape. A permanent solution to the pain. I looked down at my wrists, wondering if I'd be able to stand the pain. Probably not. My eyes flickered to the scissors in my makeup bag on the night table. Without giving it a second though, I sucked in a deep breath, and ran the edge along the back of my wrist just to see what it felt like. My stomach lurched in pain as a squeal escaped my lips. Nope—no way I could pull that off.

But there were other ways, I thought; it'd be like drifting off to sleep, and I'd never have to tell anyone, or face the failure my life had become. Blood trickled warmly down from the back of my hand from my 'test' cut; I moved slowly towards the bathroom to run it under the tap, still very much beside myself, not functioning normally.

A ringing from my purse made me jump, bringing me out of my haze. I glanced to the screen wondering, hoping but dreading at the same time, that it was John. No—just Tricia.

"Hello?" I said, unable to hide the melancholy from my voice. I sounded hoarse, gravelly; no chance that would go unnoticed either.

"What's wrong? Are you okay?" she asked, picking up on my mood immediately.

I sniffed trying to pull myself together. But even still, I knew it was hopeless. "I'm okay," I lied.

"You're not. You sound even worse than you did last week. What's going on, Rachael? Tell me—I want to help."

"There's nothing you can do."

"Let me worry about that part. Where are you? I'm going to pick you up and we can go out for a coffee, or just come back here and figure this out."

I paused, unsure of my answer. I knew I didn't really want to see anybody, but strangely, for the first time in days, another part of me actually thought it might be a good. "Um. Okay, I guess," I answered, still hesitant.

I shook my head as I ended the call, knowing I was a mess in every way. A minute ago, I'd been contemplating suicide—I needed to get help. I needed to sort myself out. And fast.

6

Thankfully, before there was time for my thoughts to turn darker once more, I heard a knock at the door.

Hi," I mumbled, unsliding the lock and letting Tricia in, feeling too wiped to care about the state I was in. With ending it all on the table, how I looked was the least of my worries.

"Rachael, honey—how are you?"

"I'm good," I said, automatically.

Tricia looked at me, her eyes seeing through me in an instant. "Come on. Talk to me. How are you really doing?"

And she meant her question but we both knew the answer, as she looked at me and then around the hotel room. How I was feeling was written all over my sloppy clothes, messy hair and puffy-eyed face. I was long past any semblance of composure. I looked nothing like the successful entrepreneur I'd been parading as for the past decade.

I stared up at Tricia, my eyes already pooling with emotion. It was impossible to look her in the eye—I was such a failure. And somehow, I was going to have to let the world know about it. That my marriage had utterly crumbled; that my life was nothing more than fiction, and to make matters worse, I'd been an unwilling pawn in some grand scheme to swindle believers out of their money for greed. And after everything

I'd worked so hard for—my marriage, my success, my family—here I was alone. I had nothing left to show for it. Nothing at all.

"Come here," she said, pulling me in for a hug.

Tears fell down my cheeks, the weight of the last month pouring out like it had so many times before.

"It'll be alright," said Tricia, rubbing my back, trying in vain to console me. "What did he do, honey? Is it really this bad?"

"Worse," I mumbled, walking across the threshold back into the hotel room. I should have guessed that she'd know something was up between me and John. I wasn't at home—it must have been obvious why. I hadn't even thought of that. Everyone probably already knew there was trouble in paradise, and immediately my stomach sunk with the realization.

"I don't even know where to begin," I said, feeling the heavy weight press upon me once more.

"Wherever you want. Wherever you need to. I'm here for you. That's all you need to know." Tricia took a seat of the edge of the hotel bed. "Now, you ready to get you out of here? I hate to see you staying in a hotel. Why don't you come to my place. Like old times?"

Old times—back when I'd first moved out to California. It was a lifetime ago; I was such a different girl back then. Thoughts of the past swarmed my head, rendering me useless to the present. I couldn't even answer Tricia, I was so wrapped up in the memories. I panned through them as best I could, wondering, torturing myself, over the details—could I have seen the signs if I'd been paying attention at the beginning? Or was I just too blind by John's charm, too stupid to ever see the truth until it was staring me right in the face on a bank statement.

"Rachael? Come on, grab your stuff. I'm making the decision for you."

I looked over at Tricia, who was already packing things up. I nodded silently, as I tried to focus on the present, concentrate on the now, but my mind kept drifting backwards. Until we got to her house and it all poured out. Everything I'd been through and seen.

"John... a criminal. I can't believe he did that, honey. That's wrong on so many levels. An evil I never knew existed," she said, compassionately.

"I know," I said, as I wiped away fresh tears. Telling her had been just as hard as I imagined. Maybe even harder. But once I began, it flowed from my soul, taking a weight off my mind. My eyes were finally open, and now her eyes were open too to the extent of betrayal that I, and our congregation, had suffered at the hands of this... man.

"Come here," she said, moving over on the couch to throw her arm around me. "Now that I know what the story is, I can at least understand a bit better. But really—I just care about you. How are you handling it? *Are* you handling it? Rachael, the people in the church are asking about you, they are all so concerned. I understand why you want to keep a low profile. This is a real scandal... a true full blown mess! This stuff is going to be all over the newspapers now the I.R.S. is involved. I hate to see Christians get a bad name because of jerks like John and his deacons! We all thought he was a true man of God, but he has shown his true colors... he's nothing more than a charlatan... a con artist... Satan's right hand man!"

I turned my eyes down to look at my folded hands in my lap. I'd just admitted how completely inept I'd been, totally blind in my marriage, and now I had to somehow find the courage to tell her I was still completely incompetent—failing to cope with this news, unable to function by any standard. The feelings inside me were black; the embarrassment, the worthlessness, all melding together to form this sickly feeling of despair and shame.

"Rachael, what are you thinking? How are you getting through this?

"I'm not," I whispered.

"What do you mean?"

"I'm not getting through it."

Tricia grabbed my shoulders and turned my body around, forcing my eyes to meet hers. She took my hands in hers. "What are you talking about? You're not thinking of doing anything drastic? Anything stupid, are you?" She spoke softly, slowly, making sure I hear every word, that it went in.

I laughed uncomfortably, and glanced down to the cut on the back of my wrist.

"What is that?" she asked, her voice steel and uncompromising.

"Just, um." I paused wondering if I should try to lie, or just cut to the chase and tell her the truth.

"You weren't trying to...?"

No matter how painful it was to share, I knew she'd get it out of me in the end. I took a deep breath before nodding. "So, ya. I thought about it today. About giving up. About throwing in the towel. But don't worry. I can't do it. I can't handle the pain," I replied with a shrug. Another thing I could pull off—I couldn't even end my own suffering and stop this mess once and for all.

"Rachael," moaned Tricia, squeezing my hands in hers. "There are people that love you. People that need you, who value you. We love you for who you are, for everything you do."

I nodded again, not really taking any of her words in.

"You can't do something like that, you can't think like that. It's never an option. Tomorrow is always a new day. Listen to me," she said, shaking my hands to get my focus. And I wanted to listen and concentrate on her words, but everything was just so hazy, as it had been for so many days now. I think part of me didn't want to hear it, though I knew I should.

"Rachael, promise me you won't do anything like that again. You need to promise me. In time, it will get better. It will. I know it doesn't seem that way, but things will work out. You'll get through this—and I'm here to help you. Promise you won't do anything like that?"

I nodded, reluctantly, pulling back my hands so they could twist uncomfortably as I spoke. "It's just, it's not going to get better. I don't think it will."

"Time will help, I promise."

I shook my head, knowing in my heart that part of me would always be broken. It didn't matter how long passed, I would always know how blind I'd been, what a fool I'd been played for, and how I'd profited from John's deception. But at the moment, all I could think about was right now. And what I'd lost. "I had everything—my marriage, my husband—they were perfect; and now I have nothing. No house. No husband. No family. It fell apart," I explained, and the words kept coming. "And it broke me. And I'm not sure I want to live in a world like this, with a life that's such a joke. He wasn't just a thief, Tricia, he stole from his parishioners—from people who trusted him, who were praying to God, through him. It's so despicable, and I was part of that."

"No you weren't. You didn't have anything to do with it, did you?

I paused, and shook my head. "Not technically. But I lived in that house, shared in the profits—and I didn't say anything!"

"But you did when you found out, didn't you?"

"Yes, but how long had it been going on? How many people did he rob? Why didn't I notice!"

"It doesn't matter. You didn't rob anybody. You've got no reason to blame yourself or feel guilty."

"But how? How could I have not seen it? I was married to him! What kind of marriage did we even have—I don't even know him."

"He's someone who tried very hard to hide that side of themselves from you—from the whole world. This isn't your fault. It isn't, Rachael."

"Then why do I feel so guilty? Why am I like this?" I said, looking at myself, knowing I looked a mess on the outside, but even still that was better than what I feeling like on the inside.

"No one cares what you look like. You don't have to be perfect all the time; you're allowed to be human."

"I don't think I'm even managing that. I'm not sleeping, I'm not eating. I can't even concentrate anymore. On anything. I'm a mess. Just worthless, really." I sniffled as I wiped away the tears from my chafed cheeks.

Tricia put her arm around me pulling me close. She stroked my hair, letting me cry it out.

"I just want to die," I whispered, feeling overwhelmed once again. No matter what she said, there was no obvious solution, no way out, except for that—an easy way out, it seemed. And the images of death, of the sweet peace and tranquility that would bring, crept closer and closer with every day. I couldn't deny the thoughts of this escape were stronger than I had ever imagined possible.

Tricia pulled back away from me, her eyes emblazoned with determination. "No. No you don't. I know you and I've known you for years, longer than John. I knew you before him and you're more than him, more than this. You hear me now, Rachael, you are not going to let him take your life, or ruin it like this."

"He already has," I blubbered, my words marred by the weeping.

"We can fix this. We can deal with this, one step at a time. This is doable, Rachael. Of that I'm sure."

I nodded my head, not wanting to argue, but what she was saying was simply untrue. In that moment, no part of me believed her words.

"Let's look at this a different way," she said, straightening up. "Do you love him? Still?"

I shook my head. "No." I didn't love John. I never could have; I loved the man who I thought I'd married. I'd fallen for the image he'd presented, the fictional perfection I thought I had been spending my life with. But he wasn't real. I didn't even know the real John, but from what I'd seen, there was no way I could love him.

"So you don't want to patch things up?"

I shook my head.

"Then this stops today. All this guilt, the sadness, and grief. No—it's done. He's not worth it. He's not. And nothing that has happened is worth it either."

I stared at Tricia, her energy, her determination commanding my attention. "But you're talking about years of my life—just throwing that away?"

"Do you want to go back to him?

"No."

"Then you've already made that decision. There's nothing to be gained from wallowing in it. If you're sure you're finished with him, which it sounds like you are, then you can't just waste your energy looking at the past, feeling sad or sorry for how things have turned out."

"You make it sound so easy," I mumbled.

Tricia shook her head. "No, it's not. But I don't care how long you've invested in the relationship, or how much you thought you knew him, or loved him—it's just not worth it. You can't throw away the rest of your life for what might have been or should or could have been. It wasn't meant to be. And since we can't turn back the clock—you've got to find a way to let it go, to live with it and move on."

My head bobbed in agreement, but words and wisdom were much easier to preach than to live by.

"So, you agree?" Tricia concluded. "We're moving on."

I paused, trying to absorb what she was saying. The logical part of me knew she was making sense but I was still too emotional to take it all to heart. John had been my whole life—I wasn't even sure I knew how to live and love without him.

"I don't know how," I whispered.

"One step at a time. That's all there is to it. He hurt you, honey. So you need to heal first. We need to get you back to a healthy place, build you up again. But we can do it. You can do it."

"But everything's so messed up. I shouldn't be in this situation. I should have seen it coming."

"First things first you need to forgive yourself for any mistakes you may have made, or think you've made. It happens—but to get caught up in them, to dwell on them, is helping no one. Forgive yourself. Learn from what happened, and move on."

I nodded, listening to her advice. Tricia was always on target with how to fix things—absolutely I should listen to her. If anyone could get me sorted, it was probably her.

Still, I didn't feel remotely ready or strong enough to heal myself. But thankfully Tricia wasn't waiting for me to agree. Before I knew it, she was giving me a road map of sorts for the days and weeks ahead.

"Can we do that? Forgive yourself? The first step is always the hardest. But I need you to get on board. You can do this," she told me.

I looked up at her, feeling old and tired, and it was as if she were asking me to do manual labor. But I could try, I could do at least that. I nodded to her, willingly myself to find the inner strength to give it a go. A fresh start. A new leaf.

"Okay, then we're going to focus on letting go. Since you can't go back and change the past, there's no other option really: you must let it go and figure out a way to move forward. You have to allow yourself to find joy and contentment in the happenings of today. I know how easy it is to get caught up in what ifs, or what might have beens, or playing things out, all the different ways they could or should have gone, but none of that matters, honey. What's done is done—we've got to look forward, and move forward—happiness is ahead of us, in the future, not the past. If you spend all your time dwelling and reliving it, you'll never be able to let it go and see the happiness that might be up ahead. Okay?"

Tricia spoke passionately, as if her words could inspire me to tackle this head on. And I wanted to. But in my heart, I didn't feel ready to dive headfirst into this new way of thinking. There was still too much to figure out, to come to terms with, to reconcile with.

"I don't think I can do this," I said quietly, backing down again. "I want to, but I don't see how I'm just supposed to move on. How do I let go of the past when that's everything, my entire life? I'll never get it back. I've been so blessed—it won't happen again. It just can't."

"You've got to count your blessings, Rachael. You still have so much. Yes, there's no denying you're in a bit of a situation right now, but you still have so much to be thankful for."

I looked at her, my eyebrows raised—how could anyone possibly believe that? "Seriously?"

"You need to learn to count your blessings and be thankful. I'm serious."

"Like what?" I challenged.

"Easy—you've got most of the important ones covered. You've got your health, your family—your parents, I mean. And you've got good friends, and a job. You're lucky, Rachael. I know it's easier to look at everything else that's gone wrong, at what you think are problems or issues in your life, but compared to a lot of people, you're still blessed. And you have options of where to go from here. Not everyone has those things."

"You're right," I sighed, knowing in my heart that she was completely correct. Of course she was—and I knew that. Only that made me feel all the more guilty that I was wallowing at all, or considering taking my life with a blade. I felt the tears start to build in my eyes; I wiped them away, as discreetly as I could.

Tricia handed me a tissue. "You can't stay down in the dumps, either. It's not helpful, and it's not healthy. But I'm guessing with all the guilt and confusion going on, it's more complicated than just making time to do something nice, something fun. I'm betting first off, you haven't really found yourself smiling or happy since this whole mess started?"

I nodded.

"But I bet if you did feel happy, or enjoyed something, you'd feel even guiltier. Because part of you would be thinking about the past, or thinking about the loss, or telling yourself that you should be thinking about it. That you don't deserve to be happy?"

I blinked, wondering how she was pinpointing my emotions like this.

"Let me tell you it doesn't work like that. You're allowed to be happy. You're allowed to take pleasure in life, to enjoy things, to be content. You're not forsaking anything—you have no reason to wallow in guilt, or chastise yourself forever over things beyond your control."

"What am I supposed to do? Just fake a smile all day, is that what you mean? I'm not happy. I can't exactly change that."

"Not in every way, but there are things you can do. You need to seek it out; happiness doesn't always come to you. But you need to allow yourself to have simple pleasures in life—I'm sure that means something different to you than it does to me, but it could be reading uplifting and positive books, having a nice meal, listening to music or the laughter of children playing in the park—whatever will bring a genuine smile to your face, that's what I'm talking about."

I smiled, or tried to rather. It was half real, half fake at best.

"You're going to have to do better than that," Tricia laughed. "My suggestion, and it's the last one, I promise: stop focusing so much on your misery and start looking beyond yourself. Kind of like seeking out happiness, look for the world beyond you, look to see how you can contribute to it. Maybe go and volunteer and do something that fills your heart with joy."

"You've got it all figured out, haven't you?"

Tricia laughed. "I wish."

"Well, you seem to know what you're talking about. How'd you get so smart?" I teased.

"You're not the only one this has happened to. I've seen what it does to people, and I've seen what works. You don't have to do anything, Rachael—you don't have to listen to anything I've said. And you'll still be okay. I swear to you, as time passes the pain will lessen. My suggestions are simply a way to make that time easier for you, more enjoyable, more pleasant. Will they make it always be sunshine and roses? No. Nothing can. Will it take away the pain and depressing thoughts right away?" She shook her head. "I wish it could, I wish I could take it away, but I can't. But that doesn't mean every day needs to be torture. It doesn't have to be this way."

And so, I nodded my head and Tricia left me to lie down on her couch. But instead of retracing all the problems in my marriage or stumbling through all her advice; amazingly, I fell asleep, a deep restful peaceful sleep.

When I woke up, I remembered what she said about reading uplifting books and, call it fate or divine intervention, the first book that I found was on Tricia's shelf and it was the Bible. Without a pang of guilt or remorse, I opened the good book and read the following passage:

> "Therefore I tell you, do not worry about your life, what you will eat or drink; or about your body, what you will wear.

> Is not life more than food, and the body more than clothes?
>
> Look at the birds of the air; they do not sow or reap or store away in barns, and yet your heavenly Father feeds them.
>
> Are you not much more valuable than they?" ~ *Matthew 6: 25- 26.*

Taking these words to heart, I took the next steps in my life. My eyes wider than before of some of the ways that betrayal can creep into a relationship, and yet determined not to allow the shadow of one man to cast darkness over the rest of my time. I still knew how to love and no matter how burnt, or broken or disappointed you are, I learned that you must remember your worth, your value on this Earth.

Give yourself a chance to start over – you owe yourself that. And you owe it to the next man/woman to give them a chance at love, too! Being older and wiser seems to go hand-in-hand with being more cynical and jaded, but I've promised myself one thing – not to let a bad apple spoil the whole bunch.

John was wasted sperm, to put it mildly... a burden on society. And I wouldn't let someone like that steal another day, or even another minute, of my life.

So, I'm thankful every day for moving on from my marriage; no longer a Mrs., but still very much the real me.

Marilyn

1

The picture of my parents on their wedding day, hanging on the wall of our front room, represented the epitome of love to me. "She looks so beautiful," said Sarah, my older sister.

"I know. And happy. Look at her smile, and her eyes—she's glowing," I said, staring up at the framed photo. "They'd have been married for how many years today?" I asked, knowing Sarah had such numbers stowed somewhere in her head.

"Well, they were married 15 years before she died. And it's been six years since then. 21 years, I guess."

I turned to the window of our small farm house, easily spotting our father in the fields. He hadn't mentioned their anniversary today, but he rarely mentioned her at all. I was nine when my mom died—my father was never the same. "He loved her so much," I murmured, knowing it was completely mutual. They were perfect together. They had a bond that was unbreakable, even in death it seemed.

"'This is what life's about'. Do you remember her saying that?" asked Sarah.

I turned back towards her, smiling. "Mom said it almost every day. It's all about love." And I believed her, as you do when something is repeated, reiterated, and demonstrated on a daily basis. Love was everything, the ultimate goal of life, at least my life. Falling in love, being in love—it had been my dream for as long as I could remember.

"Think Dad'll ever find someone else?" I asked, knowing in my heart that I hoped he wouldn't, just to further highlight the undying love between him and my mother.

"I don't know. He's got all of us running the house for him. Six kids buzzing about doesn't give you much time to start dating."

"We're not exactly kids, Sarah. I'm the youngest and even I'm already 15," I said.

"Okay, Marilyn. But I'm not sure he wants to. It's not easy finding the perfect person. And he found her once. What are the odds he'll find her again?" said Sarah, shrugging her shoulders.

I nodded, but really didn't understand her rationale. If life's purpose was to love and be loved, then how could he not seek out someone else? It was a tricky situation—I couldn't understand it, but was relieved by his decision. For myself though, love was all I wanted in my life—and thankfully, I'd finally found it with Jack Winston, my high school sweetheart.

The crunch of tires on the gravel driveway drew our attention towards the window again. My heart sang as I recognized the car and the familiar silhouette behind the wheel—Jack was here.

"Be careful, sweetie," said Sarah, kissing me on the forehead.

"What do you mean?" I asked, running my fingers through my hair to freshen it up.

"Exactly that—be careful. Love isn't always cut and dry. And it doesn't always play out the way you expect," Sarah warned, playing the older—and wiser—sister.

I shook my head, laughing off her concerns. I was naive. Back then, I had no idea of the complexity involved in loving someone or the heartbreak that follows when the relationship ends. It simply isn't a lesson learned from others; it must be experienced to be fully understood, unfortunately.

Sure, I knew what grief felt like, but not the pain of a broken heart. Yet even when love is strong, like I saw with my parents in their marriage;

there's really no good way for it to end. And it always has to end. But at that point in my life, I was immune to the reality of a broken heart. I had no concept of how all-encompassing, painful and scarring it could be, how conflicted and doubting it can make you feel.

Regardless, the allure of connecting with a partner on every level, of sharing your life with someone, working together, growing together, raising a family was strong inside me; even the threat of a broken heart couldn't sway the urge I had to love and be loved.

Besides, no one goes into a relationship thinking about the moment when they'll get their heart broken. But, of course it happens—sooner or later.

"I love you," I said, leaning over to whisper in Jack's ear, fighting the tears that were threatening to spill out. He was the first boy I'd ever said those words to. And it felt like I'd never get to say them again.

"I love you too, Marilyn," he said, holding my hands in his. "I wish I didn't have to go. I wish there was some other way." He squeezed my hand, before pulling me in closer for a hug. His arms were warm around me. My heart pounded with the closeness of our bodies. I felt safe there, so secure. I couldn't let myself think about what tomorrow would hold, or that this would be the last time I'd be in his arms.

"Oh, Jack. I'll miss you so much."

"I'll miss you more," he whispered back.

I smiled, looking up to meet his eyes, feeling my cheeks blush at the same time. Love was such a complicated feeling, so powerful—it was like some supernatural power had overtaken all sense of reason in my mind; though I knew in my heart Jack really had to go, it was as if I was simply unwilling to accept that reality. "Are you sure you have to leave? Isn't there any way out of it?" I pleaded.

Jack shook his head, his eyes taking on a steely, determined look. "I know you don't mean that. There's nothing more important than defending our freedom; someone's got to go. Someone has to be ready to fight."

I sighed, knowing full well that this was happening, whether I liked it or not. But even still, did it have to be the boy I loved that was shipping out this week? "It's just, Germany is so far."

"It's where they need us," he replied matter of factly. "They don't exactly ask my opinion."

"I know," I sighed again. I couldn't help the onslaught of despair that was creeping into my thoughts—two years apart, separated by an ocean. It sounded like agony.

"Marilyn," said Jack, pushing me back a little so he could look deeply in my eyes. "I'll come back to you. I promise you. I love you and no distance in the world will separate us. It's not possible," he said, doing his best to reassure me.

I tried to smile, but it wasn't convincing. Even if everything was well between us, despite the distance, two years was still an incredibly long time to be apart—to miss him and worry about him, to long for the day when we'd be reunited.

"Sweetheart—it'll be okay. I promise. Never in all my 18 years have I ever loved anyone as much as I love you. I know we'll be together again. And just because I'm not here with you doesn't mean I'm not in here," he said, touching my heart with our entwined hands.

"Will you write to me?" I asked. I admit that I sounded like a child, so much younger than I was.

"Every week."

I stared into his eyes, wanting, wishing I saw in them what I saw in the wedding picture of my parents—pure, unfaltering love. Without that, there's no way we'd be able to last two years on opposite sides of the ocean. "Jack, I do love you," I mumbled again. "I know you have to go. I'm just afraid, that's all. I feel like I'm losing you."

"It won't be forever," Jack looked down, his eyes suddenly focused on his feet.

"What is it?" I asked, feeling even more nervous. What wasn't he telling me?

"I know I'll come back. But... what if you're gone when I do? What if you move on, Marilyn? Will you still be here, waiting for me?"

I sighed in relief. "I'll wait for you forever. I love you. There's nothing I want more than to be with you. But you... won't you forget about me?" I asked, nervously.

"How could I? You're the love of my life," said Jack, leaning in to kiss me.

"And you're mine."

Silence filled the room, as we simply held hands, knowing this was our final night together. There were so many words unsaid, so many feelings simmering just beneath the surface.

Jack took my hand and brushed it against his cheek, holding it against his warm skin.

"Mmmm," I murmured unconsciously. Being in love felt wonderful. I never wanted the night to end.

But it did. And Jack left for Germany. The heartache began almost instantly.

"There's a letter for you!" cried Sarah, running in from outside. "Open it, open it!" she said, thrusting the envelope into my hands.

I looked down, sighing in relief to myself. He'd remembered.

For the first three months, there'd been a letter every week, but not last week. It was the first time there had been no letter. Like any other girl who missed her boyfriend like crazy, I'd checked the mailbox religiously but to no avail. And I couldn't help but wonder if it had finally happened—had Jack finally moved on and forgotten about me.

"What's he say?" asked Sarah, ever supportive.

I scanned the letter quickly as I always did, before reading it back over, savoring every word. "Nothing really." I stifled a sigh, not wanting to let even my sister see my disappointment.

"Did he say why he didn't write last week?"

"No." I shook my head. In truth, he barely said anything. He loved me, the weather was getting colder, he missed me—he said all the right things, but something had shifted in his tone. I couldn't put my finger on what had changed, but I could feel that something had.

And something had changed. Over the next few months, the letters came less and less regularly, until they came no more. A month passed and then another without one letter.

There was no formal announcement or decision to end it between us. Yet, looking back at his last letter, the signs were there. There'd been no talk of his return, no mention of his unyielding love for me, no mention of anything other than the weather really.

'You'll always be part of me, Marilyn' is how he'd signed off. In retrospect, there was an air of finality to his last words. But I hadn't wanted to believe it then, any more than I wanted to now. But with two months and no word, it was all too clear that our relationship was over. All that was left was my broken heart.

"Is that it then?" asked Sarah, after she found me crying on the bed. "He's just going to let things fade away? No closure, no end—he just wants it to fizzle out?"

I sniffled, wiping the tears from my eyes. "He probably doesn't even think that much about us anymore to even have a conscious thought about ending things. He's halfway around the world—what does it matter to him? What does he care if I still love him?"

"He *should* care! And he should do the right thing by you! If he wants to end it, that's fine, but he should at least tell you, like a man, instead of leaving you dangling, waiting to see if another letter ever shows up!"

I shook my head, the tears pouring in a steady stream now. "I don't matter to him anymore. I'm not part of his life—I mean, we're not even in the same country. Who were we kidding?" I sobbed, pausing to catch my breath. "It just feels so horrible though. And there's nothing that can make it better. I know there isn't."

"Time," said Sarah quietly.

"What about it?" I murmured

"Time will make you feel better. Time will mend your heart."

I didn't believe her, not even a little bit. My heartache was so severe, so breathtakingly intense; the emotional pain had turned into physical pain as well. I was beside myself with my emotions as the heartbreak turned to anger.

"No," I said, arguing more with myself than Sarah. "No, it won't! But I don't care; it doesn't matter!" I sniffled, trying to use the anger to propel myself out of the crying phase.

"Marilyn," said Sarah softly, as if she could tame my emotions with just a cautionary tone.

"I'm serious. And you can bet I sure won't be here whenever he does finally fly home. I'm not just going to stay around—waiting for him like some fool."

"Staying here doesn't mean you're staying for him. You live here, remember?"

"Today I do, but not forever. I'm not going to stay in the same small town I was born in and marry whoever will have me."

"What are you going to do?" she challenged. "We barely leave town, and you've never even left the state. You're not just going to go off and..."

"Why not?!" I countered, belligerently. I sighed, wanting to believe my words but even I was unconvinced. "I don't know, but mark my words, this life—small town farming—it's not my future. And when I get older, I'm leaving. I promise you, no, I'm going to promise *myself*—I'm getting out."

"Marilyn, slow down. You're upset. Don't make any rash decisions."

"I'm not, but I'm getting out of Texas. I'm going to the city, any city, somewhere far away from country life!"

"To do what?" Sarah asked, crossing her arms.

"To work. To live. To build a nest egg. I'm going to do it all in some big city."

Sarah stared at me for a long minute before saying anything. Then, she took my hand and led me out into the front room and sat me down. "Look up," she instructed.

My eyes followed to where her hand was pointing: at the wedding photo of my parents. I turned to look at her, knowing my confusion was written all over my face.

"Look at it. What do you see?" she said.

"What are you taking about?" I snapped, my anger having not subsided yet although at least the tears had for the moment.

"Look at the picture. What do you see?"

"Mom and Dad."

"Look deeper. Not *who* but *what*," she said, her own face stern. Whatever she was trying to do, she wasn't going to give up until her point had been made.

I turned my attention back to the photo and inhaled deeply. It had been hard to look at their happy smiling faces since Jack had left for Germany. It was a reminder of the love that had gone away in my life, and now the sting was even greater. Love seemed almost tangible in that photo. My mother was stunning in her white dress, and I'd never seen my father look so smart; a special day, where two people had become one, become part of something more, something greater than themselves.

I'd stared at that picture more than a thousand times since I was a little girl, dreaming about the day it would be my turn. My tears welled once more, as I realized just how far away I was from that reality.

Yet, it wasn't the ceremony itself that I craved. While the dress and the flowers and the party sounded lovely, I wanted to be a wife more than a bride. There was so much more to a wedding than simply the celebration—it was the day your real life began, the moment you committed to sharing the rest of your life, until death do you part, with the person beside you.

I stared at the photo, feeling the emptiness inside me, knowing full well what I was missing, now more than ever.

"What do you see?" repeated Sarah, gentler.

"Love," I whispered.

Sarah nodded, running, her hand down my long hair, motherly, unintentionally so. "Don't forget it. No matter where you go or what you do, that's the bigger picture. That's what it's all about."

"But it hurts," I whispered. "It hurts so much."

"I know."

"But how can something so wonderful hurt like this?" I asked, feeling the emotional pendulum swing back once more.

"It's all part of it, sweetie. There's no easy answer, no fool-proof solution. But you've got to keep letting yourself fall in love until you find him—the right one."

I closed my eyes and nodded, unsure how I would ever survive this kind of heartache again. But even in pain, I knew I would do it again; chance the broken heart for the possibility of everlasting love.

Sarah was absolutely right—I would continue to put myself out there, for however many times it would take, because I knew in my heart I wanted to find a soulmate and get married. It wasn't that I couldn't be happy by myself, and it wasn't that I needed a man—but I wanted one. Having a husband, having that love, would make me feel complete.

But I still knew that our small farming town in Texas wasn't where I was going to find *him*. And so I bided my time, focusing on my studies, until I graduated from high school. There was no better reason to leave our town than to attend university.

"Alright, Marilyn," my father sighed. I could hear his reluctance but his eyes gave him away. My body twitched with excitement, in anticipation of his permission. "Are you sure?"

I nodded, my nerves dancing on edge.

"I don't know why you want to do this, but you have my permission to go. I'll let you go off to university, if that's really what you want to do." My father exhaled loudly in defeat.

"Oh, thank you, Daddy. Thank you, thank you, thank you!" I exclaimed, pushing up from my chair and rushing over to him at the other end of the table.

"I won't pretend to understand. You don't need more studying, Marilyn. You've just graduated high school for goodness sake. Girls just don't need all that rattling around in their heads."

I nodded in agreement though I did not share his point of view. I'd always found learning fun, but this, getting out of our little town, putting a foot into the real world—this was everything I wanted. And surely, the big city was the perfect place to meet Mr. Right.

Walking onto the university campus for the first time, I felt my heart swell with excitement. All these new faces and places. It had been a long time coming.

I stared at the big stone building, the campus engulfing me with its presence. To say it was an adjustment would be an understatement—everything in the world around me was new. New sights, new sounds, new experiences, and new feelings as it was the first time I'd ever spent any length of time away from my family and hometown. It was bittersweet gaining the independence and space I so desperately craved, but with it came an unexpected loneliness.

Thankfully, I quickly made friends and so had lots of girlfriends' houses where I could spend my free time, hanging out. Together we walked into the campus cafeteria, smiling and laughing, completely oblivious to everyone around us.

"Come on, Marilyn, you first. Get in line," one of them teased.

I dutifully stepped forward into the line, and turned around to laugh at them. And then it happened. The moment everyone always talks about: it felt as if lightning had struck my heart. I was powerless to it.

As I reached down to pick up my tray from the counter, my fingers brushed against something warm and soft.

"Oh, my apologies, miss," said a warm, smooth voice.

My cheeks blushed in embarrassment and delight as I looked up at the tall stranger. "My fault, I'm sure," I said, offering the tray to the man before me.

He laughed and shook his head. "Well, I guess it might be. I'm Tommy. Tommy Lee, actually."

"Hello there, Tommy Lee. I'm Marilyn."

He took my hand in his, shaking it with a gentleness that seemed out of place with a man of his size and strength.

"A pleasure, Marilyn. Are you having lunch?"

I nodded, my eyes downcast in embarrassment. But not before I'd managed to get a good look at him—tall, handsome, with broad shoulders and perfect smile, filled with sparkling white teeth. He was easily the most handsome man I'd ever laid eyes on.

"I am as well," said Tommy Lee, continuing the small talk.

I smiled, but still my eyes refused to meet his again.

"This is my first year. What about you?" he asked.

I could feel his eyes still on my face as I nodded. "Yes," I said, knowing I needed to keep talking. One word answers weren't going to continue the conversation and, if I clammed up, I'd have no one to blame but myself when he eventually walked away. "Are you staying in the dorms on campus?" I asked.

"I am." Tommy Lee smiled as we walked through the line together, filling our trays with lunch. "You too?"

"Ya. I love them. They're so much fun, aren't they?"

"Much better than the barracks I'm used to."

"You're in the army?"

"Just out. I did a two year term. And now I'm back to complete my diploma."

"Wow. What are you studying?"

"No major declared yet. I'm not sure what I want to do after this. I mean with my degree. I just want to be self-employed."

"Sounds like there's a story behind that."

Tommy Lee laughed and shook his head. "Nothing terribly interesting. I just promised myself after I was discharged that I'd never work for anyone else, ever again. It wasn't for me," he shrugged. "But how about you? What classes are you taking?"

"Psychology."

"Oh, so you can get inside my head," he said with a cheeky grin. "Is there a bigger plan there or did it just seem like a good choice?" he asked.

"Actually, I do have a plan. Not sure if it'll change along the way but at the moment the goal is to go into criminal psychology. Examine criminals, like how they think, and to figure out why they make the choices they do."

Tommy took a step back to look at me, as if sizing me up. "Wow—I never would have guessed that about you. What a major."

I laughed uncomfortably, not sure if I'd just blown it with this gorgeous guy. My friends gave me a quick nudge, checking us out with a knowing smile about what was going on.

"So," Tommy Lee picked up his lunch tray, "you're enjoying it here, then?" he asked as we walked together and sat down at one of the empty tables.

I smiled, happy I hadn't scared him off. "I love everything about university life. It's fantastic. And so different from what I'm used to. Small town girl, what can I say. There's just so much to see and do."

"I know. What's still on your list to try?"

I laughed, blushing a little. "I don't know, lots of things," I said, feeling suddenly shy.

Tommy Lee smiled, and his eyes squinted as if he was forming a plan. "Have you been to a basketball game yet? Our team is great, you know."

I shook my head—I hadn't.

"Well, we're playing this Friday at the athletic center. Why don't you come by and then afterwards... I can take you out? I know a great place to go dancing, if you'd like?"

My eyes widened in happy surprise. "This Friday?"

"Game starts at 6," he said, dangling the information.

I paused for another second, wondering if this guy was for real, before a smile spread across my face. "I'd love to."

2

The stands were full at the basketball game—it seemed like everyone on campus was there.

"Which one is Tommy?" asked my girlfriend, Lucy.

I smiled to myself and pointed to the boy I barely knew. He was on the court, tall and focused as he eyed the opposing team.

"Ooooo, handsome," said Lucy, raising her eyebrows in excitement.

I smiled to myself, enjoying her approval. "I know. He seems really nice, too. Too good to be true?" I teased.

"There's no such thing," she said giggling. We laughed as Tommy dribbled the ball all the way up the court and – swish! – scored easily.

"He's good," I said, unable to hide my surprise.

"That's why he's on the team," she laughed. "And he's taking you out after the game?"

"Maybe dancing?" I said, feeling unsure it would fruition. Perhaps he wasn't serious about meeting up? A nice guy—handsome, sweet, funny, successful—could I really be that lucky?

"Nice shot, Tommy!" yelled a girl a few rows in front of us.

Tommy looked over to her and smiled before scanning the stands and finding me. He grinned even wider and gave me a wink before throwing himself back into the game.

The girl in front of us turned around, following Tommy's gaze. She watched us for a second, before looking back at the game.

I shrugged, feeling Lucy's eyes on me, but I had no idea why the girl in front of us was so curious.

A whistle blew and we were fully immersed in the game once more. I enjoyed watching Tommy play, and before I knew it, the game was over—our team had won!

A rush of people flooded out of the stands en masse as the final buzzer sounded. Throngs of girls headed court side, making their way to the players before the boys headed for the locker room.

I watched with Lucy from our seat, unsure what to make of it all.

"Aren't you going down to congratulate him?" she asked, clearly puzzled.

I shrugged, unable to shake off the uneasy feeling in my stomach. I was torn. It all seemed very public, going down to the players' bench to fawn over him like a groupie. I liked him, and there was no denying the butterflies in my stomach, but I wasn't looking to be one of a group of admirers. And at this stage, it was completely up in the air as to where things stood between us. We weren't dating by any stretch of the imagination; it wasn't even certain that we were even supposed to be going on a real date, though it felt like we both shared a mutual connection.

With a deep breath, I walked slowly from our seats, watching Tommy standing with his friends. He grabbed a drink of water and gave a high five to another player. There were girls everywhere, surrounding them all. Mostly surrounding him.

"I think he's got enough people to chat with—" I mumbled to Lucy, suddenly feeling silly for coming at all. Maybe I wasn't the only one he had invited. And maybe he invited them to go dancing, too.

I watched as the girl from a few rows in front of us ran right up to Tommy. She was so loud and gushing I had no trouble overhearing her.

"You were amazing," she said, her eyelids batting excessively.

I looked down, not wanting to see any more of the scene; we passed by as quickly as we could.

Thankfully Lucy wasn't one to push. "Come on, honey," she said, grabbing my hand. "We can still go dancing, you and me?"

"Hey!" a voice called out.

Just one of the many people yelling across the gym.

"Marilyn, hey!" the voice called again.

I stopped, not positive but pretty sure I had heard my name. I looked at Lucy who nodded, eyebrows raised, before I turned around to look back towards the thick of things.

Tommy smiled and waved towards us, before jogging over. "I thought that was you," he said.

"Hi," I said shyly.

"Tommy, Tommy! What a great game tonight!" gushed another girl walking by.

"Thanks!" he said, smiling widely at her.

"You were amazing!" said an older girl, near us.

"It was a team effort," said Tommy, seemingly enjoying the attention.

"I'm sure you have stuff to do," I said, feeling very much like the groupie I had no intention of becoming.

Tommy cocked his eyebrow teasingly. "Well you're right, I do have to run through the shower and get changed. But afterwards I thought we were going dancing? Was that not the plan?" he said, slightly confused.

"Hi, Tommy!" said another chorus of girls. "Will we see you out tonight?" they called out from the other side of the court.

Tommy smiled and waved back at them before returning his attention to me.

"What do you say?" Tommy asked. "Am I taking you dancing, Marilyn? I think we're gonna have a good time together," he added, letting his words drift off.

It was funny, and strange really—even with these other girls obviously dying to go out with him, he was putting himself out there, like he was betting it all on asking me out and potentially getting turned down in front of everyone.

I pursed my lips, unsure if I really wanted to be just one of the many adoring fans, before Lucy elbowed me to give him an answer. "Okay.

Let's do it," I said, clinging to the possibility that Tommy really did want to get to know me and that he really did have feelings for me. Was it even possible that this guy was Mr. Right? Somehow, even just thinking that could be a real possibility made me all the more excited to go out with him tonight. "We'll have fun, won't we?" I replied, trying to hide any hesitation from my voice.

"Absolutely! That's great! Just give me a chance to get washed up and then we'll be set. Do you want to wait here or should I come by your dorm to pick you up?"

"Hey there, Tommy!" shouted yet another girl before I had a chance to answer.

"I'll wait with her here," said Lucy quickly,

Tommy smiled and nodded at Lucy before he turned and winked to me as he headed for the locker room. "I won't be long," he said, calling out over his shoulder.

We walked back towards the stands and took a seat near the bottom. There were a few other people still there, milling about but only a handful left on the bleachers. I didn't even think to whisper, and neither did Lucy.

"Did you see all those girls? They were practically falling over themselves to get his attention," chuckled Lucy as we waited on the stands for Tommy to reemerge.

"Ya, I know. He's very popular."

"You two talking about Tommy?" said a girl in a black t-shirt a few rows up. "I'm Mikey's girlfriend. He's the point guard," she said, as if that should somehow matter to me.

I nodded shyly, feeling like we had just been caught gossiping. So, I didn't say anything else but the girl didn't need any encouragement to keep talking.

"He's a real ladies' man."

"What?" said Lucy, her shock echoed in the expression on my face.

"Well, in the sense that he's flirts with everyone," Mikey's girlfriend continued with a shrug. "He says he's not and that he's just being friendly. But he's not fooling anyone. Voted best dressed and best dancer on campus last year. He's something alright," she said, trailing off. "Mikey!" suddenly she exclaimed, running over to her boyfriend who had just left the locker room.

I looked at Lucy and shook my head, not knowing if there was anything I could even do with that information, if I even believed it. "That was... interesting," I said.

"Ahh, you waited," said Tommy, looking relieved as he walked out of the locker room.

"We said we would," I said, managing a smile.

"You did. And I'm glad you did. Are we all set then for a night out?" said Tommy, holding the door open for us.

"I think so. Do you have a place in mind?" I said, knowing full well that we were probably headed just to the other side of campus.

Tommy looked at me, unsure if I was serious or not. But, Lucy interrupted before he could say anything else.

"You guys have fun!" she said, casually stepping away from us as we headed across the lawn of the athletic complex.

I felt my eyes widen in her direction, but said nothing. I wasn't against going on a proper date with Tommy, just the two of us, if she didn't want to tag along. And this way, it would probably get much clearer a lot quicker if we really were going on an actual date, or if he simply wanted to add me to his harem of admirers.

"So, Marilyn. How come I've never seen you before now?" said Tommy, watching me closely as we walked under the moonlight.

"You saw me this week. That's before now," I teased.

Tommy smiled. "Before then?"

"It's my first year; I thought I told you that."

"You did. But still, it seems unfair that I am only just getting to meet you."

I laughed, almost nervous by his flattery. "So, where are we going?" I asked, changing the topic.

"Are you not having a nice walk with me?" Tommy teased.

I smiled back at him, "I am. I'm just eager to see your moves on the dance floor. I saw them on the basketball court—impressive, and I heard you were also a pretty good dancer. I thought it'd be nice to see for myself."

"Who told you that?" asked Tommy, a mix of genuine curiously and confusion.

"Just a girl at the basketball game. Voted best dancer, that's what she said."

Tommy laughed. "I can't imagine what else she told you. Don't believe everything you hear!"

"It's not true then? I thought you might be too good to be true," I teased.

His eyebrows raised, impressed by the compliment. "Well, I don't know about that; I do my best. But yes, best dancer on campus–they gave me the title last year. Not sure if it's true, not sure if I agree, but," Tommy shrugged. "There's more to me than just dancing."

"Oh? That sounds promising. Tell me something interesting about you. I'd love to hear it."

Tommy smiled and shook his head. "Just like that?"

I smiled back and nodded, looking up at him. His eyes were sparkling in the moonlight, as our walk had slowed to almost a standstill.

"I like you, Marilyn. How's that for interesting?"

I felt my stomach spin with nerves at his forwardness; my feet stopped dead in their tracks. I looked down to the ground, too embarrassed to meet his steady gaze. "I," I stammered. "I like you too," I finished quietly.

Tommy reached out for my hand and gently took it in his own. "Well, that's good. Because we're going dancing together. Come on," he said, with a playful tug.

I felt myself blush as his hand gripped mine, the contact electrifying.

And the rest of the night was more of the same. Although I was just one in a sea of girls around him on the dance floor, Tommy made me feel like he only had eyes for me.

"You really are a good dancer," I said, as he walked me back to my dorm.

"You're not bad yourself," Tommy smiled.

"Hi, Tommy!" called out a random girl walking nearby. "You were great tonight!" She giggled. "At the basketball game, I mean," she said, giggling some more.

Tommy nodded and smiled to the girl but his hand stayed firmly in mine.

"There's a lot of that?" I asked, wondering out loud.

"What?"

"Attention."

Tommy smiled and laughed. "Sometimes. But it's not all like that."

"What do you mean?"

"Well, sometimes it's got a bigger purpose. Like tonight–did you see the scouts at the game?" asked Tommy.

"Scouts? What do you mean?"

"Recruits, you know–the guys who watch the college games and find the best of the best. It's how they figure out who should be playing in the professional league."

"And they were there tonight? Watching you guys play?"

Tommy nodded. "I mean, that kind of attention is pretty good. It's the only way to get picked up by the big teams, so you're hoping to get noticed."

I shook my head, my eyes wide in shock. "I could see you were good on the court, but I had no idea that anyone was looking at you for that! Wow," I murmured.

Tommy smiled easily, swinging my hand as we walked. "It's not a done deal or anything." He laughed, "Far from it actually. The odds of getting picked up are crazy, but who knows. I can dream, right."

I smiled up at him, seeing for the first time a glimpse of what was underneath the polished, glossy exterior. A boy with a dream.

"Is that the big goal then? Professional basketball player?" I asked, more curious about the real him than the projected image.

"One of them."

"Tell me about the other ones," I said, genuinely interested.

Tommy looked into my eyes before pulling us off the path towards a wooden bench lit up by a lamppost. "Seriously?"

I nodded. "Only if you want. You don't have to or anything," I said suddenly wondering if I was scaring him off.

"No, no. I don't mind, it's just no one has ever asked me before."

"Really?"

Tommy smiled. "It's true. It's either basketball or business. But never the bigger picture, just dollar signs."

"What do you mean?"

"How much will I make, how big will I get? Sometimes it seems like everyone thinks I'm going to strike it rich and they're already lining up to get a piece of it."

I felt my eyes widen in shock and horror. "Really? They're trying to stake a claim on future earnings?"

Tommy nodded. "Well, that and they think I've got money now." Tommy shrugged.

I looked down, wondering how conflicting that must be–people wanting you for money, or fame, but being so desperate for it that they're gambling on your potential, pursuing you on the hope that your dream will come true.

"I don't, really," said Tommy, interrupting my thoughts.

"Don't what?"

"Have any. I mean, I have money but not the kind these girls are after. If it works out, sure, I might one day, or if one of my business ideas take off, the potential is there," he said, quite humbly. "I mean, don't get me wrong, I hope it turns out that way; I really do. I've got lots of ideas to try out, but..." his words faded off.

I looked up at him, a sadness there behind his eyes. There was so much more to him than just being a basketball star, or a great dancer, or a potential business leader. And I felt lucky I was getting to see Tommy's other side. The real him.

"What would you do with it? If you got rich?" I asked, teasingly.

Tommy laughed, a playful glint in his eyes. "I'd out it all on red." He laughed.

I felt my mouth drop open in shock.

"I'm kidding, obviously. Kind of," he quickly reassured me. "But you know what I mean—you work hard, you play hard. But it's all about luck. Luck will make you rich, make you successful. I mean, life is one big gamble anyway, isn't it?"

I paused, having never thought of life in that way before. He was right in a sense—picking a career, picking a partner; there was never any certainty, no guarantee you were making the right choice, or even a good choice. I could see his point—luck, fate, whatever you wanted to call it, played some part in it. "Well, I guess so. Thank goodness I'm not here for the money, or any future money."

"I can tell," said Tommy with a smile. "It's what makes you so refreshing. I had a really nice time tonight, Marilyn."

I looked down, feeling my cheeks blush. Even knowing that it didn't have any effect on me, it was still surreal to think that of all the girls who'd been throwing themselves at him, here he was with me—he'd picked me to walk home, to spend the evening with. But there wasn't time to overthink it; in the same breath, Tommy leaned down towards me and kissed me. It felt like the first night of the rest of my life. And it was.

We fell in love—it happened quite quickly actually. We cared for each other, learning and growing together, sharing our hopes and dreams for the future. And we stayed together; the happiness we found there led us to the altar and then blessed us with four wonderful daughters.

My life was complete. I had found my partner and had been blessed with a wonderful family on all accounts. Life was good. Not perfect, but then it never is.

I looked up to the old photo of my parents on the wall of our front room, knowing that despite our troubles, Tommy and I had it good. Of course, after all these years there'd been hiccups along the road, but thankfully, nothing major. And marriage was never meant to be easy—it was a decision to love someone, until death do we part. It was a commitment to be made objectively, not just emotionally. And I tried to remember that whenever things got tough.

I'd known long before I'd signed up that there would be sacrifices to be made along the way. But the trade-off was having a man by my side forevermore, a comfort in knowing I was complete, I was whole. And those reasons seemed like more than enough to justify working together on this marriage, compromising with each other even when it wasn't what I really wanted to do.

"What are your plans for the day?" I asked Tommy as I was packing up lunches for the girls to take to school.

"Not sure. I've got a meeting with that guy. You know that new idea I was telling you about?"

I nodded as I raced about the dining room, buzzing around, trying to get everything organized, and everyone out the door, myself included.

"Well, I'm going to pitch it to him today, see if he wants to invest in it."

"Sounds good. If that's what you want to do," I said quickly, not really able to take in what he was saying. It wasn't the first time he'd tried to get a business idea off the ground. And it wouldn't be the last.

"Are you even listening to me?" snapped Tommy.

"Of course I am," I answered, still flitting around the ground floor.

"You're not looking in my direction. You're not even staying in the same room as me, Marilyn!" His irritation was growing by the second. But the clock was ticking.

"Honey, listen this isn't a good time for me right now to hear about this latest idea. How about when I get home from work? Okay?" I offered.

Tommy huffed, but said nothing. Still, from the other side of the room, I could hear him mumbling under his breath. "It wasn't meant to be this way. I was supposed to be the breadwinner. That's how it's supposed to be."

I closed my eyes and stopped for a second. There was no need to have an argument with him. And he surely didn't want my sympathy or pity, not after all this time. But he kept dragging up this issue; the muttering, the self-pity, the frustration.

"This next one will work," he continued to himself. "We'll make that quick buck and then they'll all see. It's going to happen this time, it has to."

I sighed as I finally buckled my seatbelt, the girls out the door and on their way to school. There was no resolution with Tommy before I'd headed out to work, but there never would be. He wasn't happy. And even when I supported him, emotionally, or financially, it wasn't enough.

I tried to stay focused on the road as I drove to work, not letting my eyes and mind wander—but they did. They always did. And I turned, like every morning, towards the playground as I drove by. The basketball courts—like a permanent reminder of what our life could have been. What if Tommy's career had taken off.

It wasn't the money I longed for, or even to share the responsibility of bringing home a paycheck; but rather, that success would have made Tommy happy. Or at least it might have.

But, life hadn't played out that way. Nor had any of his backup business ideas. He resented the fact I was the main breadwinner in our household, but even still, he never changed his ways. An old dog, new tricks—it felt like my hands were tied.

Instead of playing the short game, always looking to make a quick dollar, Tommy needed to focus on the long game. He really needed a plan, and one that he could stick with. Even just an idea he could build upon and turn into a solid business. They rarely worked out that way though, and it was like a revolving door of hopes and dreams followed by crushing disappointment.

I felt truly sorry for my husband, once so successful and confident, the center of attention—his place in the world felt like a sure thing. And now, I thought, spinning my wedding ring on my finger, now he'd lost his way.

I could feel the drive inside me, this overwhelming need to help him. I had to do something. I was his only teammate left.

Later that day, after the girls were tucked in bed, I started, "Tommy..."

"Marilyn, honey," he said, oblivious that I had something to say. "I've been thinking."

My eyebrows rose subconsciously, knowing, dreading almost, what was going to come out of his mouth next. I'd heard this opening so many times. So many ideas, so many dreams. But I wanted to be supportive. He deserved at least that. "What about?" I asked.

"I think I know what we should do."

"About what?"

"About you having a job."

My jaw dropped in shock and confusion. This was not the course of the conversation I had expected. "I'm sorry, what?"

"Come on. Realistically, I can't have you being the main breadwinner indefinitely."

"What are you talking about? I'm the only one with an actual job! And surely someone needs to be bringing in some money. To pay for things–like the mortgage, food, the car–they all take money."

Tommy pursed his lips in frustration. His patience was limited these days, non-existent on others. "I know, trust me, Marilyn, I know."

"Then how are we going to pay the bills?"

"Didn't you hear me this morning? I had a meeting today. You know I've been working on a way to make some money for our family. Some way for us to get rich–make a quick buck."

"Umhum," I nodded, nervous with his tone. To say nothing of the fact that I like my job. Being a psychologist was everything I had hoped it would be–fulfilling, challenging, and I was helping others. Working at the prison, there was no denying the positive impact I was having on the world.

"Well, I think I've got a plan. I want to open a supermarket."

I looked over at him, frozen in shock, my mouth slightly agape. "Supermarket?" I said, unable to hide my confusion or surprise.

"I want to have a supermarket. Just a little one, on the corner. And I want you to help me run it."

I smiled, trying my best to be supportive, but it felt like the rug had been pulled out from under me.

"Me? You want me to help run it?"

"Absolutely. I want to do it as a team!"

I felt my head shake before the words even got out. "But what about my work? My job? It pays the bills, Tommy."

"But you won't have to anymore. We'll do it together."

I sighed out loud, feeling more than a little frustrated and annoyed at the idea that I had to sacrifice my career, my ambitions for his idea – born only moments ago in his head.

I stared into his eyes, seeking some greater insight in them–confirmation or desperation maybe, I wasn't sure. He stared back at me, his commitment locked on this latest venture.

"And we can't just work on it together, like a side project, at nights or on the weekends?" I asked, already knowing the likely answer–stores were a full time project–and we needed to do this full time if we wanted to have any chance of making it a success.

I looked down, trying to summon the determination to help him that I'd had at the start of this conversation–here was my husband, asking, begging me to help him. An opportunity to get him out of the rut he'd been in for too long now. But it meant giving up my dream, my career, my ambitions.

I inhaled deeply, my eyes glancing over to our wedding photo on the wall as I looked back to him. "Okay," I said quietly. "Let's give it a shot. We can do it. We'll do it together."

3

"Tommy?" I called out, as I walked in the house. It was almost 5:15pm. I closed my eyes and shut the door behind me, praying my husband wouldn't answer me. And at the same time, knowing that he would. But he wasn't the same man who I'd married.

I ran my hand across my face, pushing the wisps of hair away, rubbing the exhaustion from my eyes. I didn't have the strength to deal with anything else right now. But I knew what was coming. It was like clockwork...

"What are you doing here? Who's at the store?" yelled Tommy from the kitchen.

I took a breath, fighting the instinct to cower at his harsh tone. I closed my eyes again, forcing myself to be calm. There was no reason for the aggravation in my husband's voice. I hadn't done anything to deserve it, I told myself. Still, these days, it was as if every interaction was charged with aggression. Despite all the deep breathing, the nervous energy still sent a shiver down my spine. Somehow, over the ten years we've been together, it had turned into this: I was scared to death of my husband.

"I've just finished for the night. Steve's working the rest of the evening shift, remember?"

As I stood in the entrance way to our modest home, I could hear his footsteps coming nearer. They were loud, fast-paced and seemingly stern.

"It's early. I can't believe you're done," Tommy said, doubt lacing his words. He took a long swig from his beer bottle and stared at me from the other side of the foyer.

I tried to steady myself for another lashing from his sharp tongue and the barrage of questions that were coming. "Well, I am done, what can I say?" My words were quiet, like the whisper of a terrified child.

"Did you place the orders?" he barked.

"Yes."

"And you brought the money to the bank?"

"Yes.

"How about the bills? Did they all get paid? They're due at the end of the month, you know."

"I do know. I remember–you told me at the start of the week. And yes, I paid for everything when I was at the bank. I stopped there on the way home."

Tommy nodded. "Was it a good day? Did we take in a lot?"

"Yes. A good day, sure," I said, not overly concerned about the precise figures. We had sales, that was all I was concerned about.

"What does that mean? Was it a good day or not? You need to know that kind of thing. I'm counting on you to step up. To take responsibility. Did you hear yourself? 'A good day, sure,' like you don't care. It doesn't even sound like you have a clue about what's going on."

My eyes shifted to my feet, my fingers twitching of their own accord.

But my husband kept at it. "Honestly, you've got no clue, do you? You have no idea how we did today or ever. Did you even check the figures? I mean, specifics–for today–what were they?"

His words cut into me. Though the acerbic nature of his tone was devastatingly familiar, it still hurt. And it pained me even more to admit I was getting used to it.

"I don't know, Tommy," I said, still fixated on the ground. "I'm sorry, I just don't remember."

"How can you not remember?" he said with a roll of his eyes.

"I don't think I checked the numbers, not the specifics. I mean, I checked what we were depositing, but—"

"Great. Just great. You can't even handle that. I thought you were going to be an asset, a partner in all this..."

I nodded, biting my lip as my husband admonished me, like I was a naughty child.

"Forget it," he finally said. "Explains why you're home this early—doesn't take a lot of time if you're not doing the job properly." Tommy shook his head before turning on his heels, slugging back his beer as he headed for the front room without another word.

He was two rooms away before I'd even had a chance to regain my composure. Silence enveloped me; I just stood there, for the longest time, in disbelief. I should have checked the figures. He was right. But I hadn't. I didn't make a note of those kinds of details anymore. We'd been turning a healthy profit for months now and, since then, I'd not been as concerned about the daily take. We could afford to have an off day.

I chided myself, second-guessing my judgements and abilities, as Tommy's words played over and over in my head. Somewhere deep down, I knew this wasn't my fault, and I'd done nothing wrong, but it was so much easier to fall under his spell and believe his harsh criticisms.

Suddenly, a sound that melted my heart hit my ears. A broad smile spread across my face—squeals and giggles rushed in my direction, pushing aside every other thought.

I grinned at my little girls who were running towards me for a hug. With desperation, I grabbed them in my arms, giving my sweet little ones a solid squeeze. It felt incredible. My anxiety disappeared instantaneously; everything felt right. I was home.

I stroked my daughter's hair, letting the joy of being with them take over. And it did so quickly. Gone were thoughts of Tommy, of the confusion and anxiety. Gone was the worry and fear, pushed aside and replaced by pure, uncompromised love. I hugged each of my girls, knowing, without question, they were my world. Nothing else mattered so long as they were okay. I could get through anything for them. And I would. No matter what. So long as I had my girls, everything was alright.

"Love you, Mom," whispered the youngest. And as quickly as they had appeared, they were off again, running up the stairs to continue whatever game they'd been playing.

As their laughs faded, the fears of reality resurfaced. I could hear my husband, back in the kitchen now, still cursing me under his breath as he muttered on his way to get his next beer.

I sighed, knowing it was only going to get worse. Much worse. There was never a good way to bring up a problem at work. Even on the best days, my work was never enough. And on the worst days... my body cringed, just thinking of them.

I slipped off my shoes, as I fought with myself on the inside—he didn't mean to sound like this. No, he did. And you just don't treat people this way! No, this was a phase. It'll get better. It had to. But it won't and you can't live like this! No one can walk on eggshells indefinitely! Wait, this isn't the real Tommy. He won't stay like this. He just can't. And if he does?! When will the patience finally run out? When will you get to snap back?

The internal dialogue was rapid-fire, a continuous conflict between both sides of myself, almost an argument between loving and fearing my husband.

I shook my hair out, trying to clear my head, to sum up my inner strength. But there was no easy solution. And there were no other options, no clear way to make the situation between Tommy and I any better. I'd signed up for both, better and worse.

Even still, my legs weakened as I walked into the kitchen; it felt like I was walking into a lion's den, rather than entering a room of my own house to ask my husband a simple business question.

"There was actually something I need to speak with you about, Tommy, if that's okay?" I said, feeling like a shy school girl once again, as opposed to an equal partner. It wasn't right, but even still, it felt like the safest approach to take.

"What? What do you need from me? Can't you handle it?" he said.

"I can handle it. It's just while I was at the bank–" I started, almost unable to continue, knowing that this conversation couldn't possibly end well for me.

"And?" said Tommy.

"And it looked like we were missing some money. I mean I'm sure it's just a simple bookkeeping mistake, or maybe a miscalculation on the bank's part, an easy fix," I said, rambling through my explanation, not wanting to cause any panic, or upset him.

Tommy's eyes narrowed, the anger in them unmistakable.

"I can ask them of course, but I was just wondering if you knew anything about it. I just wanted to check. Did you see it when you made the deposits yesterday?" My legs twitched, as did my hands. I forced myself to look at my husband, fighting the urge to look away from him.

Tommy glared at me, as if I had somehow just personally attacked him.

"It's okay if you didn't," I said, giving him a way out.

"What are you saying, Marilyn? That I wouldn't notice something like that? That I'm not smart enough to, or that I don't pay attention to my own accounts? What exactly are you getting at?"

"Nothing. I'm sorry. Really, Tommy, I was just asking."

He shook his head, his fingers squeezing themselves into tight fists at his side. My heart raced with anxiety–it was like poking a bear–I shouldn't have bothered mentioning it. Asking him wasn't worth it. Nothing was worth this.

"Sorry, Tommy. I'll call the bank tomorrow and sort everything out. It's just I didn't want to get into things with them if there was an explanation, that's all." I felt myself shrink down in size under his gaze. It was instinctual, though I knew deep down I should have held my own. Still, it was like part of me cowered for self-preservation. I eyed the doorway, wishing one of the girls would call out for me so I could escape.

"Well, it's all gone. No point asking them where it is," mumbled Tommy.

My head snapped up, my shock and confusion genuine. "I'm sorry, what? So you do know something about it then? And it's gone?" I spoke slowly, trying to process the idea that Tommy had just berated me for not paying attention to the finances, when in fact he had been responsible for these missing funds all along.

"Damn right it is," said Tommy, standing up tall. He was arrogant and unrepentant. "My account—my money. And I took it."

"But there's a thousand dollars missing–what did you do with it? What did you buy? It was something we needed, right?" Panic set in as my mind filtered through the countless ways I would have spent it—food, clothes, mortgage payments, savings—even though we were in the red, money still went far too fast these days. "Tommy?" I prompted.

"We always need money."

"Yes. But," I paused, trying to figure out what he was getting at. Yet I couldn't. "That makes no sense," I said quietly. "Sorry, Tommy. I don't understand."

"I spent it."

"Right. I get that part, but how? Where did you spend it? On what?" I asked, knowing I was on the edge–his patience with me had to be almost gone.

"You gotta spend money to make money, Marilyn. You should know that by now." He looked at me, his eyes on fire, enraged that I was still questioning him.

"I do. Of course, Tommy. And I agree with that. It's just–" but instead of pushing the issue, I felt my resolve weaken. His intense stare, his razor sharp tongue–there was no point. The money was accounted for, on some level at least.

"You still want to know, don't you? Like you're my mother."

"No, I don't need to know. You're right, it's your money, our money. It's there to be spent," I said trying to diffuse the tension that had built up.

But it didn't work. Maybe I wasn't convincing enough. Tommy glared at me, his lips curled in anger. "I made a bet, that's what I did with it. I bet it all."

I stared at Tommy, my jaw slack in disbelief. Words ran through my head: You're kidding. You have to be kidding, please tell me you aren't that reckless, that you're not that irresponsible! But these words never came out of my mouth. Instead, I stood there, like a gormless shell of a person and let it go.

"I'm going to make it big one day. You watch me, Marilyn. Someday I'm going to win big."

I stifled a sigh and closed my eyes for a second, trying to understand and accept that our hard earned money had been tossed away so foolishly. "I–" I started, not knowing what combination of words I could say to make this not happen again. "Is there any way we could talk about it before you gamble away our savings? I don't think, I mean, for the girls and I, I just want to make sure we have enough, without risking what we need to get by. What do you think?" I asked, my voice trembling with every word.

"I don't know about that. I provide for you, don't I? And it's only my name on the account. You've got to trust me–luck is going to make me rich. Maybe not today, but someday. Someday one of these bets will pay off."

My eyes widened in fury; I quickly turned my back to him, taking a minute to compose myself. He was treating our money like a ball in his hands, shooting for a hoop when he feels lucky. My hands curled up in frustration, though I said nothing.

The floor creaked; I looked back over my shoulder, and saw Tommy smirking as he left the room. He'd won, a point on the scoreboard, was that how he saw this, I wondered. I shook my head again; this was so much bigger than winning an argument, this was our life. Our livelihood.

But as I headed to the stove to start dinner, my head raced with the new information. We needed that money. Maybe not all of it, but a significant portion for sure. And he'd just gone and gambled it away. Nothing to show for it except the hole in our account where it used to be. And this wasn't the first time either, and he implied it wouldn't be the last.

Tears ran down my cheeks, the emotions coming out of nowhere. I stomached the sobs building in my chest, knowing there'd be no sympathy from him, and that if I was caught weeping, it'd only be worse.

Get a handle on this, I ordered myself. But it seemed like it was just one thing too many. The exhaustion wasn't helping much either. It made everything harder, including getting some perspective and reigning in my emotions.

In that moment, it felt as if my world was shattering all around me. It wasn't just that Tommy had gone into our account and gambled our money away. And it wasn't just the way he spoke to me. And it wasn't just the long hours–I'd put in plenty of those. No, something in my core knew this ran deeper. And I knew who to blame—me.

This wasn't the way I wanted to live my life. I'd given up everything for Tommy, for him to chase his dreams, while mine were relegated to the background.

Manning a grocery store—that was never my first choice. Nor second or third. This wasn't a career path I had ever envisioned for myself. Nor was it still.

But I valued my marriage and my husband. And when he asked for my support, I gave it to him willingly. I had agreed to try, while foolishly assuming that Tommy would be taking the lead. And at least some of the responsibility as well.

Nevertheless, it hadn't played out that way. And now I was in over my head, alone, and unfulfilled while Tommy spent more and more time working on his own ventures, gambling away whatever little money we had left over.

"Dinner," I called out, having taken the time it took to cook the meal to pull myself together. I had to; I had to make it work–for the girls if no other reason.

I repeated that to myself day after day, time and time again–make it work, you're in this together. And I prayed it would get better, that Tommy and I would find a better path. But it never happened.

Driving away from the bank, my hands were already shaking. Our accounts had looked healthy just last week, but today they were virtually empty. It had to stop. This ridiculous gambling had gone way past the point of rational. It was dangerous and left me wondering how we were going to be able to pay the bills if we couldn't get it under control.

The voices were back in my head though as I fought with myself over what to do next to straighten this situation out.

You can't talk to him about it. He needs you to be supportive. I am being supportive! He's being reckless and needs to come back to the real world. But he's always been a dreamer. You knew that when you married him. For better or worse. And it could be worse still, right? Do you hear yourself?! This isn't about being supportive, or kind, or worrying about his feelings. It's about putting food on our table, and paying the mortgage! I'm there putting in the long hours, while he just takes the money and throws it away. But this isn't you –you don't raise your voice, you don't look for a fight. You treat others the way you want to be treated. You weren't raised in the street—educated people don't speak to others like this. Maybe not, but nothing else is working... It's gone on for months! And what good has being polite and refined done?! It's done nothing.

Anger erupted inside me; the weak, passive arguments that had led for so long now we're losing magnificently inside my head. It had to stop. A line had to be drawn. And I was the only one who could do it.

"Tommy," I said quietly, after the girls had gone up to bed. I took a deep breath, knowing in my heart that it wouldn't be an easy conversation for either of us. But it wasn't optional–we needed a better, safer plan for our finances. So regardless of how it went over, things needed to get sorted.

Tommy looked over from his chair, a glass in his hand. He rattled around the ice cubes, just a drip of liquor remaining. He raised an eyebrow, but every part of him looked at me with contempt.

"We need to talk about the money," I said calmly. I watched his eyes narrow as the words came out of my mouth. He stared with such intensity, as if he were daring me to continue. But today, I wasn't backing down.

"We're turning a profit at the business, which is great. Really, the store is doing so well, but there's nothing to show for it."

"Well, that's just how it is sometimes. We've got to keep at it. Sooner or later something will pay off."

I nodded, vowing in my head to stay strong, to not back down. "Actually, that's the issue; work is paying off, but I'm pretty sure you're taking the profits—all of them, right?"

"We're going to get lucky one of these days. I mean that. And you're lucky to have me. Not everyone would be able to go big like this. But I am. I can just feel it—sooner or later I'll hit the jackpot."

"Okay, so we're on the same page–you've been sneaking profits, right, Tommy?"

"I told you this before–how dumb are you? No wonder we're not making more."

I sucked in a breath, refusing to buckle under his harsh criticism. "I don't think you should be gambling it away any more. We need that money."

"We need it to invest, that's right," he agreed, slugging back the last drop of his drink. "Get me another one, will you? A double."

"No. You need to listen to me—this has got to stop. You've got to stop clearing us out. How are we going to pay the bills? How are we going to buy food? What happens if we have an emergency?" I said, feeling my voice get louder as my frustration grew.

Tommy's eyes opened wider, surprised, shocked by my outburst. His nostrils flared, and he slammed the glass down on the side table.

"This is your fault, Marilyn. You got us into this mess. All of it!"

"What did you say?" I asked, stunned by his accusation.

"This isn't what I was supposed to do with my life—some average guy, married to an average girl, in an average house, average kids," he exclaimed, shaking his head, looking around at things, our life, with disgust. "I was going to be someone. I was going to make something of my life. And look at me. I have nothing!"

"Nothing? You have a wife and four wonderful daughters. That's a far cry from nothing."

"Is it? What's that worth, really? None of it pays the bills. None of it gets me rich. And you're sitting there, trying to control every little thing I do. Do this, don't do this. I hate it!"

"Is that what this is about? Control? Money?" I asked, grasping at straws.

"Whatever you want to think, sweetheart. Don't try and read me with your little psychoanalysis—it isn't going to work," said Tommy, his tone dripping with contempt.

"So what is it Tommy? You regret marrying me? You regret our life? Our choices? Or does it all come down to wanting it all–and you think if we struck it rich, we would be happy."

"Don't think you know me. Don't think you understand me. Everything is about money. Getting ahead, getting more–and I was going to have it all." Tommy stood up, pacing as he spoke. It was as if his anger increased with every step.

"You still can. Hard work pays off, Tommy–"

"It doesn't. Not with you. I mean, maybe that's it—it's you."

"Me what?"

"You're to blame. You're responsible for this life I have. This is your doing," he said, stepping up to me, pointing his finger in my face.

Instinctively I stepped back. "I've done nothing but be supportive of you!"

"You're holding me back. You've made it impossible for me to be who I really am," Tommy yelled, his frustration growing by the second. He continued to step closer, little by little until he was right in my face once again.

"Who you really are? And who is that?" I challenged.

"A business man. A successful business owner. Before you came along, I was going to make it."

"And what exactly did I do to hinder that? How is this my fault?" I said, feeling my own anger fuel my confidence. In that moment, all my inhibitions were absent—and it felt so good to finally stand up for myself, for our life, for what was right.

"You're holding me down. You're holding me back, like you always have."

I shook my head, in awe of his ridiculous claims. "This is unreal. You're drunk, that has to be it. You can't be this delusional, Tommy. We're on the same team."

Tommy slammed his hand against the wall, right next to my face. "You're dead weight. You're a liability, not an asset. And I need someone who can get behind me. You're supposed to support me, support my ideas."

I jumped as he punched the wall again, and I stared at my husband, my own hands balled into fists by my side. I knew there was no truth to his words, yet hearing them out loud combined with the physical aggression, made me freeze for a second. Did he actually believe that? He must.

I stood there, staring at him as that realization sunk in. He'd never considered me an equal. He'd never believed I could help him, that I was talented and skilled in my own right. And that was why he could ask me to quit my job to help with his dream. I'd have never been able to ask that of him. But he had no trouble.

And maybe that should have been my first clue. I watched him now, his body rigid with tension and anger he looked like a man on the edge.

"That's fine, Tommy. Think what you want. But we're in this together. And since I'm working shifts at the store and helping run it, it's my money too that's going into that account. You can't gamble it away anymore. Not my share anyway." I shifted my body to the side, away from his imposing stance, determined to not back down.

And then his hand came up. Fast, firm, unrelenting. Tommy slapped me; a stinging blow across the face.

4

My hand clung to the side of my face, my eyes glassed over in shock, in horror, at what my husband had just done. It was as if I were living someone else's life. My body shook ever so slightly, as if it were trying to waken me from a dream.

But the look in Tommy's eyes told me this was no dream. This horror was too real to be a nightmare. The rage burned in his eyes, fierce and uncontrolled, just like his anger, fresh and raw.

The world seemed to slow down around me, the seconds dragging out as my mind struggled to catch up. It was like I couldn't cope with what had just happened. Even though I could still feel the sting on my cheek, and I could still see the fire in Tommy's eyes; I couldn't process it – any of it. It just didn't make sense. Not my Tommy. Not my marriage. This wasn't what we were about. This wasn't him.

But at that moment, the man staring back at me didn't look like the soulmate I had married either. The anger, the fury, the overwhelming frustration in his face—a far cry from the happy man I'd said "I do" to.

I blinked, trying to get my head back in the present, instinct forcing me to pull it together. My eyes darted around the room, uneasily, as if looking for a safe place to rest. But they flickered back to Tommy, desperate for some sign this attack was over, that he'd been taken over by some other force and my real husband was still somehow waiting to escape and come back to me. But there was no reassurance, no easy way to explain the violence that had suddenly erupted in our home.

Tommy clenched his hands into a fist on either side. His knuckles white with pressure, his body still trembling with anger or adrenaline, or both. He wouldn't do it again, I thought, as I subconsciously took a step away from him. But there was no conviction in my mind. I could feel it inside me–every ounce, every measure of knowledge and understanding I had of my husband melted away in an instant. Maybe he would hit me a second time. Maybe the man who had just slapped me across the face was just getting started.

I took another bolder step and then another back away from him. The terror plain to see in my face, I'd never felt more alone or afraid than in that moment. This wasn't who I'd married. This wasn't who I'd fallen in love with. This wasn't the man I'd spent over a decade with.

Still, I stood there, paralyzed in fear and disbelief, unable to run only retreat in slow-motion, shock etched on my face. But I knew that I had to move faster, further. I had to create some sort of physical distance between us. I had to keep myself safe.

I watched Tommy, not saying a word, as the two sides in my head quarreled and my feet moved backwards, in small calculated steps. No sudden movements. Don't open your mouth–the instructions to myself were like a command, my instincts taking control. These instructions were to be followed. No questions asked. I could feel the weight of the orders–and the stakes. If I didn't extricate myself from this situation, there was a possibility this could get worse. Much worse. I slid my foot behind me, again and again. Five steps separated us now.

My eyes darted furtively between Tommy's face and his hands, still clenched in rage, as he paced in front of me. He was so big, his arms so long, his stride so wide. There was no getting away from the fact I was still within his reach.

My heart pounded, I could feel the blood coursing through my veins, my adrenaline high.

Get out. Let him cool down, I ordered myself. I knew how to do this and I would do it, I said, trying to convince myself. But though the orders were firm and unwavering, it was impossible to ignore the other voice in my head. It whispered to freeze my position, not wanting to enrage the man before me. Don't keep looking at his hands. You're being ridiculous, Marilyn. He won't punch you. He wouldn't. Not you. Not the mother of his children. He couldn't. He wouldn't hurt you like that.

And though the voice was adamant, and it believed what it was saying, everything about the situation contradicted that. From the tension in the room, through to the anger in Tommy's face–and the sting in my cheek–this wasn't a safe place anymore.

No others words were said, internally or externally. No other movement made except for my slow and steady retreat until I was out of his sight.

I crept up the stairs and hid in the bathroom, desperately trying to pull myself together, to figure out what had just happened. What had I done to trigger this? What had I said that set him off?

Tears pours down my cheeks; the pain, the realization of what had just happened hurt more than his slap. Everything I thought I'd had in life was gone. And maybe I'd never even had it in the first place. It was impossible to put my thoughts into any sort of order, so scattered and random, as my emotions jumped between fear and shame, sadness and guilt. Yet still, after my eyes had run dry, and hours had passed, there was no clarity. There was no easy solution.

And so I resigned myself to believing it wouldn't happen again. In my heart, I knew him–Tommy wasn't like this. The aggression, the violence, the rage–it was a one-time thing. A misunderstanding. It had to be.

But of course it wasn't. It never is. And it went on, happening with more frequency than I'd like to admit. And it was months before I finally had the courage to speak up for myself, to defend against his irrational anger, as he unloaded his pent up frustrations on me, time and time again.

I walked into the front room and my eyes looked towards the ground even before I saw him. It was a nothing conversation, but I knew it would turn into something; I knew how it would play out.

It shouldn't have been like this. But it was. And as I cowered inside myself, the anxiety mounting with every step closer to him, I hated myself for staying, for excusing his behavior, for tolerating the violence.

What he was doing was wrong. And I knew it. But I stayed, regardless. Foolishly, it was for the girls; they deserved a loving home. By some twisted logic, I convinced myself that somehow our crumbling abusive marriage was still that.

"What do you want?" snarled Tommy, taking a swig from his bottle.

"Actually, I've noticed some issues at work. At the store. And I just wanted to chat with you about them, so we can get on the same page," I said quietly. Even as the words came out of my mouth, part of me still didn't want to actually say them. It felt like I was walking into the lion's den. Because I was.

"Things you've noticed? Who the hell do you think you are? You think I care what you think? Or do you think you're in charge now? Stay out of my business," Tommy snapped.

I took a deep breath, steadying my nerves. "Tommy, this was a joint venture. Remember? So no, I don't think I'm the boss, but you're not either. We're in this together and there are some things we need to talk about."

"You're crazy! You work for me. My idea, my store, my business. So - back off," his voice gaining volume with each word.

"I can't and I won't do that," I said quietly. There was no need to raise my voice. I'd been brought up better than that, I thought to myself. Funny, how even knowing I was probably just moments away from being hit by my husband, I stood there, calmly, peacefully, quietly reassuring myself that yelling was not the answer. It was as if I somehow stepped outside my body and was separate from what was going on, from what was about to happen.

Tommy glared at me, his face getting redder by the second. "What did you just say?" he spat, his voice dripping with disbelief, his eyes bulging with anger.

"Nothing to merit that reaction. Or over-reaction, Tommy. It's our company, and I want to talk about it. I don't think that's too much to ask, do you?"

Tommy stared at me, dumbfounded for a second as I stood up for myself. It had been a slow process these last few months, but I was becoming more and more assertive. Even if that assertiveness eventually led to violence.

But what was the alternative? Even if I was sweet and quiet, obedient and loyal, Tommy would still beat me. I had been all those things when it first happened. So, I figured, was there really any point to not standing up for myself? It didn't seem like there was. And I was done being a doormat, done being second class to him, done being meek and mild.

"What the hell has happened to you, Marilyn? You used to listen to me. You used to follow my lead."

"No, actually. I used to follow you. To a fault. And I'm not going to anymore."

Tommy stood up abruptly, as if his body were moved by his level of anger and frustration.

"Don't," I said quietly as I saw Tommy's features ripple with anger. He looked enraged. But that didn't have to turn violent, I told myself, knowing all the while it still would. There was no connection to be had with his eyes. No sign of rationale, no modicum of self-control or composure. I felt my body brace myself, my muscles tighten in anxiety and anticipation.

"What did you say to me?" he growled, inching his way closer, the intimidation growing with every step.

"I said, don't. Don't get angry, Tommy. Don't shut me out of our company. And please don't yell at me," I said quietly. "Now, if it's still a good time, can we go through those numbers I was talking about?" I said, trying to stay on point, while stifling my own inner fear that was mounting by the second.

Tommy stared at me, his eyes dead and cold. Still they continued to flicker with intense outrage, anger, and disbelief. "Get out while you can, Marilyn. I'm not kidding. You've got no idea who you're dealing with. This is my business. My idea, my venture. And don't you dare think you've got any claim to it – you've rejected all my ideas, all my ventures, Marilyn. I'd be a millionaire over and over again, if it weren't for you."

I bit my lip trying to steady my nerves before responding. "I've ruined all your ventures? Unreal. Not a chance, Tommy. You're not going to pin that on me. You've got into this mess by yourself. And as for no claim to the business? I've put in the same hours. More hours actually, than you. I run the shop while you sit here and complain about it. Complain about your lot in life. You sit here doing nothing while I'm out working. Tell me that's not true? Come on, tell me?" I said, pausing to give him a chance to answer, but he said nothing.

"That's right," I said confidently, feeling oddly successful and assertive without any real reason to feel that way. But it felt good to stand up for myself. Even though I'd have to pay for it in a few minutes. "You can't deny what I've done for the business."

There wasn't even four feet between us, but his approach seemed like an eternity.

"It's just work, Tommy. That's all, I said calmly. And the money isn't just your money, the business isn't just yours—it's..."

Tommy's face was red, from both anger and alcohol. "None of this is yours. Not my business, not my profits, not this house. You've done nothing but ruin me. You took it all away from me. I wouldn't be here right now–home, alone, ruined– if it weren't for you, you selfish, stupid bitch."

Tommy closed the gap between us, his fingers clenched into fists, tension and rage emanating from his core. I recognized the signs of what was coming next.

I stepped back instinctively. And even though I knew better, knew this would be the straw that broke the camel's back, I opened my mouth once more. "I've done nothing but help you. How dare you say I've held you back. You're the one who asked me to quit my job. And I did. I quit my job for you."

Tommy's eyes slitted and he gritted his teeth. Yes, I knew what was coming. And there was no way to avoid it. It was only a matter of time.

"You're a damn idiot, Marilyn! Who do you think had the idea? This is my baby. The store is mine – you just work for me."

I shook my head, not about to give in to his bullying. "You can't possibly think that. You don't believe that. We built this together from the ground up. And I'm here to stay, Tommy," I said firmly.

"Shut your mouth," said Tommy. "I mean now." And with that, his hand struck my face for the last time.

"Mom?" said a quiet voice, in the next room. Tommy and my eyes shot over towards it. And in that instant, I knew this had to end. I had to leave, had to end my damaged relationship, break my marriage vows. The girls were getting older every day. If they hadn't already, they'd soon figure out what was happening.

"Sweetie?" I said, turning my back on Tommy as I rushed out of the room to find my daughter.

I sucked in a huge gulp of air when I found her, and all my daughters, perched in anxiety on the stairs.

"Your face?"

"Mom?"

"Are you okay?"

And my youngest just stared up at me, her sweet innocent eyes utterly confused.

The girls knew. They might have suspected before, but they definitely knew now. And the older they got, the more they'd see and hear what was going on. And worst of all—this kind of abuse would become normal for them. And what if they were on the receiving end of it? That was unacceptable to me. Tommy was out of control and this needed to end.

And in that very moment, I knew it was over. As much as I wanted to give my girls a loving family; a safe and healthy, happy family, regardless of its makeup, was much more important.

So, we left. The lump in my throat grew as I stared back at the house. I tried to swallow it away, to muster up enough courage to let myself believe that this was the right thing to do. In my head I knew it was, I knew there was no other way, no safer way. But my heart ached at what we were about to do.

A hand tugged on my arm, gently pulling me away from the sidewalk.

"Come on, Mom. This isn't making it easier on any of us."

I turned to look at my little girl, who was long past being little anymore. Where had it all fallen apart, I wondered. "What could I have done differently?" I asked myself, time and time again.

"We don't have to do this," my second oldest said to me. "It's going to be okay, I promise, Mom."

"I know. It won't be if we stay. Trust me. For your sake, for your future, not just mine." Tears streamed down my face, as I realized what had just occurred. I was divorcing my college sweetheart. After living with a monster for the past decade.

And if I wasn't careful, it would be my daughter following in my footsteps, wondering how she ended up with a similar life, full of eggshells and deceit, full of tension and abuse.

Initially, I had wanted to stay with Tommy for the very reasons I was leaving him. I cringed at the thought of my girls believing that any of this was real. Seeing the abuse, the before, the middle and the aftermath was intense. I shook my head, knowing that even just staying in that kind of hostile environment would have a lasting, negative effect on them. It would normalize it. It would tell them this behavior is acceptable. And that was a future I never wanted for my girls.

Yet, despite everything - the abuse, the fear, the drama - I loved Tommy, or the Tommy that I remembered. It hurt to walk away from him, to walk away from our marriage and life.

We were starting over and starting small, just me and the girls. My eyes roamed the tiny kitchen, as if unable or unwilling to accept that this was now our home. It felt wrong. It felt empty. It felt like our family was incomplete. Because it was.

I grabbed the kettle before it had a chance to whistle, careful not to wake anyone. It was late; the girls were asleep, everyone settled. I was the only one having trouble sleeping. And there was no need for them to suffer with me. Of course they were having a hard time adjusting, too. But it was different. The divorce happened to them. It was out of their hands. Whereas I had made this choice. I had chosen this course. And the responsibility was heavy.

But this was the better of the two options, I told myself. This was the best chance I had of raising healthy daughters–girls who respect themselves, who love themselves, who are strong enough to stand up for themselves, even if it means walking away. I knew it was the right decision, but it didn't make it any easier.

My responsibility, my duty, was always to my girls. And it trumped everything else. For who else could show them what a true partnership was supposed to look like, if not me? Or model a healthy relationship, an equal marriage? Who could show them what real love was?

It was my job to do all those things. And I'd failed. Even if it wasn't all my fault, I had hadn't managed to keep my marriage together. More tears fell as my eyes scanned the bare walls of the dull room, desperately looking for any sign of this being our home. But there was nothing; nothing to signify this rental unit was our space. Nothing personal, nothing of ours. Not even any pictures.

I sighed, closing my eyes in defeat. Of course there were no pictures. No one celebrates a broken family. And that's what we were now. Because of me. Because I had decided to take the girls and leave.

It was an impossible reality. My life was so far from the picture perfect family I had always dreamed about, I had always aspired to. The one I'd had for so many years.

I wiped away the tears that had wetted my cheeks for long enough, letting the sorrow settle in for a moment, the emotions take hold. And they fell and fell, until my eyes were dry.

Where had it all gone wrong? The violence was the obvious catalyst to our divorce. But it hadn't always been that way. We'd been fine for years, even good for some of those years. We'd loved each other; at least I had. Tommy had been my world.

But maybe that's not enough. Maybe love alone can't sustain a marriage. Or maybe the reverse is true—maybe marriage itself doesn't sustain love? Is that possible, I wondered, trying to find something in the ashes of our relationship.

If I could only pinpoint when it all started to fall apart, maybe that would give me the answer. Though, it was futile and foolish – what did it matter now? Once Tommy decided to physically hurt me, it was over. Regardless of the why and when. Sure it took months to get up the courage to leave, but there was no coming back from that slap. I'd known that the minute it happened; somewhere deep inside, he must have as well.

Pictures of our past, of the decades we shared, flashed before me, the memories flickering through my mind like my very own slide show. We had been happy. At least I was happy.

And then I realized it. I realized what I could see now with perspective and objectivity. I'd known all along who Tommy was, at least I thought I did. I'd tried to see the real him, and accepted who I did see. It was a pure love, a genuine love, an unconditional love.

And maybe that was why my love for him endured longer than his love for me? Because to love someone, and for that love to endure, you need to see that person with clarity. And I had. Even in the very end, seeing this new side of Tommy, which I hated so much.

I shook my head, realizing what had been painfully obvious for years now. While I had loved Tommy unconditionally, Tommy had never even taken a look at me. He'd had no interest in finding out who I really was, or what I was all about. He'd decided I was a good enough match, and that was that. And for that reason, it didn't take much to get the sheen off the apple.

I dabbed my eyes, not wanting to believe my words to be true. But how else could someone change so much? How could someone who had once loved me, now not? How could someone fall out of love to such an extreme that they start physically abusing them? The only answer that made sense to me was: he never truly cared about me – only himself.

Conclusion

With the stories of Darla, Rachael, and Marilyn up front and center, it's clear just how quickly things can fall apart. Is it just enough to say they were unlucky in love? Or is it something more, something deeper than just that?

While looking at our own relationships can often be a challenging experience, self-reflection demands the ability to look critically, introspectively, objectively at oneself, which can be difficult for many. Yet, it is markedly easier to see the flaws in someone else's relationships as we are taught to step into the shoes of other's, rather than step out of our own shoes.

No doubt, each of these relationships in this book had its unique hurdles. Darla walked into a marriage with a man she didn't really love, and into another with a man who was leading a double life, and then she entered a relationship with someone who was trying to cling onto her, pressuring her into more than she wanted.

Rachael, on the other hand, went after the man she wanted, someone who seemed perfect on screen and in the pulpit, and she assumed the image he presented matched with the person he was behind closed doors. Unfortunately, this was not the case. And it's a common issue for many, though not necessarily in such a dramatic fashion as Rachael experienced.

As is often the case in matters of the heart, life before marriage can be a bit of a game—where both sides might be playing for different purposes. Is one person trying to hide their true nature in an attempt to gain love and affection, either emotionally or physically? Or is someone turning a blind eye to warning signs, as they're so focused on walking down that aisle to achieve the bigger life goal of getting married? Or maybe the relationship's flaws are as clear as day, but someone is willing to say and do whatever it takes to seal the deal with an 'I do'?

Every relationship is different, as are each partner's individual motives. However, Rachael's situation highlights just how important it is to take off the blinders and look at the 'love of your life', your soulmate, with a critical eye, to make sure that your view and reality are in sync. Is it easy to do this? No. But necessary? Absolutely.

And finally, we met Marilyn. By the end of her marriage, she was left questioning her entire relationship from the moment they both met. How had it all fallen apart so spectacularly? Were there signs she should have seen in advance that her husband would turn abusive toward her? What was her role, if any, in his change in behavior? And was there anything she could have done, any choice she could have made that would have given her the 'happily ever after' that she so desperately wanted?

And, ultimately, isn't that what each of these women was looking for—their own happily ever after, a story book ending for themselves? On paper, it can seem naive, or even contrived to hope for a happy ending such as this. And some may even want to question how, in this day and age, a long-lasting happy marriage can still be a priority or even a reality. But while some are choosing to ignore the pressures of society and family to meet Mister or Ms. Right and get married, and ignoring the allure of being a Mrs.; for many, this idea of finding a spouse – and ideally a soulmate, a true life partner – is still held in high regard, as the ultimate goal in life. Marital success can feel necessary for being fulfilled, or considered whole.

Despite the rising rates of divorce, both men and women continue to flock to the altar, knowing full well that for many 'till death do us part' is not guaranteed or even all that common. And for Darla, Rachael, and Marilyn, that was exactly the case.

But why, and how, do relationships fall apart for so many people? Where did the relationships begin to deteriorate? Or were they doomed from the beginning?

Although there may have been a moment that crossed the line, possibly a point where the relationship became unsalvageable, what led the couple to reach that point? What choices or actions, decision and concessions, took them in that direction, towards falling out of love, towards a path of divorce, uncoupling from the marriage and going their separate ways? And why did they go down that road, instead of another?

Unfortunately, things are rarely clear cut; there are no easy answers or even an agreement on what went wrong. Relationships aren't black and white and, in most cases, neither person is solely to blame.

But when you take a step back, is it really any wonder that so many relationships fail? People never learn how to sustain a loving relationship. The reason is simple: nobody ever showed them. There's no instruction book, no class in school, no online course. The fact that a man and a woman feel love toward each other is natural, instinctual, but does not guarantee they will be able to create a happy and rewarding life with that person. Love does not automatically teach a person communication skills. Love does not teach a person how to resolve a conflict. Love does not teach people how to weave that love into the rest of their life.

But, even knowing that, it doesn't stop us from wanting it that way, from desperately craving these fairy tale endings, without any reasoning as to why it will work out in the end.

More often than not, these happy endings that we are taught from a young age are in fact an unrealistic goal, created by fiction. And for the most part, today, in the Western world, neither men nor women are forced to stay in a relationship that isn't working out. But that doesn't deter us from trying to find 'The One', from wishing and hoping that they are out there, waiting for us, ready to sweep us off our feet, settle down, and propose marriage.

And while in the past, these marriage vows were binding, and a woman's options severely limited should she leave the relationship; nowadays things are considerably more complicated. Though someone may claim to be in love, or committed to another for the rest of their life, often their actions portray a different sentiment, whether they present themselves differently after marriage, or new information is discovered once married, or perhaps something has shifted in the relationship, creating an unhealthy or abusive environment—whatever the case may be, women today are in a position to stand up for themselves, for their rights, for their independence, and for their happiness.

However, despite all of that, even in this day and age, marriage is still a goal or a dream for most women. And one which impacts an individual on both a personal and societal level. Whether it's family pressure to find a husband, or the fear of being alone, the desire to have kids the 'traditional way', or simply the magical fantasy of a perfect wedding; there are countless reasons why women remain fixated on tying the knot. And, sadly, these reasons, which should be secondary to the natural course that the relationship might take, have a huge impact on the outcome.

Women will go to great lengths, all for the sake of Mrs. It's a title and status, a goal and an achievement, with the prospect of marriage being, ideally, for life. To this end, there are many desperate and lonely women of all ages, races and religions in the world who would do almost anything to get married (to the right one).

And that is in and of itself the crux of the issue—in many cases, women, in their determined effort to secure a husband, make sacrifice after sacrifice, compromise after compromise, just to get that title, that position they so want.

Of course, that's not to say that compromise isn't a necessary part of a healthy, successful relationship, but it's a matter of give and take, with both sides meeting in the middle. It's not a matter of one person giving up everything, conceding every point, simply to appease the other.

Looking at the stories of Darla, Rachael, and Marilyn, it's clear that becoming a wife, or securing a husband, shouldn't mean losing your own identity in the process. At least not if long term happiness is the goal. A woman may choose to give up her faith, or be willing move to a different country; she may choose to change careers, or help her husband reach his professional goals while her's take a back seat; or she may even choose to overlook his faults, excuse his behavior and, in extreme situations, risk her own wellbeing. But, at no point should she concede who she is, or become someone else simply to appease her man. Compromises and concessions are part of any relationship, but they should be made by both sides; there must be balance.

But, unfortunately, this desire to please, to become who they think their man wants, is a pitfall that affects many women at some stage of their life. We've seen this to varying degrees in each woman's story—they put their brains on the back burner, their identity on hold, as they pretend to want everything their man wants, and agree with everything he says. If the man thinks something is great, they agree; if the man comes up with an idea, they support it. And this support and agreement, when not genuine, is the issue. This is not a matter of politeness, such as agreeing that a meal was good when maybe it wasn't; instead, this is about agreeing and supporting ideas that are potentially significant, when in fact, you aren't convinced of their merit, or don't actually support them. Consider how quickly and dramatically things could change if someone simply agreed with their partner on questions such as:

> *"I want to quit my job and go back to school. What do you think?"*
>
> *"I've been reading a lot about that new diet—I think we should cut out meat/gluten/sugar/milk from our diet. You in?"*
>
> *"I have a job offer but it's on the other side of the country. So, I think we should move! Right?"*

Obviously, when no emotions are involved, it's hard to see or understand why anyone would blindly agree to statements and situations like this. But they do, every day, so the question then becomes, why would someone feign agreement? Why would they sacrifice everything just to appease someone else?

There's no easy answer, nor one that applies to everyone. The reasons are as complex as people themselves, yet the motive and rationale is often in line with the goal of love and keeping their partner happy—that happy ending. "If I agree, then he'll be happy. If I go along with his idea, he'll stay."

Many women have been taught as children, by parents, teachers and even society that to disagree means they're being difficult. Some cultures may even still teach that men are not to be questioned. Yet, regardless of the motivation, putting your brain on hold is rarely the answer for a relationship that is aiming for the long term. Marilyn's case spells it out better than most: when a woman finally gets tired of giving up everything just to appease her husband, once she begins to speak up, it can be a monumental shock to the relationship, as the husband doesn't understand this shift in the dynamic of their relationship (in Marilyn's case, leading to Tommy's inexcusable reaction).

Giving up their identity, personality and intelligence are a common sacrifice women make in their pursuit to becoming a Mrs., yet it is not all they relinquish. For some, it is their ethics and values that are given up in their quest. Desperation can lead many down a path even they cannot truly justify. But once a woman feels like her options are limited and time is running out, they may be looser in their parameters for finding a husband, having lost focus on who their ideal man is. An "Any man will do" mentality comes into play and, as a result, they may accept anyone who is close to marriage material, even if the man is not who they really desire.

And for some women, they are willing to cross the lines of marriage, and go after another woman's husband. Though it is their motivation to get married that fuels their desire for a relationship, ironically, some woman still have no shame in helping to break another couple's marriage vows.

But while many feel this true sense of desperation creeping in more with every year they're on the dating scene, in reality this clock is simply not ticking as loudly as it used to. Objectively, in today's society, the need to marry young or quickly is in the past.

Of course, while logically the need to marry early has diminished, there's no denying the stereotypes and societal pressures that are still very real. Marilyn's story is the epitome of this–though she is a smart, educated, confident woman, she was admittedly old fashioned and felt life wasn't complete unless you were married. Did that drive her to ignoring some of the warning signs? Did that encourage her to stay in an abusive relationship? Of course, there is no definite answer, but it's safe to say societal pressures and someone's views of the world have an impact, to some degree, on their choices.

Nevertheless, is rushing into things really the right strategy? Does anyone benefit from that course of action in the end?

Imagine how different the relationship would be, how improved the outcome, if everyone came to the table with a stronger and more honest position. Not physically, or even intellectually, but with a stronger, more defined sense of self. Would someone like that be so willing to give themselves up for somebody else? Unlikely. Would someone like that be so eager to take whoever comes along out of pure desperation to marry? Probably not.

By that logic, instead of seeking out a man to complete them, a woman should take time to complete herself first. Take a recess from the dating scene, reevaluate life and one's self. Figure out what is needed from a relationship—what is truly best for themselves—and then focus on that.

But taking a step back from the dating scene, doesn't mean you have to do this alone. As women, we need to talk to each other, and look out for each other. After all, just like with Darla, Rachael and Marilyn's stories, it can be much easier to see the issues in someone else's stories than our own. We're just too close to it. Perspective is difficult when you're caught up in the midst of things—so, keep an eye open for friends as they explore the dating scene, share and learn from each other's experiences.

Yet, so ingrained is this urge to become a Mrs., many women continue to put themselves out there, time and time again, in the hopes of finally getting their happy ever after. Incredibly, even after messy breakups and divorce, women are still willing to take risks and bet everything on the next happy ending. Whether it's the urgent feeling like life is passing you by, or a loneliness in your heart that you can't seem to shake, we continue to put ourselves out there and look for love in all kinds of places. Some search the personal ads in the newspapers, others put their profiles there for all to see, and others still may dive into online dating to find a partner.

Nevertheless, remember that what you put out there is yourself. While it's easy to say, "But I need a relationship. It makes me feel whole. It makes everything better," unless you've taken the time to invest in yourself, starting a relationship on a rocky foundation can be much more trouble than you anticipated.

For many, when a relationship ends, the failure is devastating. Depression is an unspoken side effect when relationships go sour. Consider for instance, one study by the National Institute of Healthcare Research: it indicates that divorced people are three times as likely to die by suicide as those who are married.

When a relationship fails, it can be all consuming. Unlike the loss of a job, when skills or experience may be to blame; when a relationship ends, many believe it was their fault, like there is something wrong with them personally not professionally, and they shoulder the responsibility for the breakdown.

But there are strategies to get through it. There are restorative qualities to prayer and meditation. Others have found great help from positive thinking seminars, when trying to pull through a bad relationship or break-up. If children are involved, such as the case with Aila, counseling can be a helpful tool, too, as they come to terms with their new familial situation.

Ultimately though, finding and maintaining a successful, healthy relationship takes two committed people, working together as a team. And that means both people need to put themselves, their true selves into the relationship on a level playing field, with balance, as equals. No one should go into it with only half of their self—relationships are challenging enough without stacking the deck against you before you even begin.

Be honest with yourself, and be fair to your relationships—when you are ready to share your life with someone, you will get better results if you walk in as a whole self and a true self.

Really, when it comes down to it, you need to know who you are, and respect yourself, and love yourself, before you start seeking out those affections from someone else. It's certainly not an easy path to take, everything I'm suggesting—self-reflection and self-love—can be difficult, but if the end result is a healthier, happier relationship, and a healthier, happier you, then it should all be worth it.

So, for those of you seeking a man, desperate to walk down the aisle, take a step back and look at yourself first instead of looking outwards for your man. And instead of spending all that energy on man hunting, use it to build yourself up from the inside out. Truly, this is where it all begins and ends. Because you're still you, whether you're single or married, or divorced. And regardless of your relationship status, every woman is valuable and deserves to be happy.

Only once we realize and accept that reality—that we are valuable and worthwhile as individuals—can we begin to chip away at this urge so many of us have to become a Mrs.

Looking to the future, it's up to all of us to change the path so many have already taken. Certainly, the allure of being a blushing bride will continue to be a siren call, but it needn't be impossible to resist. We need to keep an eye on each other, heed the warning signs we see in our relationships, not be afraid to pause a relationship, or take a step back to slow things down, not allowing ourselves to get caught up in the moment, in the whirlwind of all those dreams of romance and nuptials. And we need to stop listening to the societal pressures around us, which are fleeting in the big scheme of things.

Indeed, the future is ours as individuals. Whatever happens, you have who you are to fall back on. Learn who you are, what your priorities and goals are as an individual, and love yourself first and foremost.

Be whole in yourself before you join in a relationship of two halves. And I can guarantee, if you do that, your future will be so much brighter for it, regardless of your marital status.

www.ingramcontent.com/pod-product-compliance
Lightning Source LLC
Chambersburg PA
CBHW060008050426
42448CB00012B/2668
* 9 7 8 0 6 9 2 7 9 7 9 2 1 *

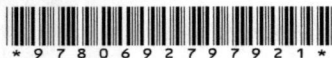